19
D/F# B7/D# B7 Em7 A/C# A7 D G/B G
Glo
-
Asus A D A/D D/G G D/A A7
22
mel.
-ri - a in ex - cel - sis De -
D5
2
1, 2
3
25
o.

AF349276

Angels We Have Heard on High

HAND DRUM

Traditional French Carol
Arranged by TOM ANDERSON

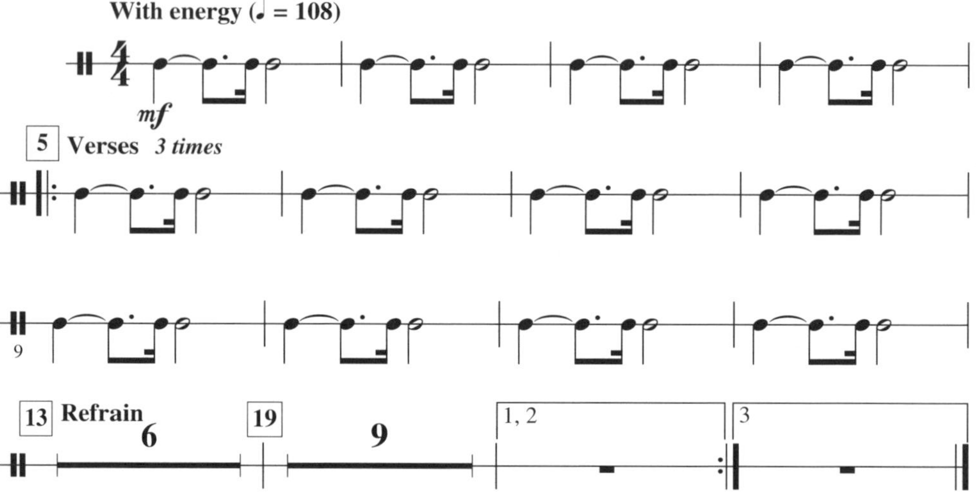

Angels We Have Heard on High

FINGER CYMBALS

Traditional French Carol
Arranged by TOM ANDERSON

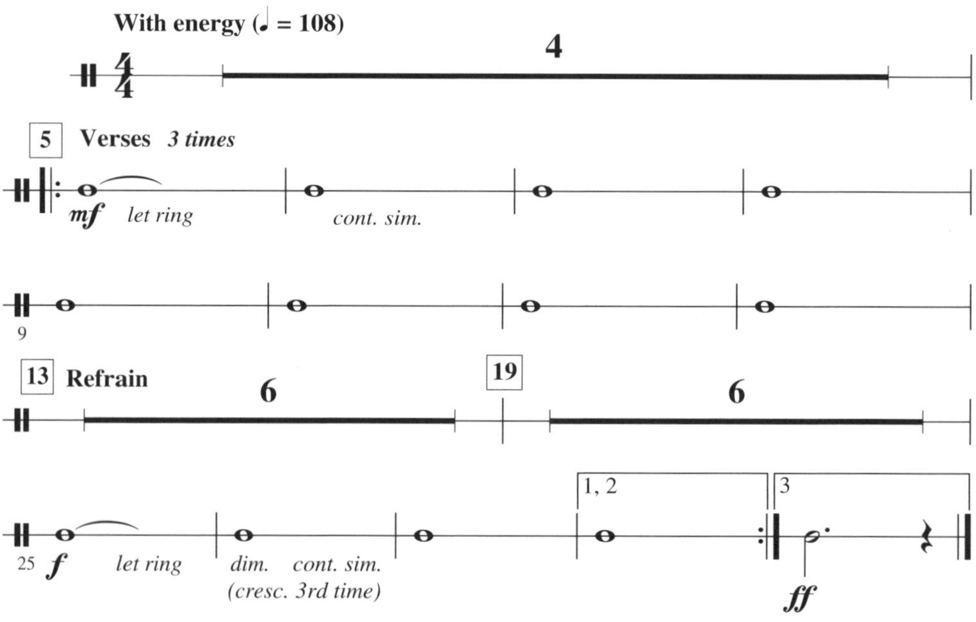

Disney
Mickey's Caroling Book

HOLIDAY FUN WITH MICKEY AND HIS FRIENDS

Table of Contents

7777 W. BLUEMOUND RD. P.O. BOX 13819 MILWAUKEE, WI 53213

Visit Hal Leonard Online at
www.halleonard.com

Angels We Have Heard on High

Traditional French Carol
Arranged by TOM ANDERSON

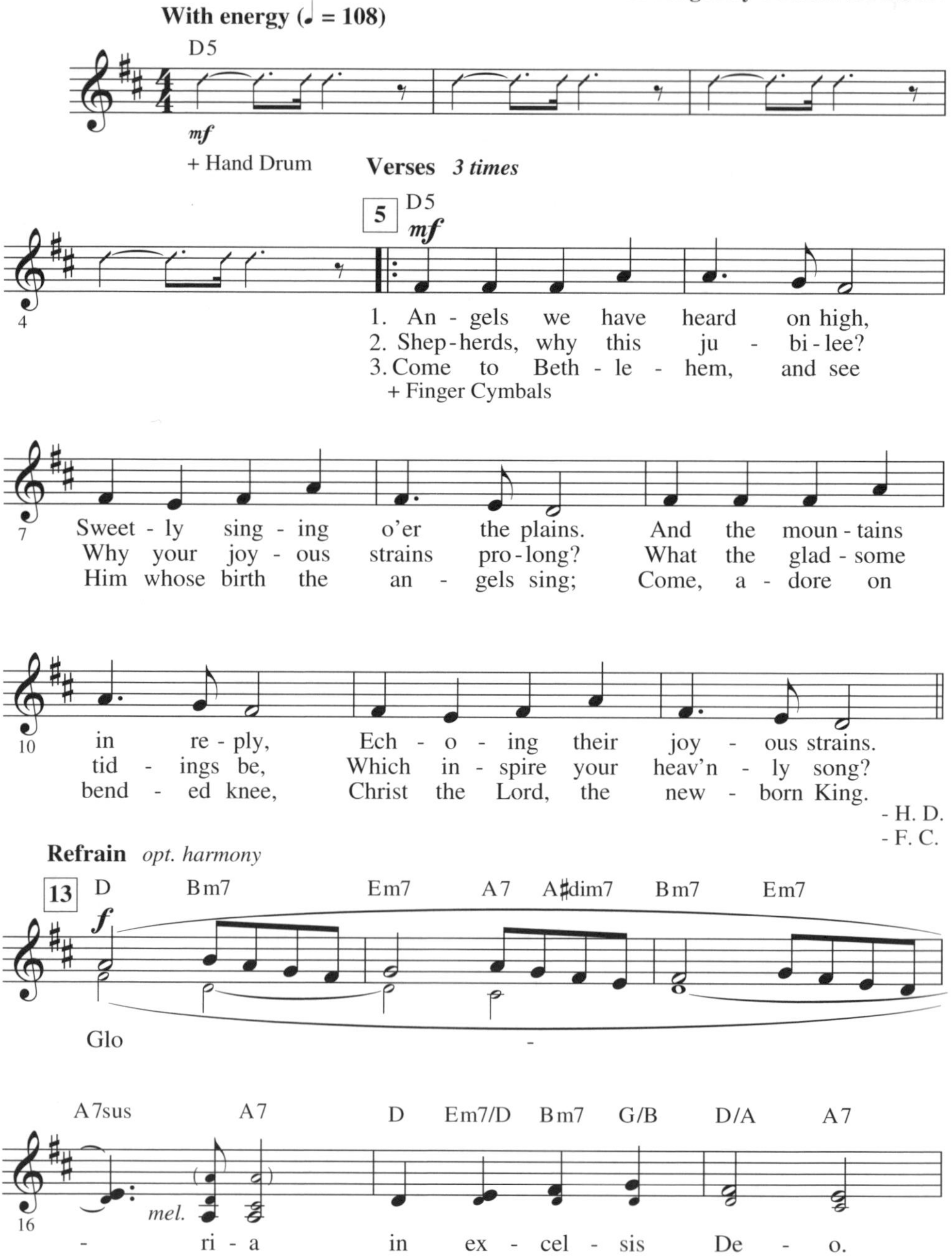

With energy ($\quarternote = 108$)

mf

+ Hand Drum

Verses *3 times*

Refrain *opt. harmony*

Angels We Have Heard on High

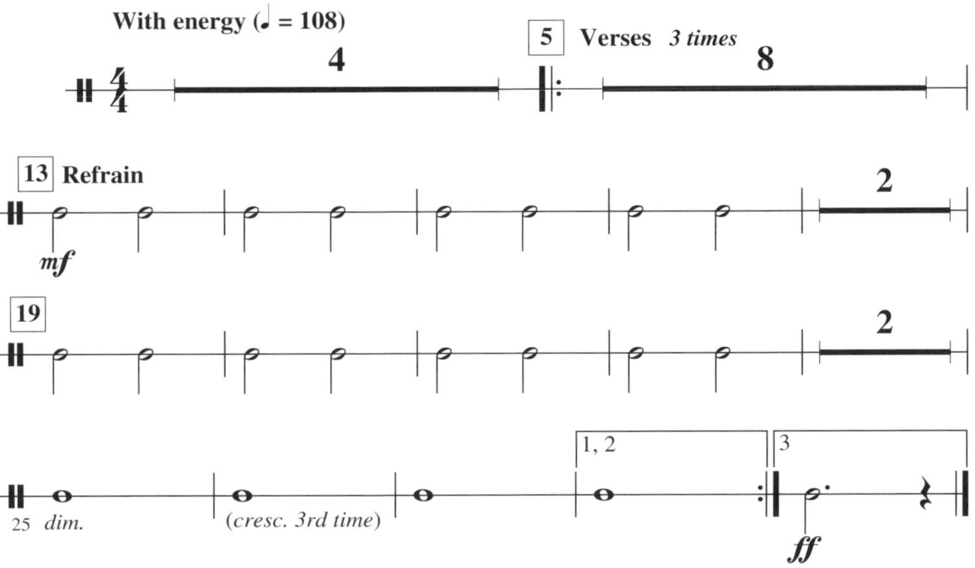

Angels We Have Heard on High

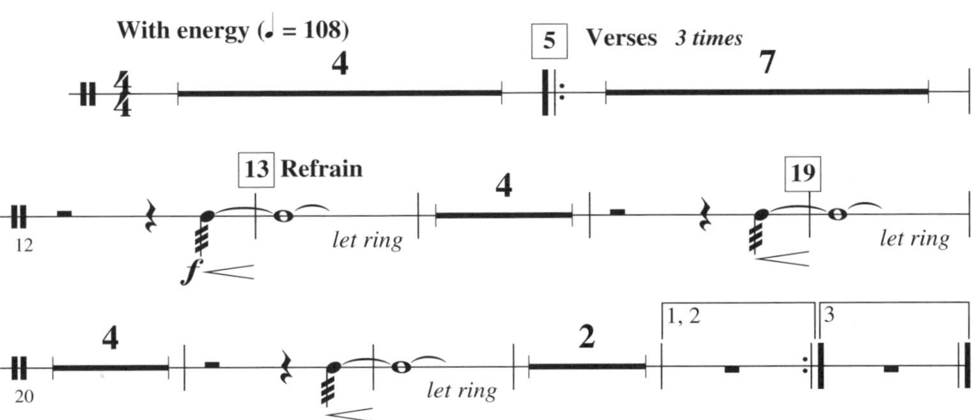

Angels We Have Heard on High

ORFF INSTRUMENTS

Traditional French Carol
Arranged by TOM ANDERSON

Away in a Manger

Music by JAMES R. MURRAY
Words, Stanza 1, 2, Anonymous
Stanza 3, JOHN THOMAS McFARLAND
Arranged by TOM ANDERSON

(5 clicks on recording)
With Motion ($\quad$ = 86)

mf

(opt. harmony, 2nd time)

1. A -

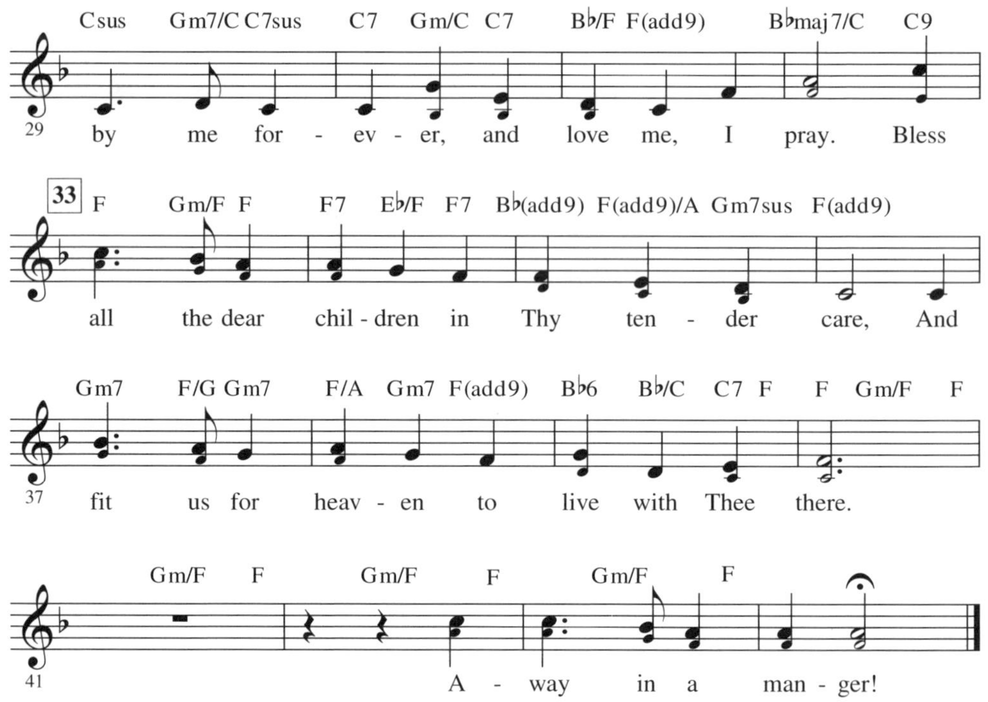

Csus Gm7/C C7sus C7 Gm/C C7 B♭/F F(add9) B♭maj7/C C9
29
by me for - ev - er, and love me, I pray. Bless
33 F Gm/F F F7 E♭/F F7 B♭(add9) F(add9)/A Gm7sus F(add9)
all the dear chil - dren in Thy ten - der care, And
Gm7 F/G Gm7 F/A Gm7 F(add9) B♭6 B♭/C C7 F F Gm/F F
37
fit us for heav - en to live with Thee there.
Gm/F F Gm/F F Gm/F F
41
A - way in a man - ger!

Away in a Manger

ORFF INSTRUMENTS

Music by JAMES R. MURRAY
Words, Stanza 1, 2, Anonymous
Stanza 3, JOHN THOMAS McFARLAND
Arranged by TOM ANDERSON

25
let ring
cont. sim.
let ring
cont. sim.
let ring
cont. sim.
33
30
35
40
let ring
let ring
let ring

Away in a Manger

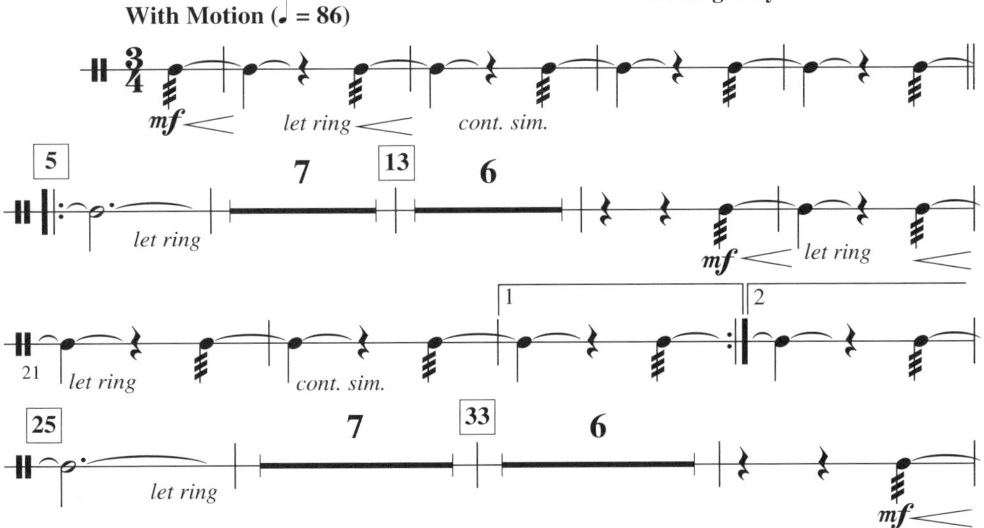

Away in a Manger

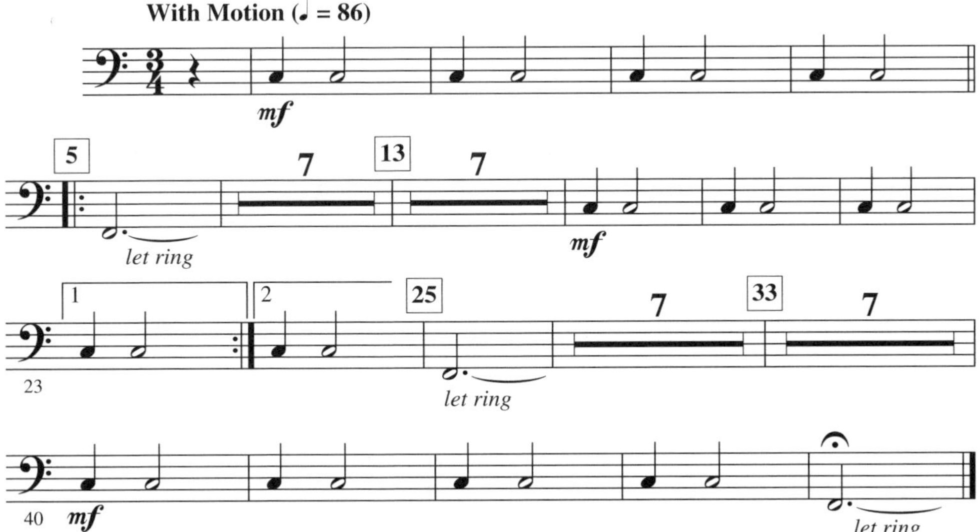

Deck the Halls

Traditional Welsh Carol
Arranged by TOM ANDERSON

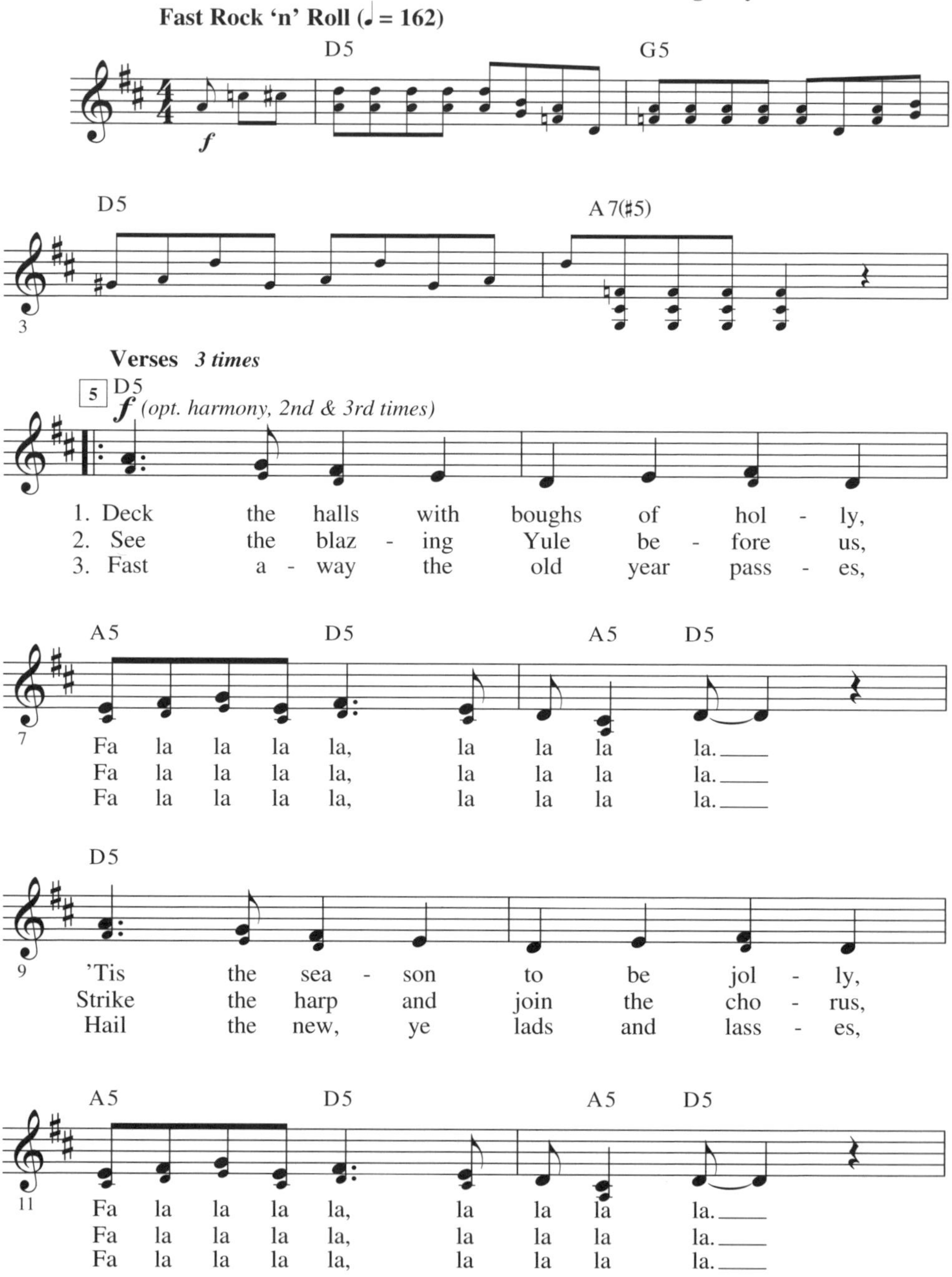

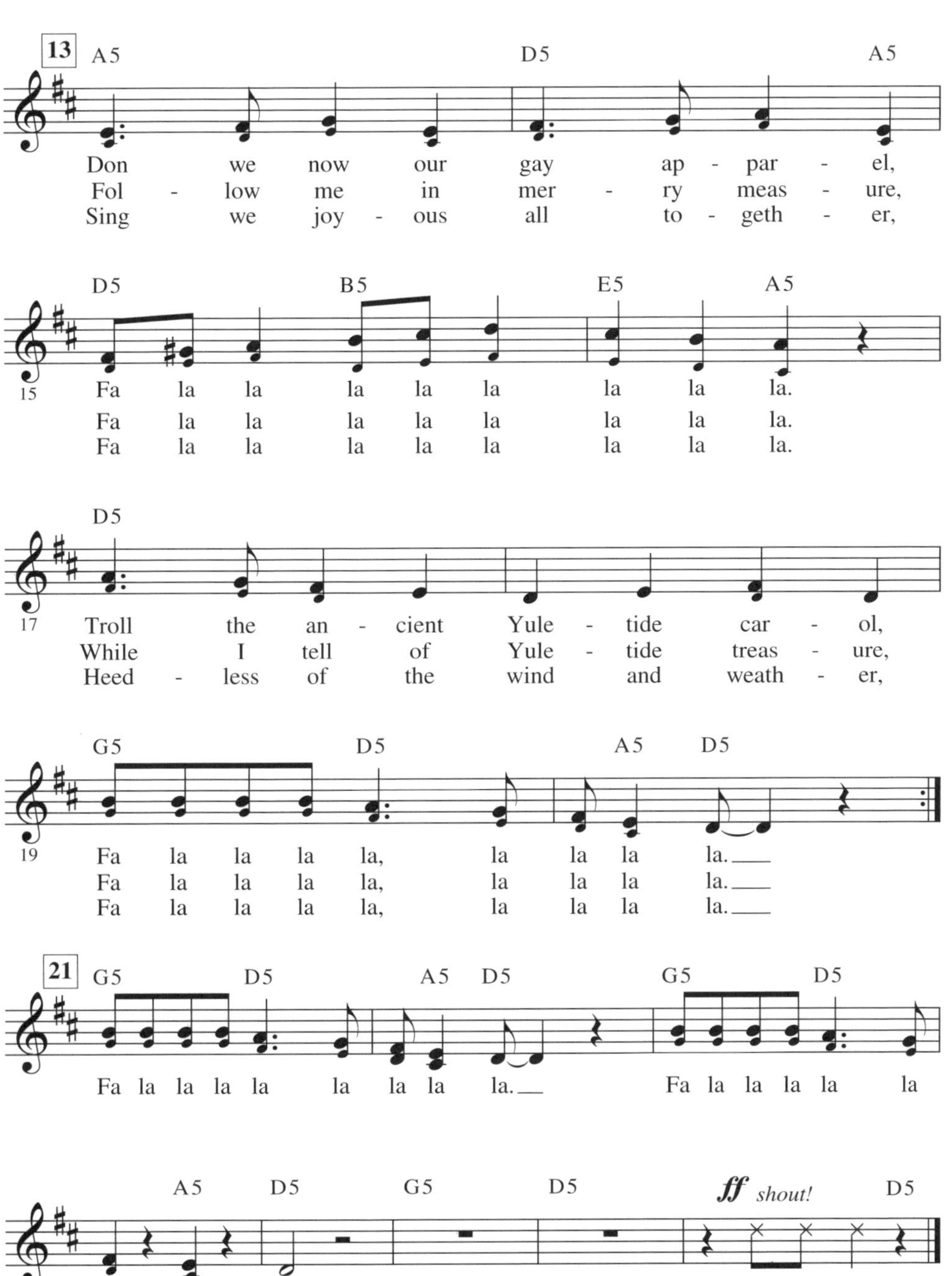

13 A5   D5   A5

Don   we   now   our   gay   ap - par - el,
Fol - low   me   in   mer - ry   meas - ure,
Sing   we   joy - ous   all   to - geth - er,

D5   B5   E5   A5

15 Fa   la   la   la   la   la   la   la   la.
Fa   la   la   la   la   la   la   la   la.
Fa   la   la   la   la   la   la   la   la.

D5

17 Troll   the   an - cient   Yule - tide   car - ol,
While   I   tell   of   Yule - tide   treas - ure,
Heed - less   of   the   wind   and   weath - er,

G5   D5   A5   D5

19 Fa   la   la   la   la,   la   la   la   la.___
Fa   la   la   la   la,   la   la   la   la.___
Fa   la   la   la   la,   la   la   la   la.___

21 G5   D5   A5   D5   G5   D5

Fa la la la la   la la la la.___   Fa la la la la   la

A5   D5   G5   D5   ff shout!   D5

24 la   la   la.   Deck the halls!

Deck the Halls

BONGO/CONGA DRUMS

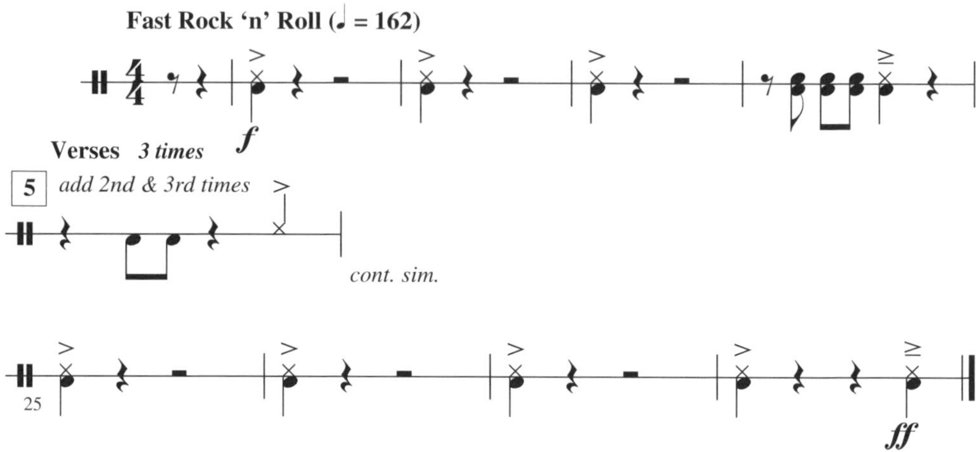

Deck the Halls

TAMBOURINE

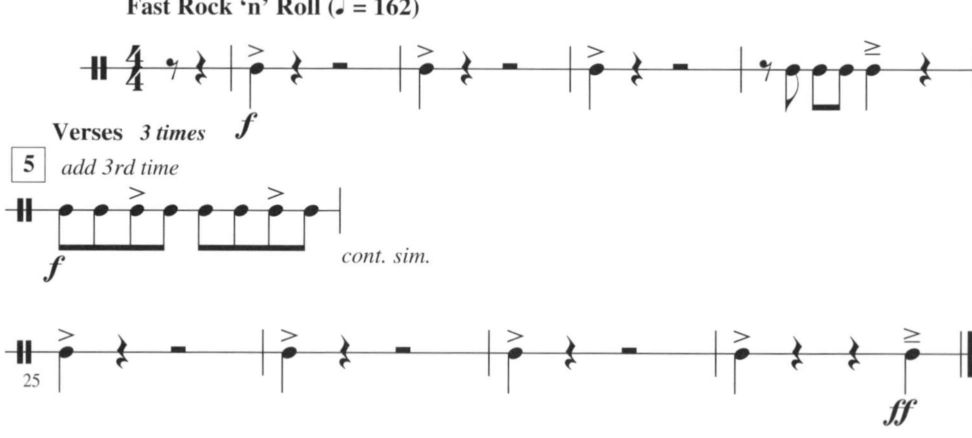

Here We Come A-Caroling

English Wassail Song
Arranged by TOM ANDERSON

Here We Come A-Caroling

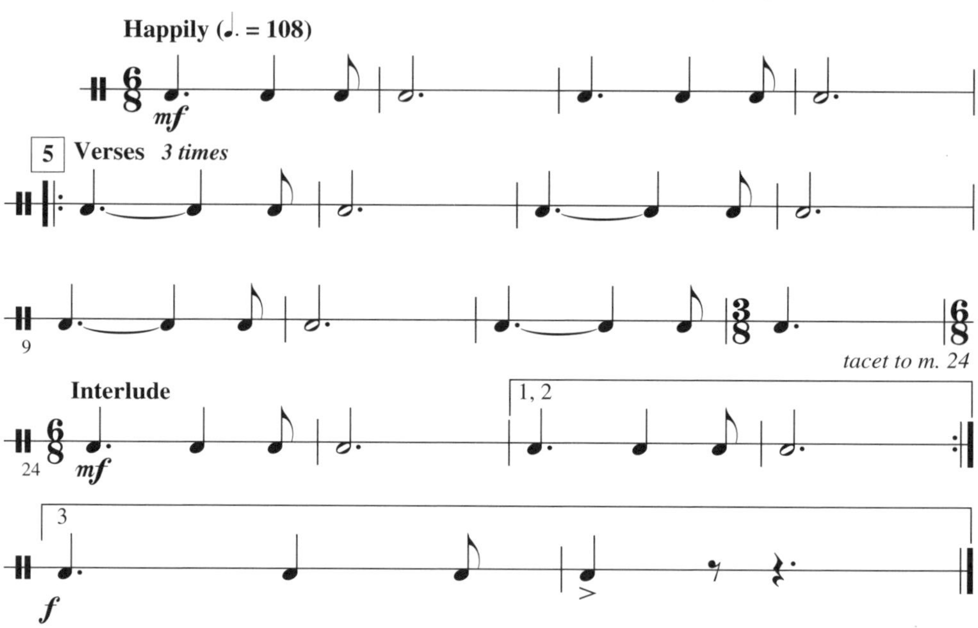

Here We Come A-Caroling

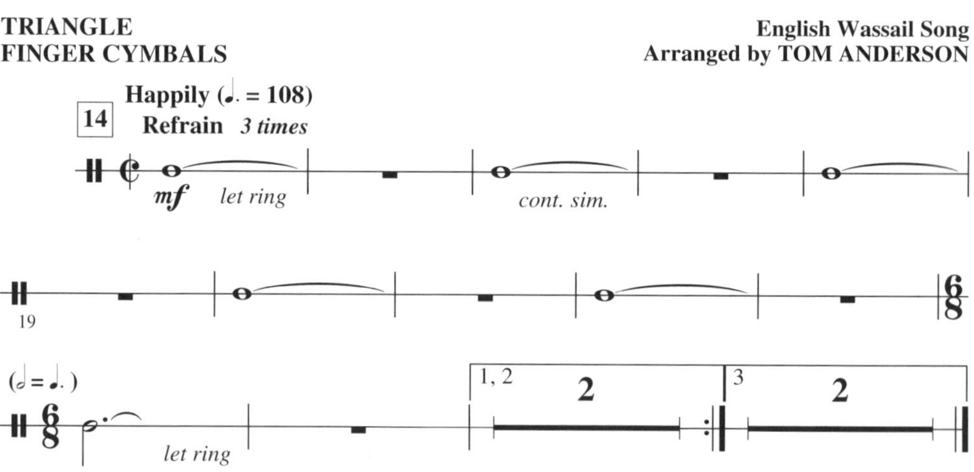

Jingle Bells

Words and Music by JAMES PIERPONT
Arranged by TOM ANDERSON

With Joy! (♩ = 106)

Verses

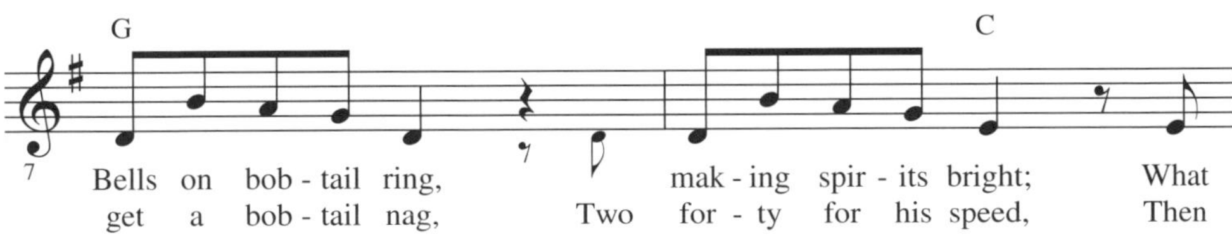

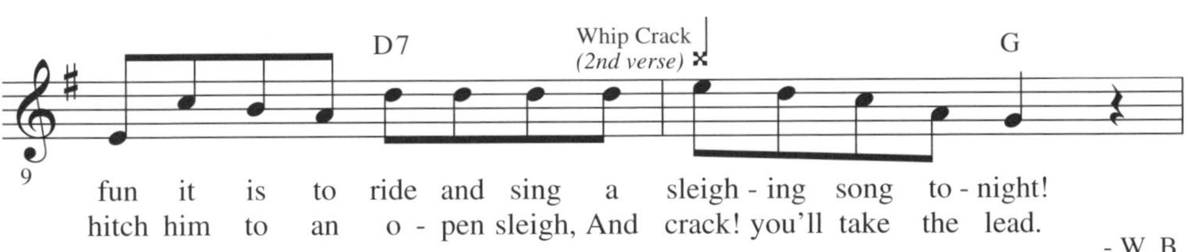

opt. harmony
11 G
Jin - gle bells! Jin - gle bells! Jin - gle all the way!
+ Jingle Bells
C   G   A7   Am7   D7
13
Oh, what fun it is to ride in a one - horse o - pen sleigh!___
G
15
Jin - gle bells! Jin - gle bells! Jin - gle all the way!
C   G   1 D7   G
17
Oh, what fun it is to ride in a one - horse o - pen sleigh!
- J. B.
2 D7   G   Whip N. C.
shout!
19
one - horse o - pen sleigh! Hey!

Jolly Old St. Nicholas

Traditional American Carol
Arranged by TOM ANDERSON

Copyright © 2012 by HAL LEONARD CORPORATION
International Copyright Secured   All Rights Reserved

21 Recorder or Other Pitched Inst.
29
27
- Recorder
32
37 3. John-ny wants a pair of skates,__ Su-sy wants a sled;__
+ Jingle Bells
41 Nel-lie wants a pic-ture book;__ yel-low, blue and red.__
45
44 __ Now I think I'll leave to you__
47 what to give the rest;__ Choose for me, dear San-ta Claus,__
53
51 you will know the best.__ You will know the best.__
55 You will know the best!______
2

Jolly Old St. Nicholas

RECORDER
or other pitched instrument

Traditional American Carol
Arranged by TOM ANDERSON

Jolly Old St. Nicholas

SUSPENDED CYMBAL

Traditional American Carol
Arranged by TOM ANDERSON

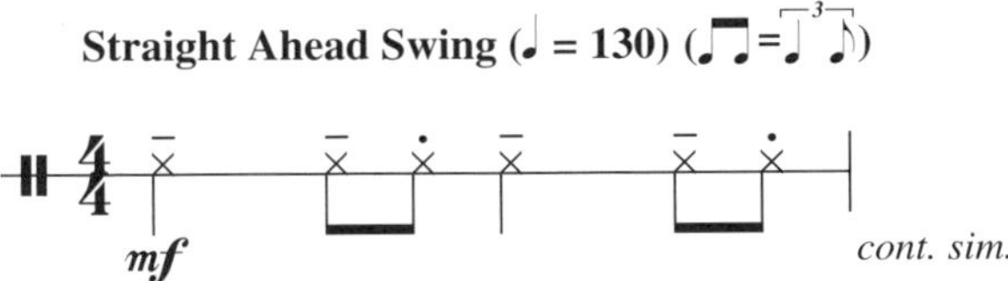

Jolly Old St. Nicholas

JINGLE BELLS

Traditional American Carol
Arranged by TOM ANDERSON

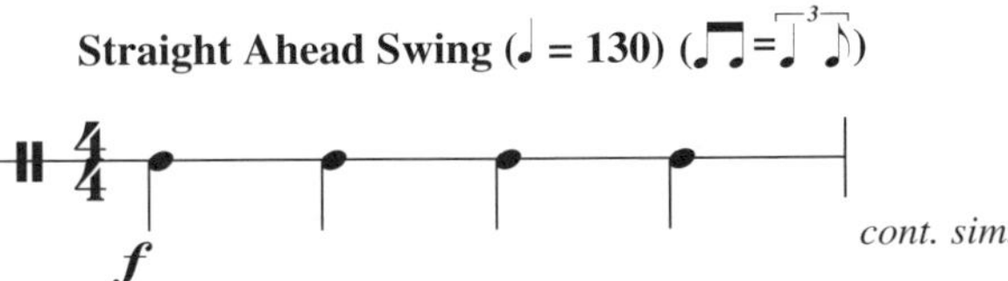

7/19

Joy to the World

Words by ISAAC WATTS
Music by GEORGE F. HANDEL
Arranged by TOM ANDERSON

(4-measure rhythm intro. on recording)

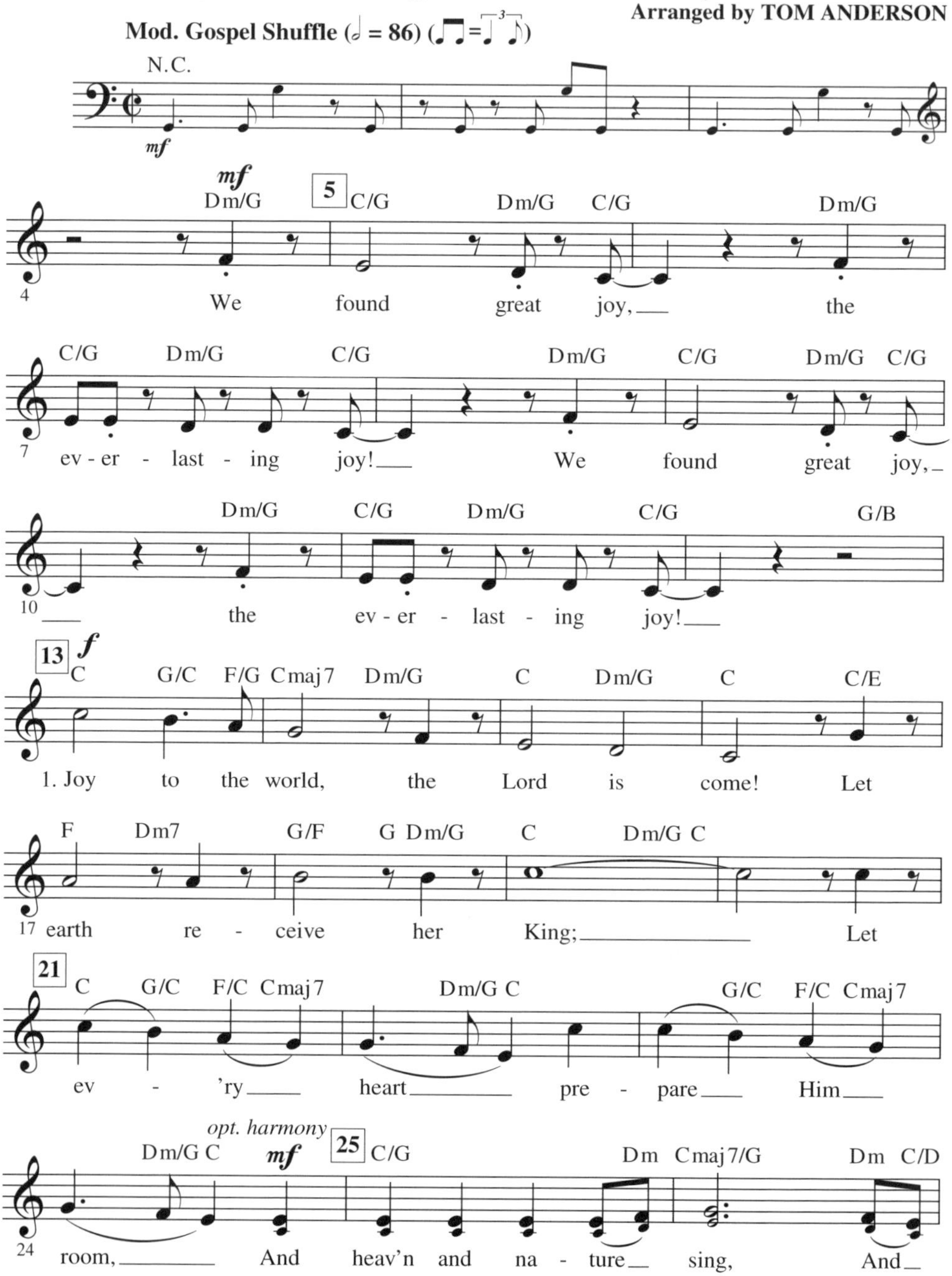

Dm7/G   C/D Dm7(♭5)/G Dm7(♭5)/A♭   Am7   Am7/G
27
heav'n and na - ture sing,   And heav'n and

F(add9) C/E F2/A C/G Dm/G   32 C   Dm/C C   Dm/C
opt. small group We found great joy, ___
30
heav'n ___ and na - ture sing.   the
mel.
+ Hand Claps on beat 2

C   Dm7(♭5)/C   C   Dm/C   C   Dm/C C
34
ev - er - last - ing joy! ___   We found great joy, ___

Dm/C   C   Dm7(♭5)/C   C   G/B
37
___   the ev - er - last - ing joy! ___   - Claps

40 f opt. harmony
C   G/C F/G Cmaj7 Dm/G   C   Dm/G C   C/E
2. He rules the world with truth and grace, And
mel.

F   Dm7   G/F   G Dm/G C   Dm/G C
na - tions prove ___
44 makes the   We found great joy! ___   The

48 C   G/C F/C Cmaj7   Dm/G C   G/C F/C Cmaj7
glo - ries ___ of ___   His right - eous -

Dm/G C   mf   52 C/G   Dm Cmaj7/G   Dm C/D
51
ness, ___   And won - ders of His ___ love, And ___

Dm7/G   C/D Dm7(b5)/G Dm7(b5)/Ab   Am7   Am7/G
54 won - ders   of   His__ love,   And__   won - ders,
F(add9) C/E F2/A   C/G   Dm/G   59 C   Dm/C   C
We   found   great   joy,__
57 won - ders   of   His   love.   mel.
+ Claps
Dm/C   C   Dm7(b5)/C   C   Dm/C
60   the   ev - er - last - ing   joy!__   We
C   Dm/C   C   Dm/C   C   Dm7(b5)/C   C
63 found   great   joy,__   the   ev - er - last - ing   joy!__
build intensity
f   Dm/C   67 C   Dm/C   C   Dm/C
66 __   We   found   great   joy,__   the
+ Tambourine on beat 2
C   Dm7(b5)/C   C   Dm/C   C   Dm/C   C
69 ev - er - last - ing   joy!__   We   found   great   joy,__
Dm/C   C   Dm7(b5)/C   C
72 __   the   ev - er - last - ing   joy!__   ff

O Christmas Tree
(O Tannenbaum)

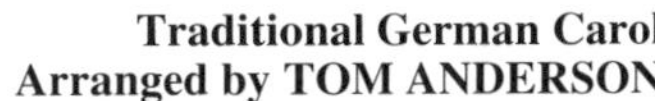

Traditional German Carol
Arranged by TOM ANDERSON

24
F2/A   D7(#9/#5)   Gm7sus Gm7   Bb/C   C7(#5)
more motion opt. harmony
sight of you   at Christ-mas-time,   spreads hope and glad - ness
- W. C.
Gm7/F F   Bb(add9)/C F6   C7(b9) Am7/D   D7(b9)
dim.
27   far and wide.   O   Christ-mas tree,   O   Christ - mas tree,   how
Gm7   Bb/C   C7(b9)   C7(b9)/F   F6   Eb13(#11)
mp
30   love - ly   are   your   branch - es!   + F. C.
relaxed
F6/9   Eb13(#11)   F6/9
33   O   Christ - mas tree!______
+ W. C.

Pat-a-Pan
(Willie, Take Your Little Drum)

Words and Music by
BERNARD de la MONNOYE
Arranged by **TOM ANDERSON**

Steadily ($\quad$ = 86)

D5

mf

+ Drums and Metals

mp

dim.

1. Wil - lie,

Verses

9 D5 *opt. harmony (2nd time)*

mf
28 E5
27
3. God and man to - day be - come close-ly joined as
B5
30
flute and drum. Let the joy - ous tune play
E5
B5
33
on! Tu - re - lu - re - lu, pat - a - pat - a - pan. As the
E5
B5
36
in - stru - ments you play, we will sing, this Christ - mas
39 Ending
E5
6
Day.

Pat-a-Pan
(Willie, Take Your Little Drum)

Pat-a-Pan
(Willie, Take Your Little Drum)

Pat-a-Pan
(Willie, Take Your Little Drum)

Pat-a-Pan

(Willie, Take Your Little Drum)

Silent Night

Words by JOSEPH MOHR
Music by FRANZ GRUBER
Arranged by TOM ANDERSON

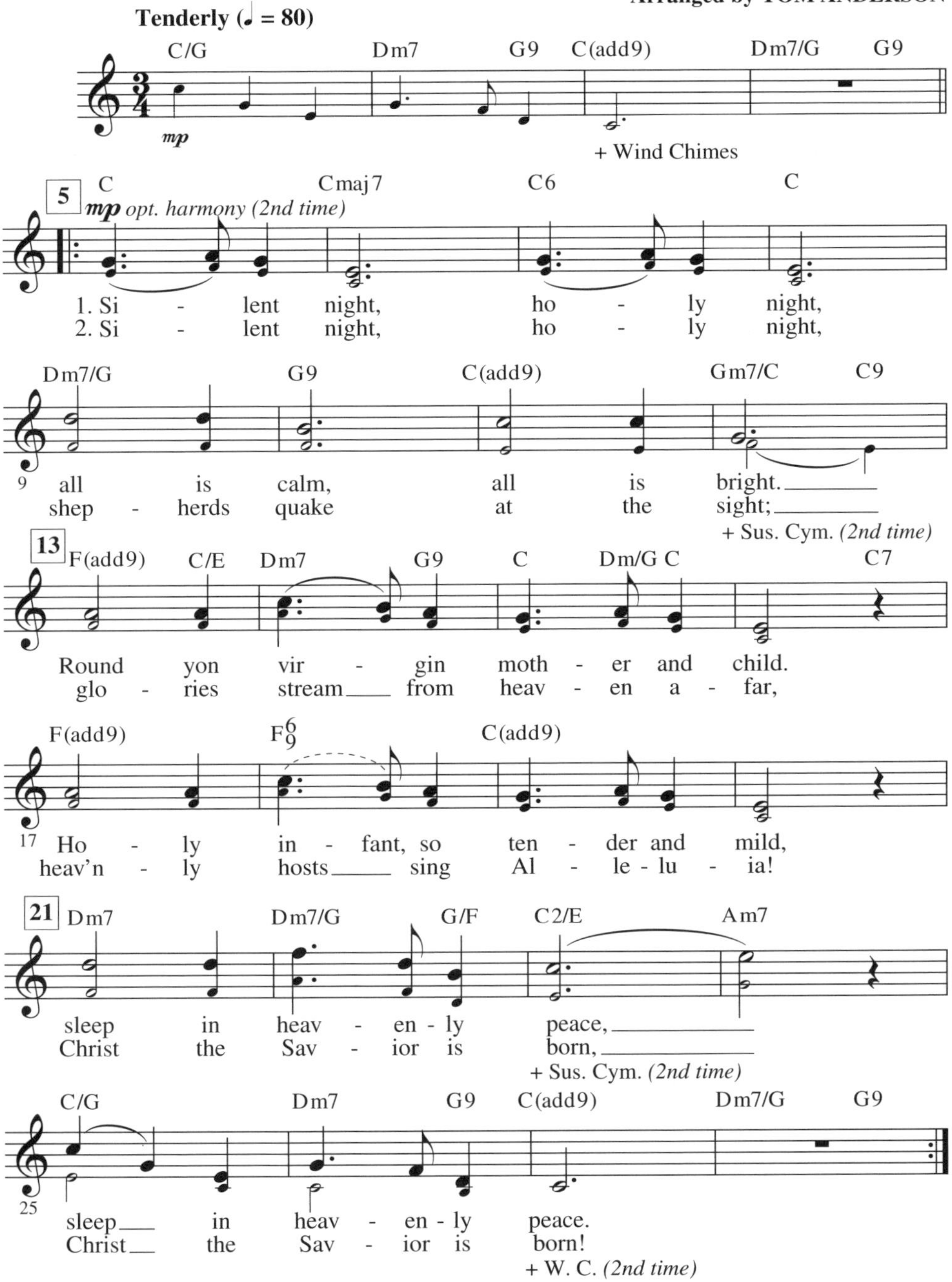

more motion
29 C mf Cmaj7 C6 C Dm7/G
3. Si - lent night, ho - ly night, Son of
+ Descant/Recorder
G9 C(add9) Gm7/C C9 37 F(add9) C/E Dm7 G9
34 God, love's pure light; ra - diant beams from
+ Sus. Cym.
C Dm/G C C7 F(add9) F6/9 C(add9)
39 Thy ho - ly face, with the dawn of re - deem - ing
45 Dm7 Dm7/G G/F C2/E Am7
44 grace, Je - sus, Lord, at Thy birth,
+ Sus. Cym.
C/G Dm7 G9 C(add9)
dim. slight rit. mp
49 Je - sus, Lord at Thy birth.
+ W. C.

Silent Night

Up on the Housetop

Words and Music by B. R. HANDY
Arranged by TOM ANDERSON

Cheerfully (♩ = 134)

21
mf
D
D/F#
3. Next, comes the stock - ing of lit - tle Will;
G
D
A7
23
Oh, just see what a glo - rious fill!
D
D/F#
25
Here is a ham - mer and lots of tacks,
G
D
Em7
A7
D
Whip Crack
D/F#
27
al - so a ball and a whip that cracks.
29
f
G
Em7
D
Bm7
Ho, ho, ho, who would - n't go!
+ S. B. and Mar.
Em7
A7
D
Em7/A
31
Ho, ho, ho, who would - n't go!
Finger Snaps
D
D7/F#
G
D/F#
Em7
Fdim7
spoken
33
Up on the house - top click, click, click,
+ W. B.
N.C.
D/F#
Bm7
Em7
A7
D
Whip Crack
35
Down thru' the chim - ney with good Saint Nick.

We Wish You a Merry Christmas

Traditional English Carol
Arranged by TOM ANDERSON

22
G   G/B   C   C/B   A7sus   A7
wish   you   a   mer - ry   Christ - mas,   We   wish   you   a   mer - ry
+ Tri./F. C., H. D., Tamb.

D   D/C   B7sus   B7   Em   G/B
25 Christ - mas,   We   wish   you   a   mer - ry   Christ - mas,   and   a
- Tri./F. C.
- H. D.
- Tamb.

C6   Am7 cresc.   Am7/D   D9
28 hap - py   New

ff G   G2/B   C   Am7   D9   G6/9
32 Year!
+ Tri./F. C., H. D., Tamb.

We Wish You a Merry Christmas

TRIANGLE/FINGER CYMBALS

Traditional English Carol
Arranged by TOM ANDERSON

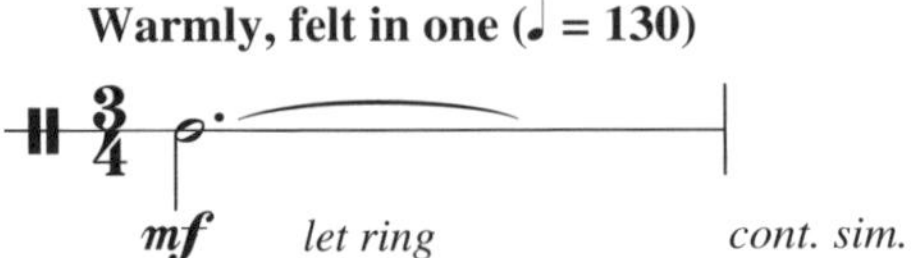

We Wish You a Merry Christmas

HAND DRUM

Traditional English Carol
Arranged by TOM ANDERSON

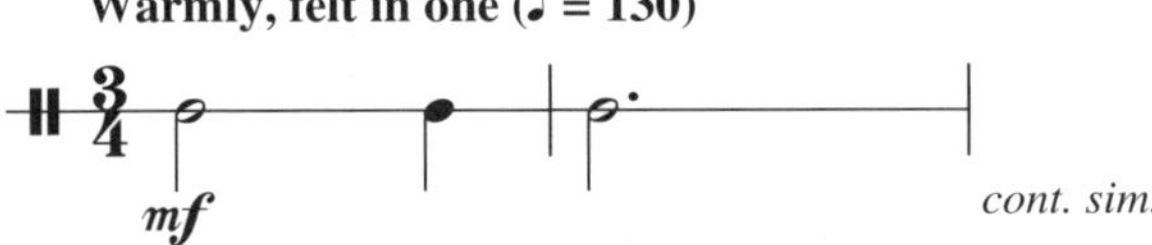

We Wish You a Merry Christmas

TAMBOURINE

Traditional English Carol
Arranged by TOM ANDERSON

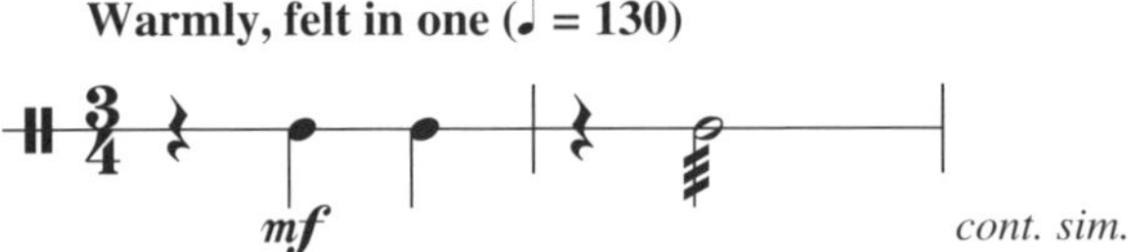

Disney
Mickey's Caroling Book

HOLIDAY FUN WITH MICKEY AND HIS FRIENDS

Table of Contents

HAL•LEONARD® CORPORATION

7777 W. BLUEMOUND RD. P.O. BOX 13819 MILWAUKEE, WI 53213

Visit Hal Leonard Online at
www.halleonard.com

1/13

Angels We Have Heard on High

Traditional French Carol
Arranged by TOM ANDERSON

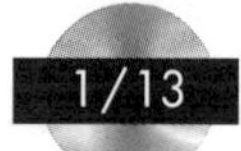

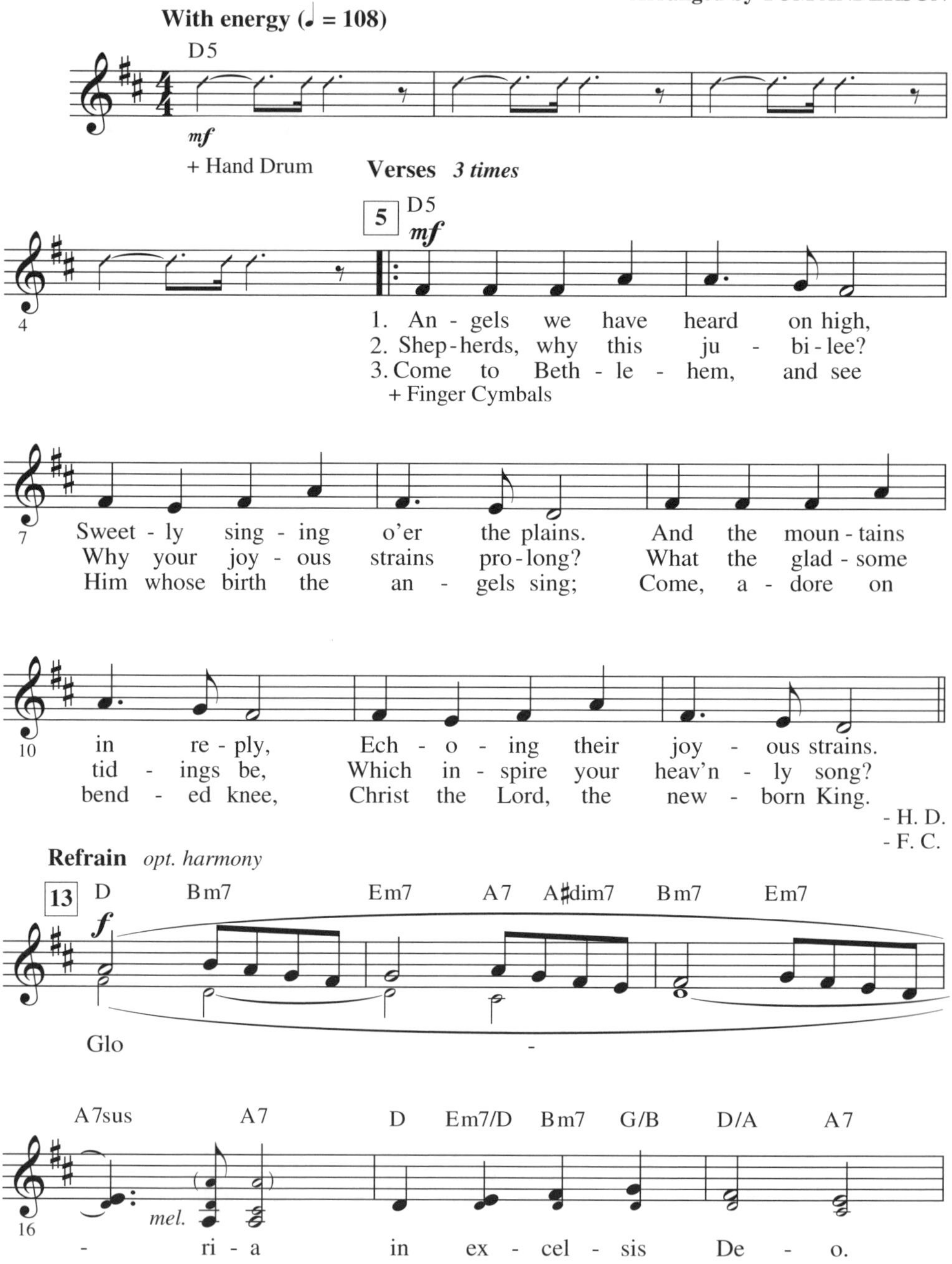

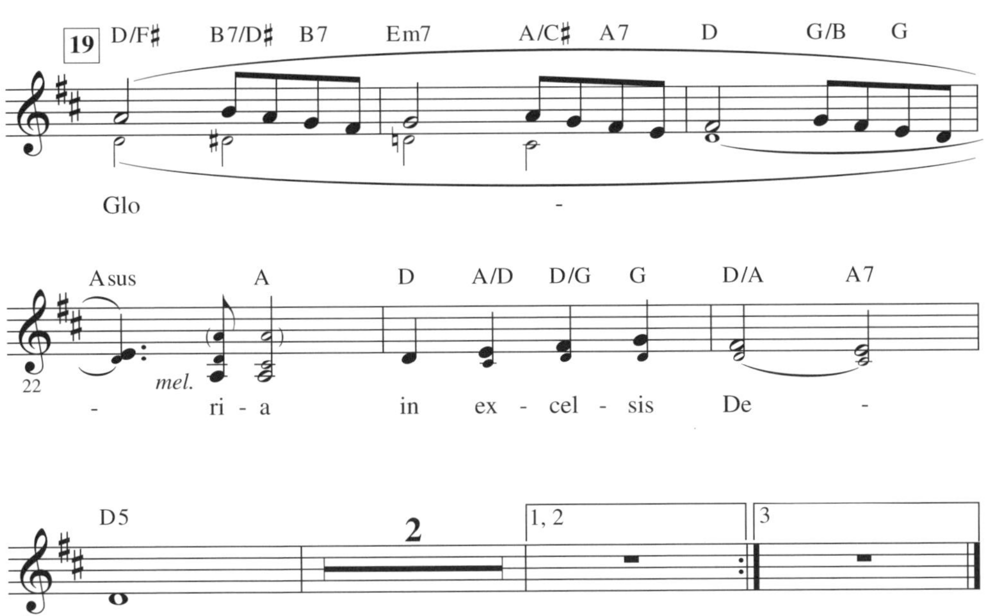

19
D/F#   B7/D# B7   Em7   A/C# A7   D   G/B   G
Glo -
Asus   A   D   A/D D/G G   D/A   A7
mel.
- ri - a   in ex - cel - sis De -
D5   2   1, 2   3
o.

Angels We Have Heard on High

HAND DRUM

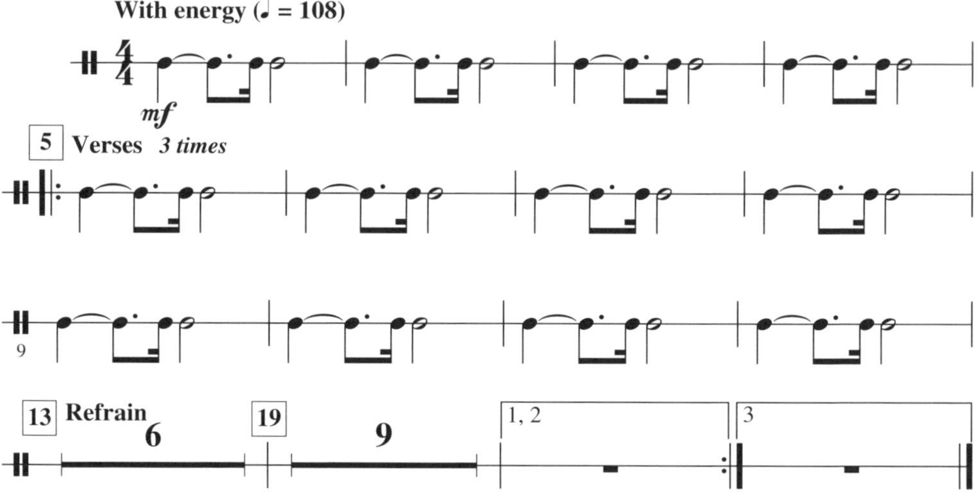

Angels We Have Heard on High

FINGER CYMBALS

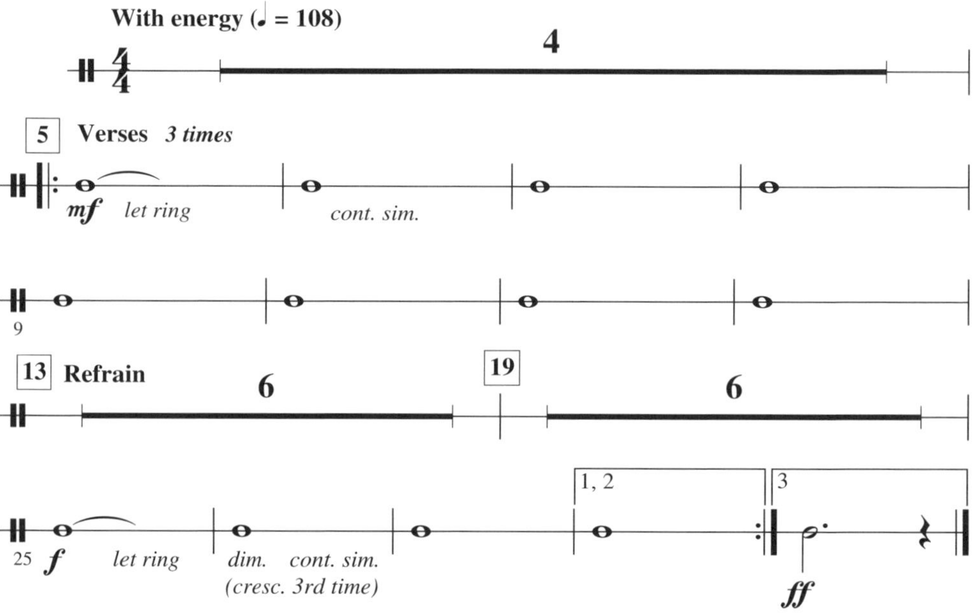

Angels We Have Heard on High

BASS DRUM

Traditional French Carol
Arranged by TOM ANDERSON

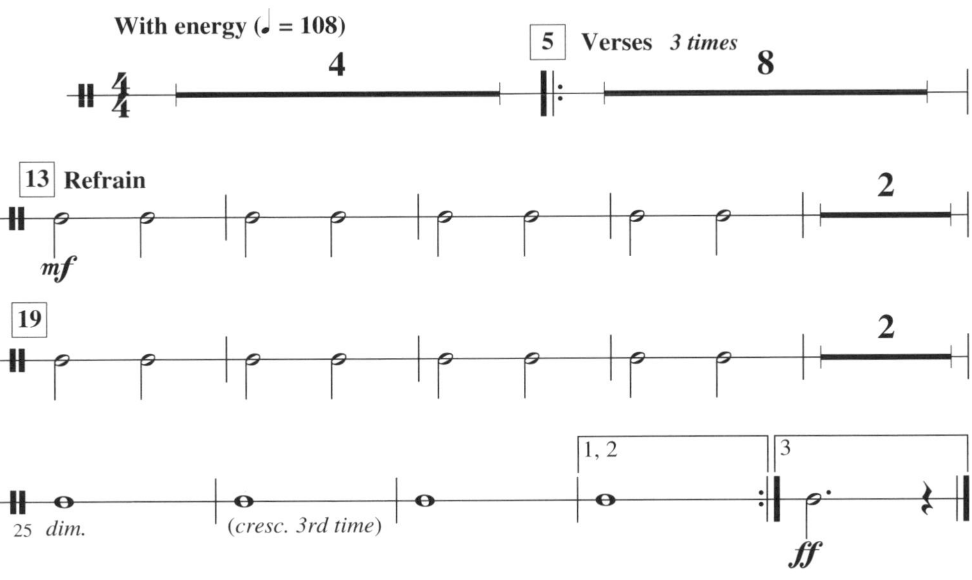

Angels We Have Heard on High

SUSPENDED CYMBAL

Traditional French Carol
Arranged by TOM ANDERSON

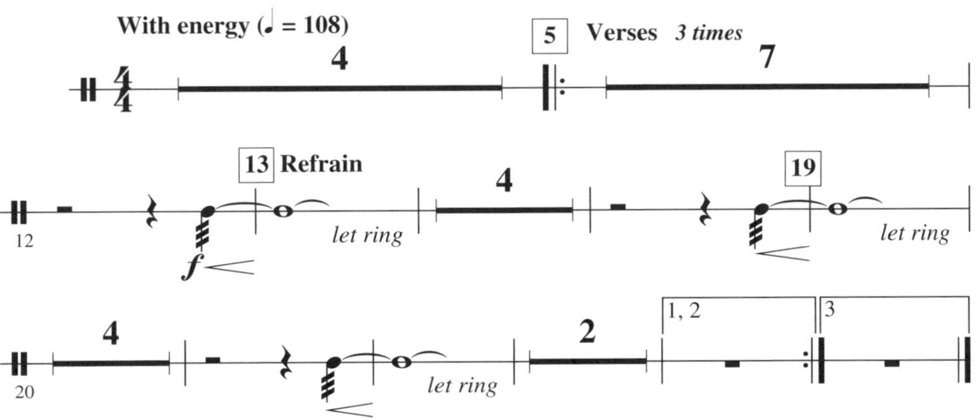

Angels We Have Heard on High

2/14
Away in a Manger
Music by JAMES R. MURRAY
Words, Stanza 1, 2, Anonymous
Stanza 3, JOHN THOMAS McFARLAND
Arranged by TOM ANDERSON
(5 clicks on recording)
With Motion (♩ = 86)
mf
(opt. harmony, 2nd time)
1. A -
way in a man - ger, no crib for a bed, The
cat - tle are low - ing the Ba - by a - wakes, But
lit - tle Lord Je - sus laid down His sweet head. The
lit - tle Lord Je - sus, no cry - ing He makes. I
stars in the sky looked down where He lay, The
love Thee, Lord Je - sus, look down from the sky, And
lit - tle Lord Je - sus, a - sleep on the hay.
stay by my cra - dle, till morn - ing is nigh.
opt. harmony
2. The
3. Be
near me, Lord Je - sus, I ask Thee to stay Close

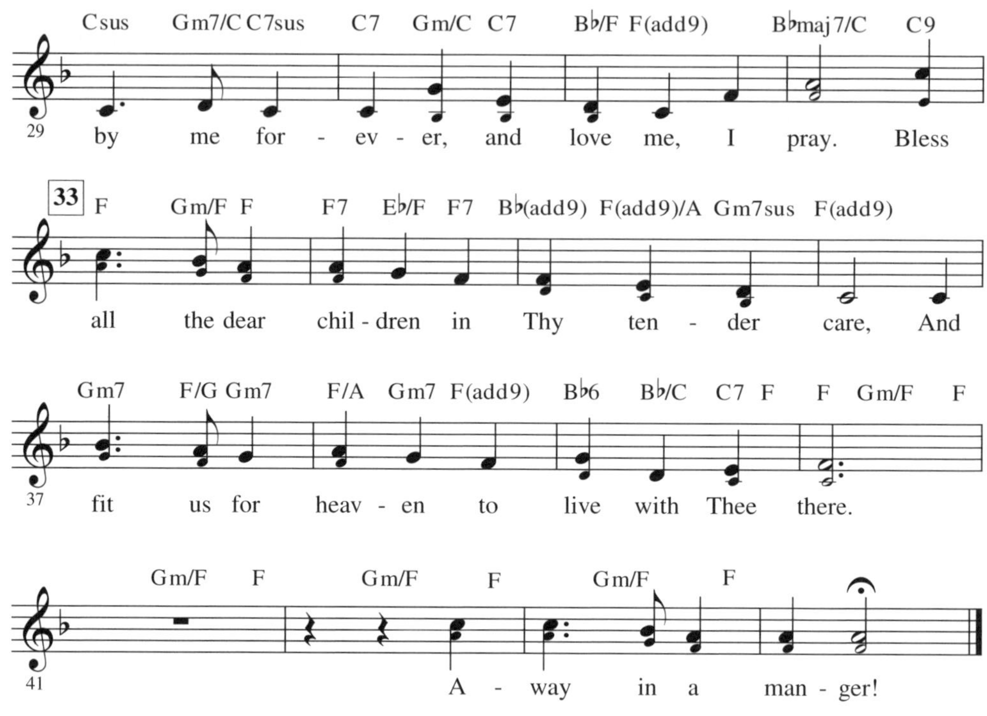

Csus   Gm7/C C7sus   C7   Gm/C C7   Bb/F F(add9)   Bbmaj7/C   C9
by   me   for - ev - er,   and   love   me,   I   pray.   Bless
33   F   Gm/F F   F7   Eb/F F7   Bb(add9) F(add9)/A Gm7sus   F(add9)
all   the dear   chil - dren   in   Thy   ten - der   care,   And
Gm7   F/G Gm7   F/A Gm7 F(add9)   Bb6   Bb/C C7 F   F Gm/F   F
fit   us   for   heav - en   to   live   with   Thee   there.
Gm/F   F   Gm/F   F   Gm/F   F
A - way   in   a   man - ger!

Away in a Manger

25
let ring
cont. sim.
let ring
cont. sim.
let ring
cont. sim.
33
30
35
40
let ring
let ring
let ring
let ring

Away in a Manger

SUSPENDED CRASH CYMBAL

Music by JAMES R. MURRAY
Words, Stanza 1, 2, Anonymous
Stanza 3, JOHN THOMAS McFARLAND
Arranged by TOM ANDERSON

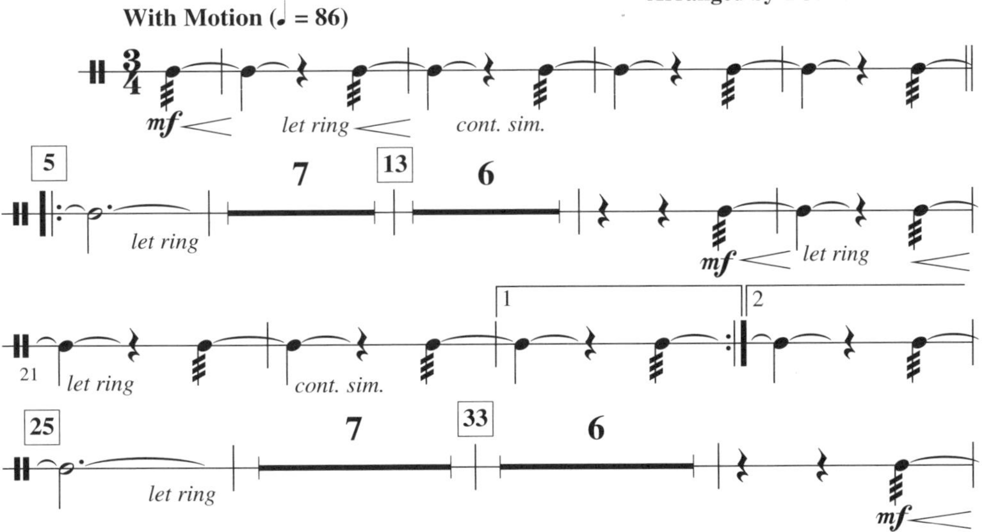

Away in a Manger

TIMPANI or TOM TOMS

Music by JAMES R. MURRAY
Words, Stanza 1, 2, Anonymous
Stanza 3, JOHN THOMAS McFARLAND
Arranged by TOM ANDERSON

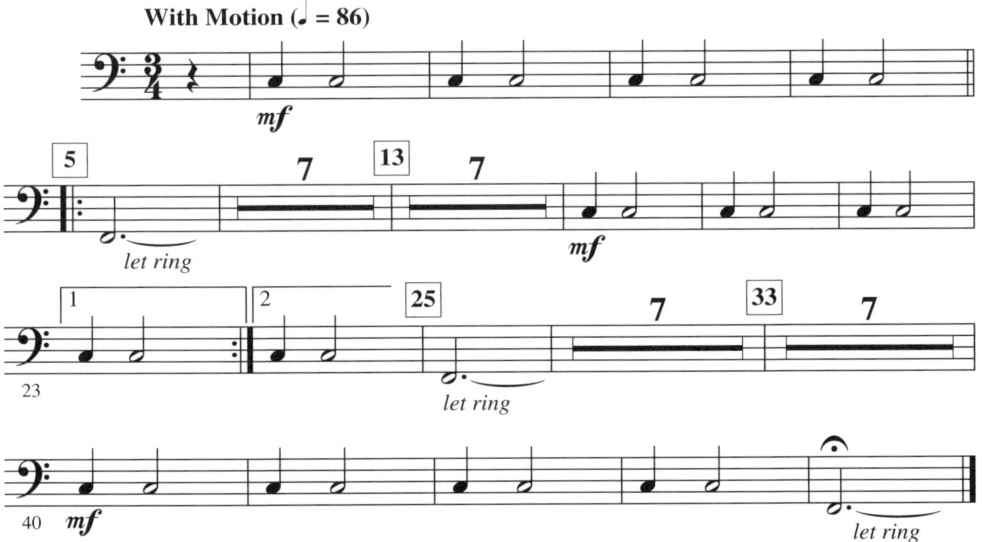

Deck the Halls

Traditional Welsh Carol
Arranged by TOM ANDERSON

13
A5   D5   A5
Don we now our gay ap - par - el,
Fol - low me in mer - ry meas - ure,
Sing we joy - ous all to - geth - er,
D5   B5   E5   A5
15
Fa la la la la la la la la.
Fa la la la la la la la la.
Fa la la la la la la la la.
D5
17
Troll the an - cient Yule - tide car - ol,
While I tell of Yule - tide treas - ure,
Heed - less of the wind and weath - er,
G5   D5   A5   D5
19
Fa la la la la, la la la la.___
Fa la la la la, la la la la.___
Fa la la la la, la la la la.___
21
G5   D5   A5   D5   G5   D5
Fa la la la la la la la la.__ Fa la la la la la
A5   D5   G5   D5   ff shout!   D5
24
la la la. Deck the halls!

Deck the Halls

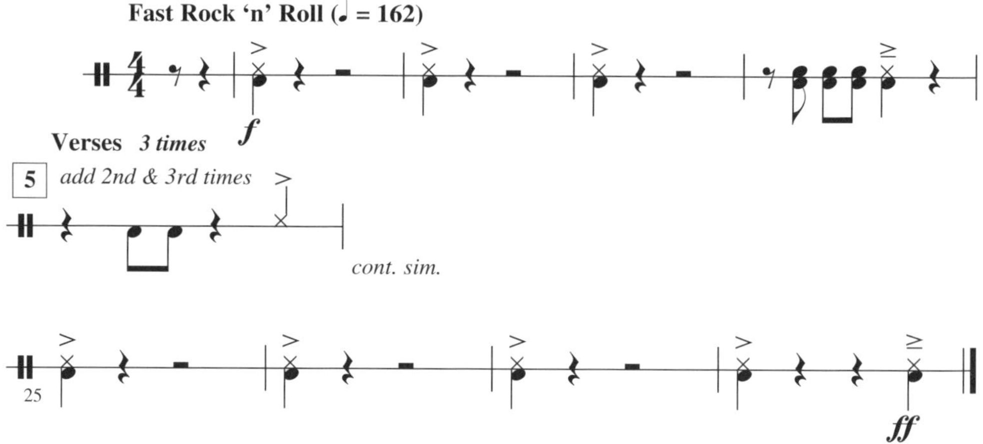

Deck the Halls

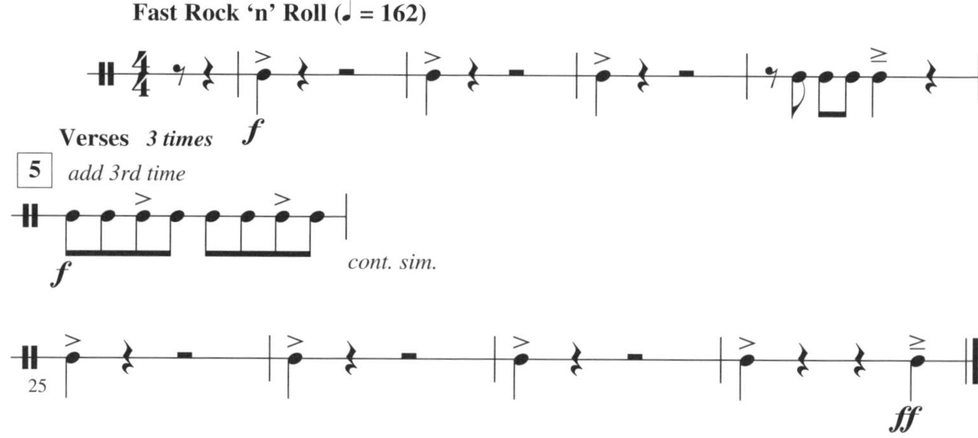

Here We Come A-Caroling

English Wassail Song
Arranged by TOM ANDERSON

Here We Come A-Caroling

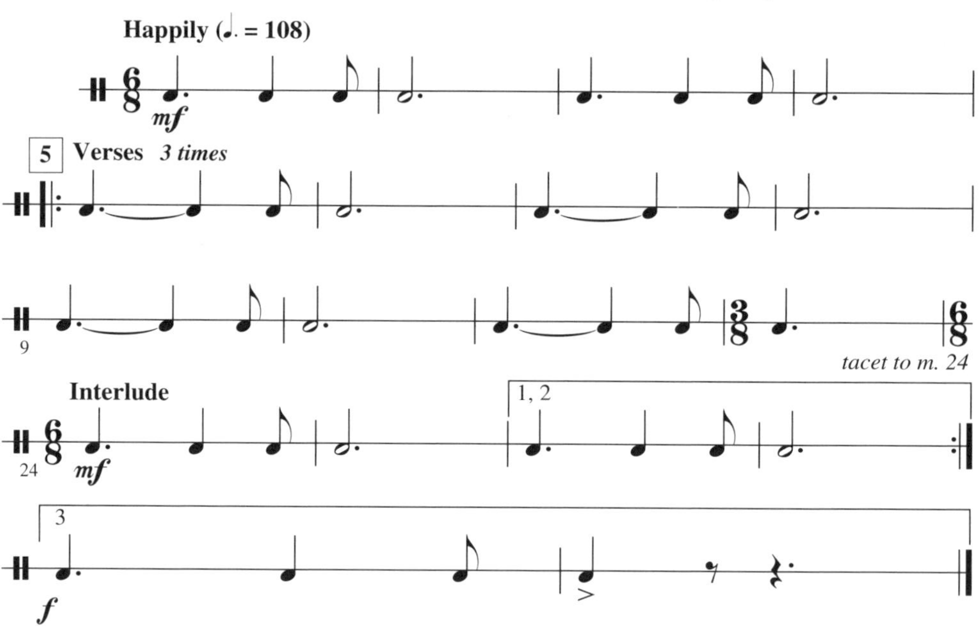

Here We Come A-Caroling

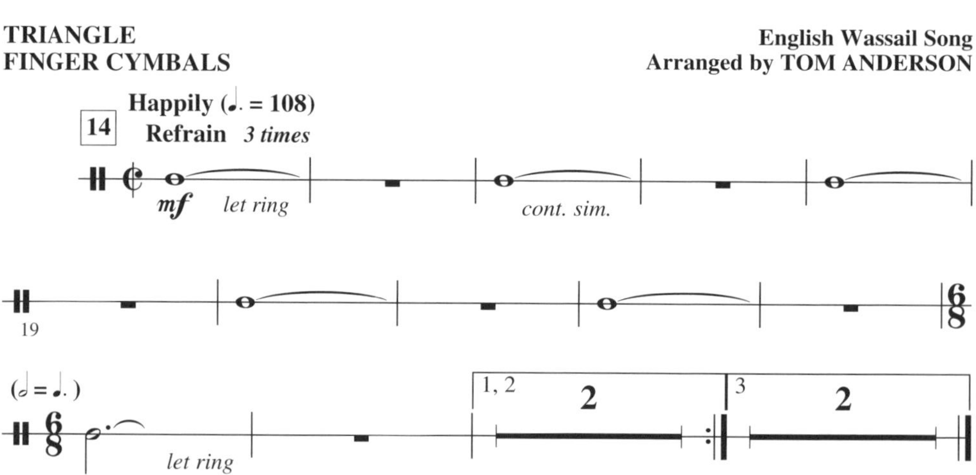

Jingle Bells

Words and Music by JAMES PIERPONT
Arranged by TOM ANDERSON

With Joy! (♩ = 106)

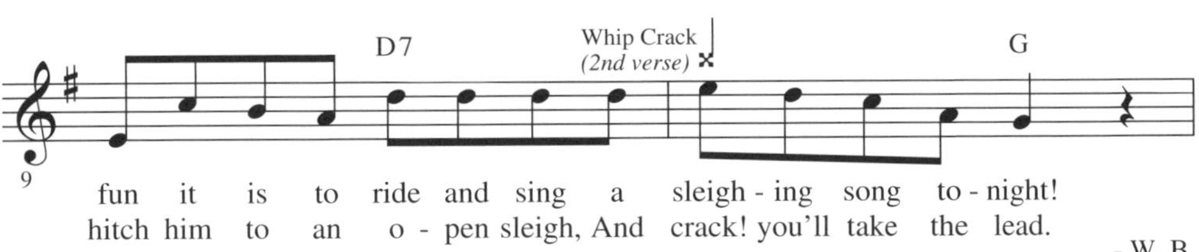

11
G
opt. harmony
f
Jin - gle bells! Jin - gle bells! Jin - gle all the way!
+ Jingle Bells
C G A7 Am7 D7
13
Oh, what fun it is to ride in a one - horse o - pen sleigh!___
G
15
Jin - gle bells! Jin - gle bells! Jin - gle all the way!
C G
1
D7 G
17
Oh, what fun it is to ride in a one - horse o - pen sleigh!
- J. B.
2
D7 G
Whip
shout! N. C.
19
one - horse o - pen sleigh! Hey!

Jolly Old St. Nicholas

Copyright © 2012 by HAL LEONARD CORPORATION
International Copyright Secured   All Rights Reserved

20   Mickey's Caroling Book – Singer

Jolly Old St. Nicholas

Jolly Old St. Nicholas

Jolly Old St. Nicholas

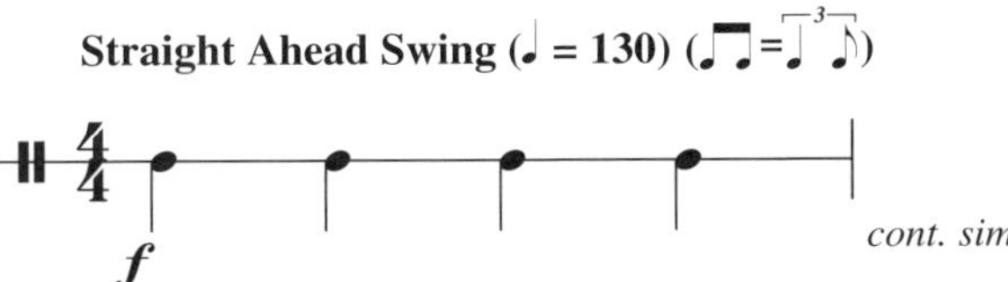

Joy to the World

Words by ISAAC WATTS
Music by GEORGE F. HANDEL
Arranged by TOM ANDERSON

(4-measure rhythm intro. on recording)

Mod. Gospel Shuffle (♩ = 86)

Dm7/G
C/D Dm7(b5)/G Dm7(b5)/Ab Am7 Am7/G
27
heav'n and na - ture sing, And heav'n and
F(add9) C/E F2/A C/G Dm/G 32 C Dm/C C Dm/C
opt. small group We found great joy,
30
mel.
heav'n and na - ture sing. the
+ Hand Claps on beat 2
C Dm7(b5)/C C Dm/C C Dm/C C
34
ev - er - last - ing joy! We found great joy,
Dm/C C Dm7(b5)/C C G/B
37
the ev - er - last - ing joy!
- Claps
40 f opt. harmony
C G/C F/G Cmaj7 Dm/G C Dm/G C C/E
mel.
2. He rules the world with truth and grace, And
F Dm7 G/F G Dm/G C Dm/G C
na - tions prove
44 makes the We found great joy! The
48 C G/C F/C Cmaj7 Dm/G C G/C F/C Cmaj7
glo - ries of His right - eous -
Dm/G C mf 52 C/G Dm Cmaj7/G Dm C/D
51
ness, And won - ders of His love, And

Dm7/G   C/D Dm7(b5)/G Dm7(b5)/Ab   Am7   Am7/G
54
won - ders   of   His   love,   And   won - ders,

F(add9)   C/E F2/A   C/G   Dm/G   59 C   Dm/C C
57   We   found   great   joy,
won - ders   of   His   love.
mel.
+ Claps
Dm/C   C   Dm7(b5)/C   C   Dm/C
60
the   ev - er - last - ing   joy!   We

C   Dm/C C   Dm/C   C   Dm7(b5)/C   C
63 found   great   joy,   the   ev - er - last - ing   joy!

build intensity
f   Dm/C   67 C   Dm/C C   Dm/C
66
We   found   great   joy,   the
+ Tambourine on beat 2

C   Dm7(b5)/C   C   Dm/C   C   Dm/C C
69 ev - er - last - ing   joy!   We   found   great   joy,

Dm/C   C   Dm7(b5)/C   C
72
the   ev - er - last - ing   joy!
ff

8/20

O Christmas Tree

(O Tannenbaum)

Traditional German Carol
Arranged by TOM ANDERSON

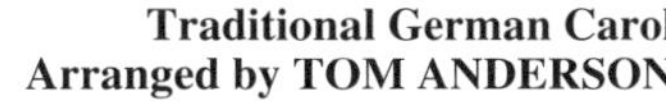

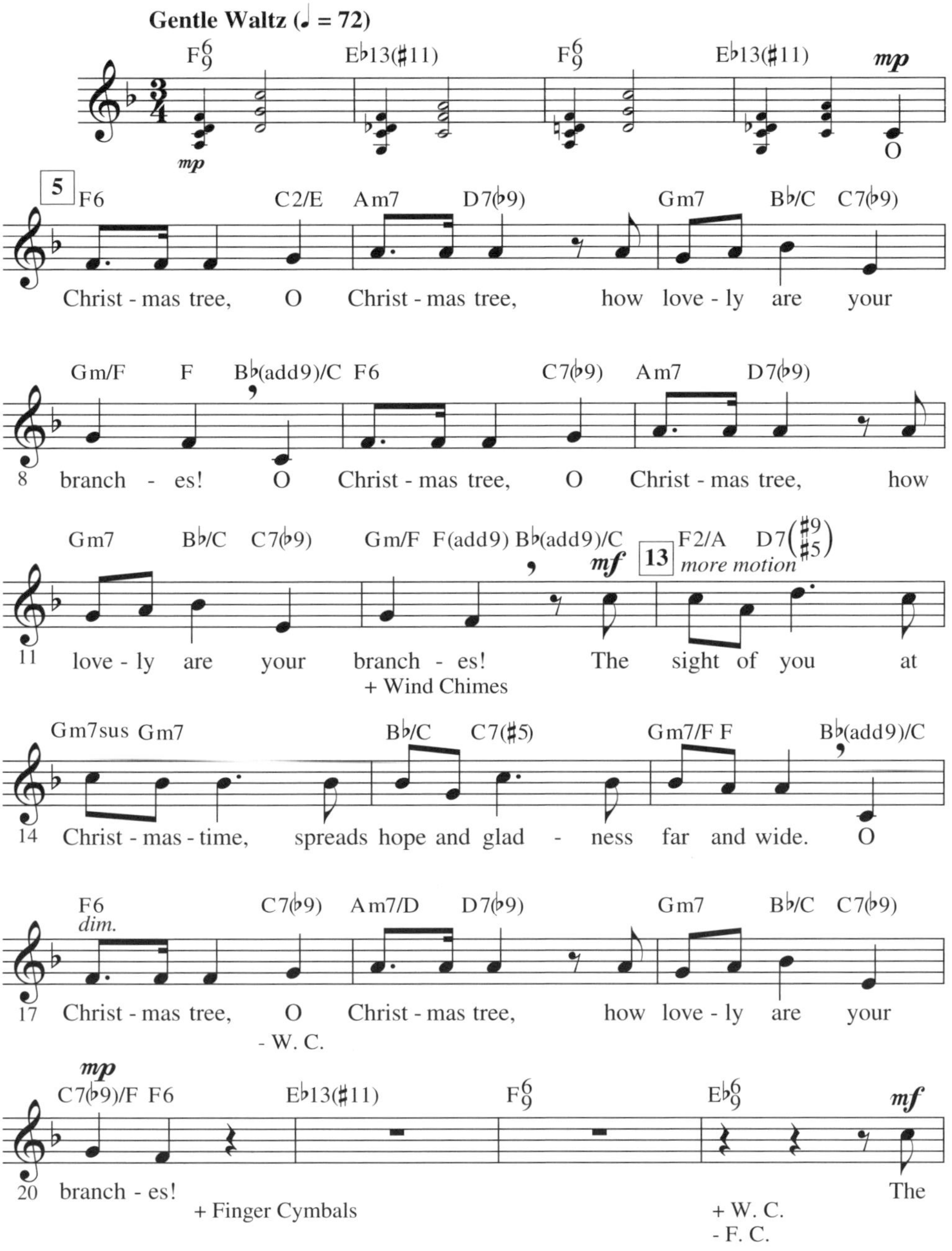

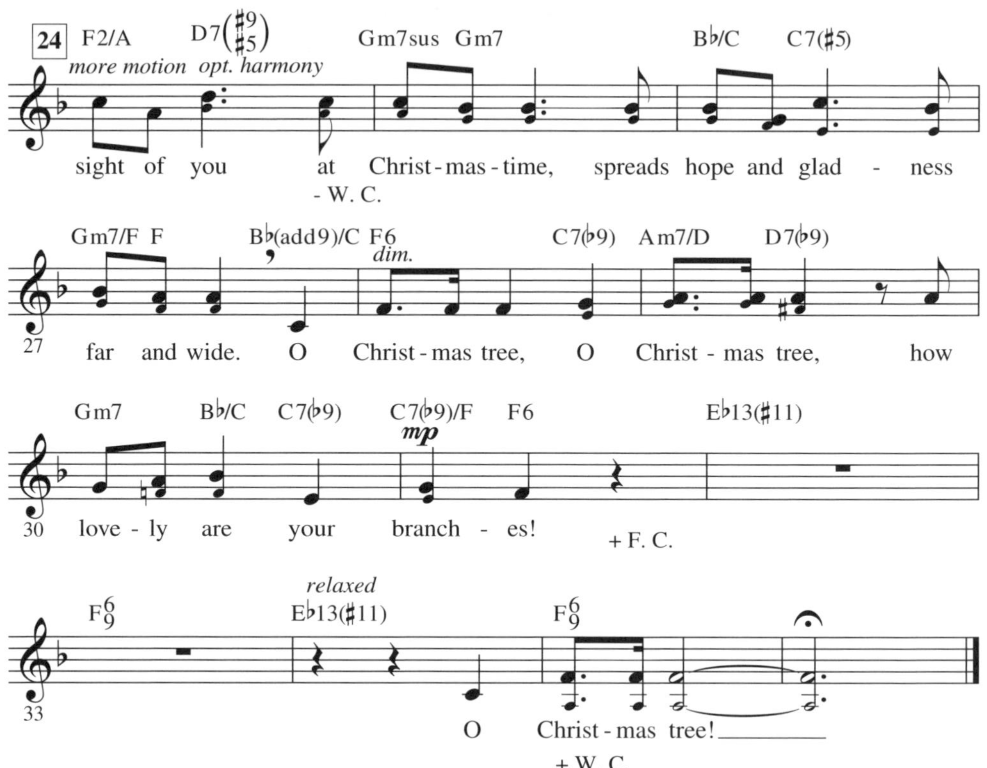

24 F2/A D7(#9 #5) Gm7sus Gm7 Bb/C C7(#5)
more motion opt. harmony
sight of you at Christ-mas-time, spreads hope and glad - ness
- W. C.
Gm7/F F Bb(add9)/C F6 C7(b9) Am7/D D7(b9)
dim.
27 far and wide. O Christ-mas tree, O Christ - mas tree, how
Gm7 Bb/C C7(b9) C7(b9)/F F6 Eb13(#11)
mp
30 love - ly are your branch - es! + F. C.
relaxed
F6/9 Eb13(#11) F6/9
33 O Christ - mas tree! + W. C.

Mickey's Caroling Book – Singer   27

mf
28 E5
27 3. God and man to - day be - come close-ly joined as
B5
30 flute and drum. Let the joy - ous tune play
E5 B5
33 on! Tu - re - lu - re - lu, pat - a - pat - a - pan. As the
E5 B5
36 in - stru - ments you play, we will sing, this Christ - mas
39 Ending
E5
6
Day.

Pat-a-Pan
(Willie, Take Your Little Drum)

SOPRANO METALLOPHONE

Words and Music by
BERNARD de la MONNOYE
Arranged by TOM ANDERSON

Mickey's Caroling Book – Singer   29

Pat-a-Pan
(Willie, Take Your Little Drum)

Pat-a-Pan
(Willie, Take Your Little Drum)

Pat-a-Pan
(Willie, Take Your Little Drum)

Silent Night

Words by JOSEPH MOHR
Music by FRANZ GRUBER
Arranged by TOM ANDERSON

more motion
29 C   Cmaj7   C6   C   Dm7/G
mf
3. Si - lent night,   ho - ly night,   Son of
+ Descant/Recorder
G9   C(add9)   Gm7/C   C9   37 F(add9)   C/E Dm7   G9
34 God,   love's   pure light;____   ra - diant beams__ from
+ Sus. Cym.
C   Dm/G C   C7   F(add9)   F6/9   C(add9)
39 Thy   ho - ly   face,   with   the   dawn   of re - deem - ing
45 Dm7   Dm7/G   G/F   C2/E   Am7
44 grace,   Je - sus, Lord,   at Thy   birth,____
+ Sus. Cym.
C/G   Dm7   G9   C(add9)
dim.   slight rit.   mp
49 Je - sus,   Lord   at Thy   birth.
+ W. C.

Silent Night

11/23

Up on the Housetop

Words and Music by B. R. HANDY
Arranged by TOM ANDERSON

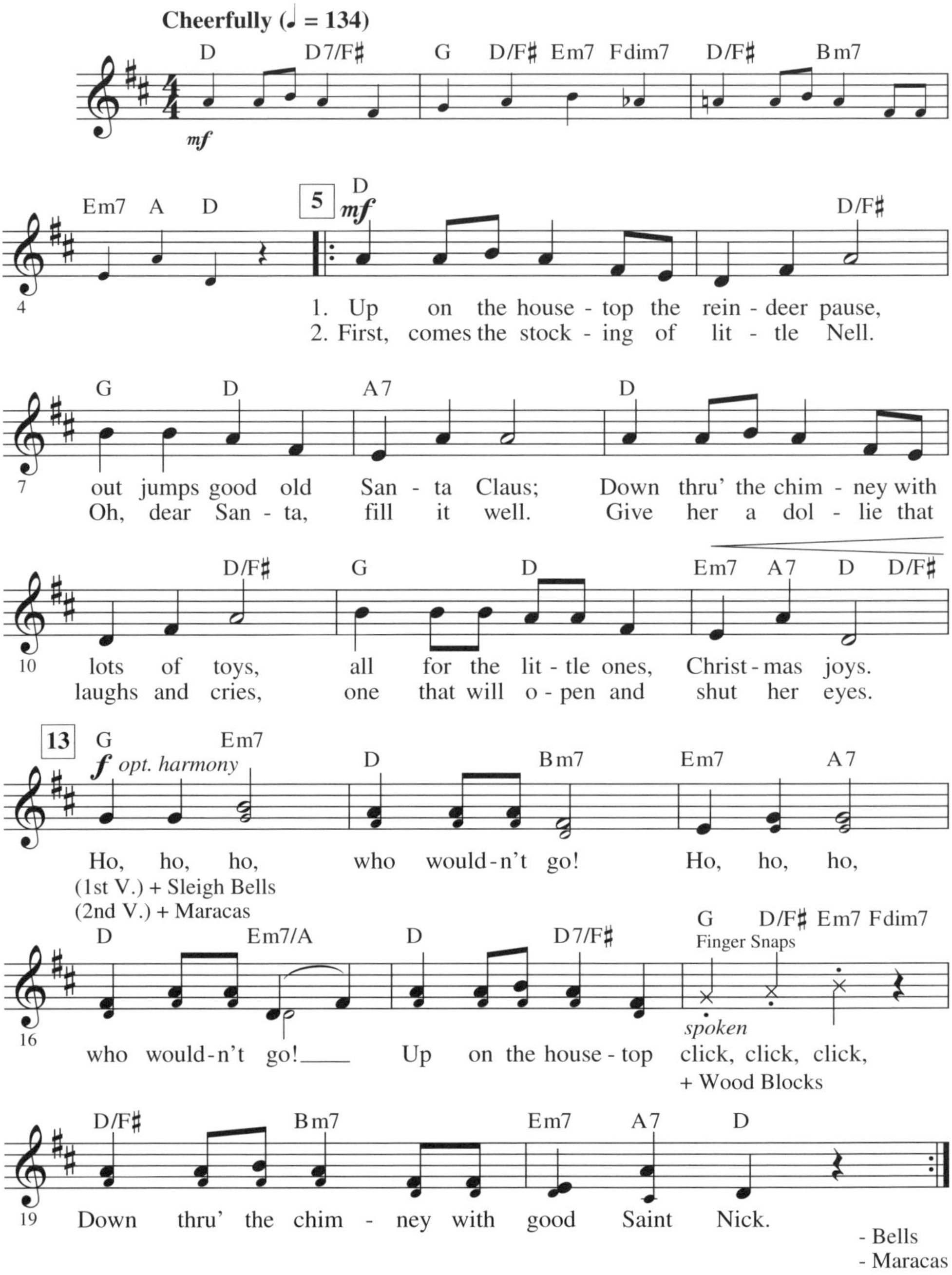

21
mf
D
D/F#
3. Next, comes the stock - ing of lit - tle Will;
G
D
A7
23
Oh, just see what a glo - rious fill!
D
D/F#
25
Here is a ham - mer and lots of tacks,
G
D
Em7
A7
D
Whip Crack
D/F#
27
al - so a ball and a whip that cracks.
29
f
G
Em7
D
Bm7
Ho, ho, ho, who would - n't go!
+ S. B. and Mar.
Em7
A7
D
Em7/A
31
Ho, ho, ho, who would - n't go!
Finger Snaps
D
D7/F#
G
D/F#
Em7
Fdim7
33
spoken
Up on the house - top click, click, click,
+ W. B.
D/F#
Bm7
Em7
A7
D
Whip Crack
N.C.
35
Down thru' the chim - ney with good Saint Nick.

We Wish You a Merry Christmas

Traditional English Carol
Arranged by TOM ANDERSON

22
G   G/B   C   C/B   A7sus   A7
wish   you   a   mer - ry   Christ - mas,   We   wish   you   a   mer - ry
+ Tri./F. C., H. D., Tamb.

D   D/C   B7sus   B7   Em   G/B
25
Christ - mas,   We   wish   you   a   mer - ry   Christ - mas,   and   a
- Tri./F. C.
- H. D.
- Tamb.

C6   Am7 cresc.   Am7/D   D9
28
hap   -   py   New

ff G   G2/B   C   Am7   D9   G6/9
32
Year!
+ Tri./F. C., H. D., Tamb.

We Wish You a Merry Christmas

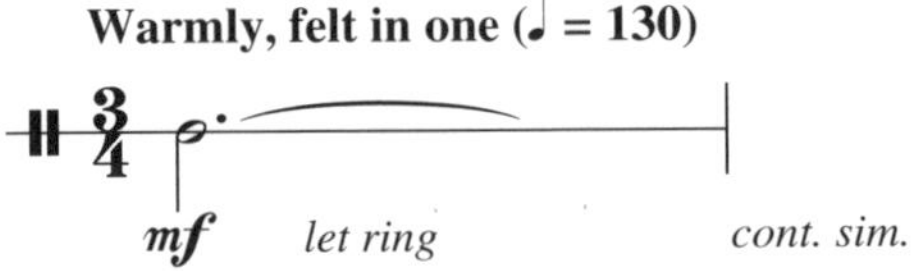

We Wish You a Merry Christmas

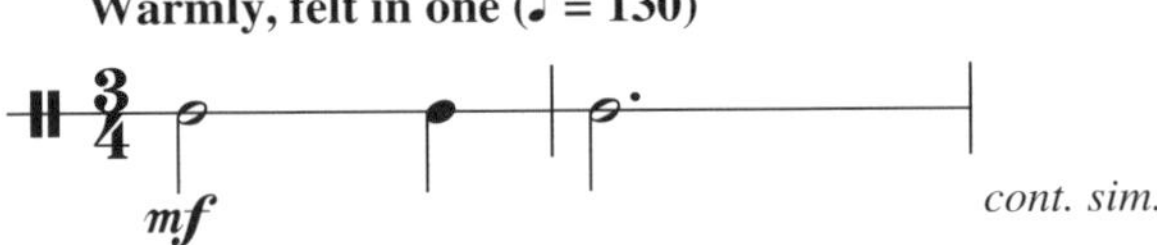

We Wish You a Merry Christmas

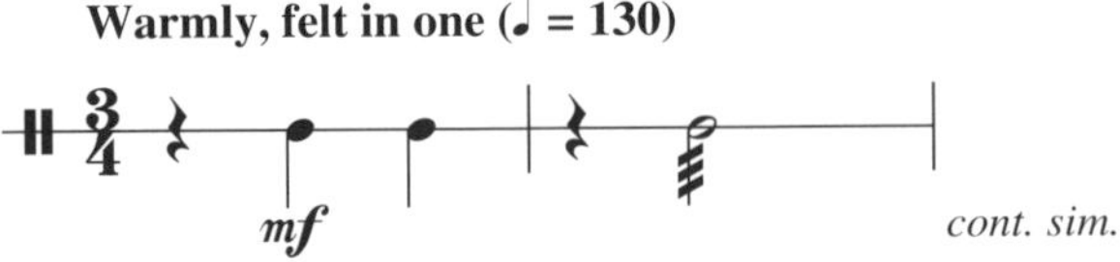

Disney Mickey's Caroling Book

HOLIDAY FUN WITH MICKEY AND HIS FRIENDS

Table of Contents

No part of this publication may be reproduced in any form or by any means without the prior written permission of the Publisher.

7777 W. BLUEMOUND RD. P.O. BOX 13819 MILWAUKEE, WI 53213

Visit Hal Leonard Online at
www.halleonard.com

Angels We Have Heard on High

Traditional French Carol
Arranged by TOM ANDERSON

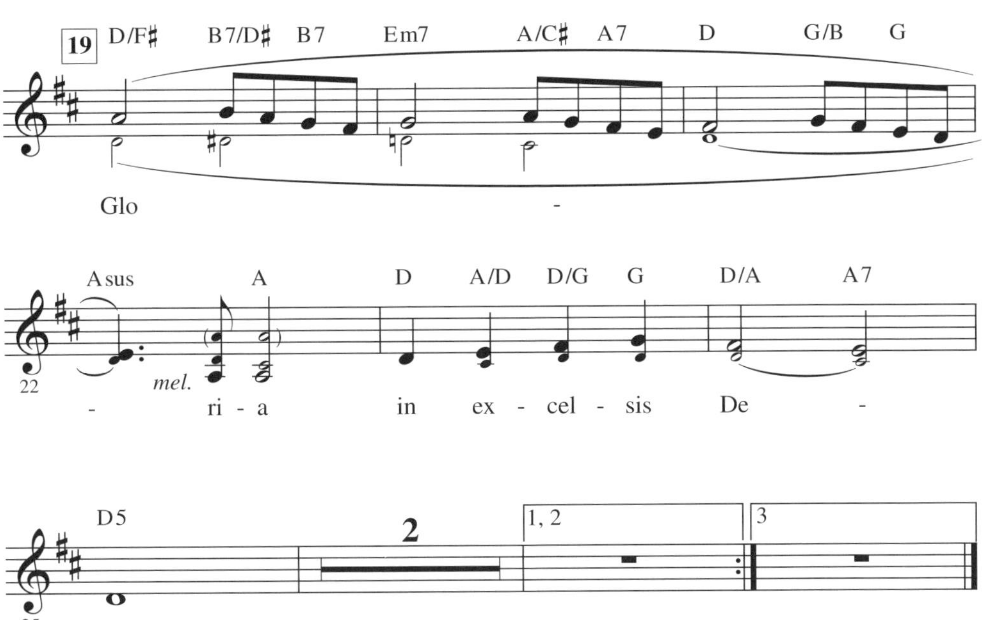
19
D/F# B7/D# B7 Em7 A/C# A7 D G/B G
Glo -
Asus A D A/D D/G G D/A A7
mel.
- ri - a in ex - cel - sis De -
D5
2
1, 2
3
o.

Angels We Have Heard on High

HAND DRUM

Traditional French Carol
Arranged by TOM ANDERSON

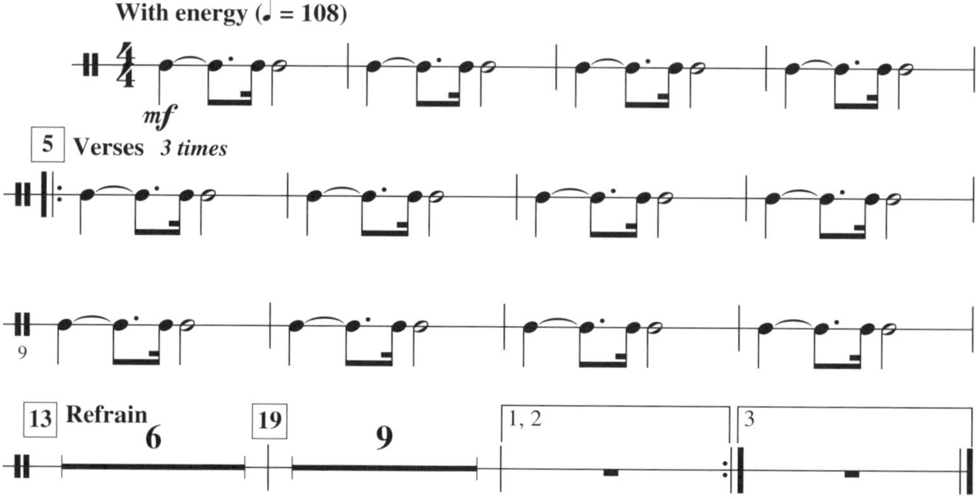

Angels We Have Heard on High

FINGER CYMBALS

Traditional French Carol
Arranged by TOM ANDERSON

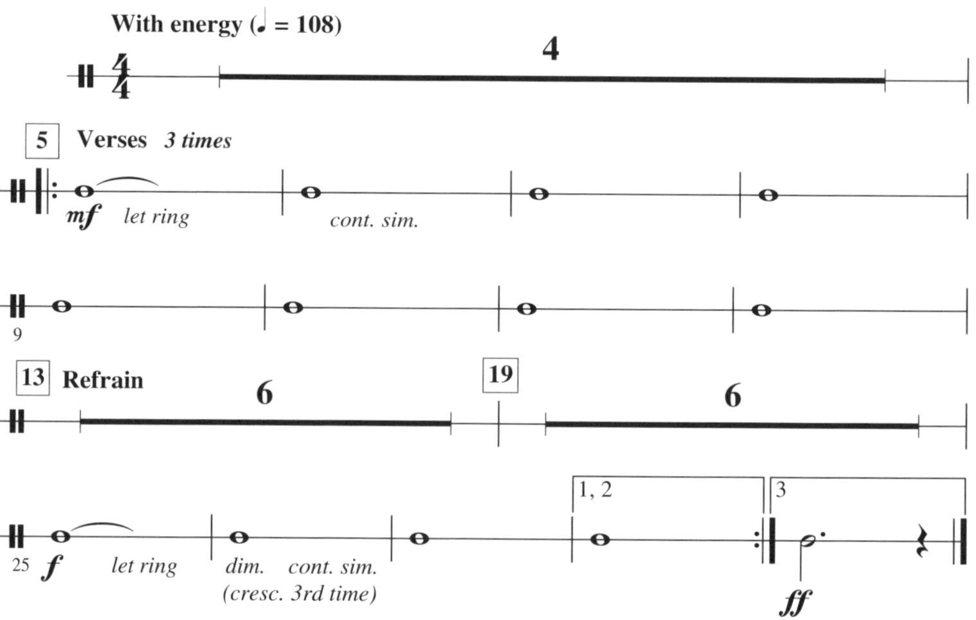

Angels We Have Heard on High

BASS DRUM

Traditional French Carol
Arranged by TOM ANDERSON

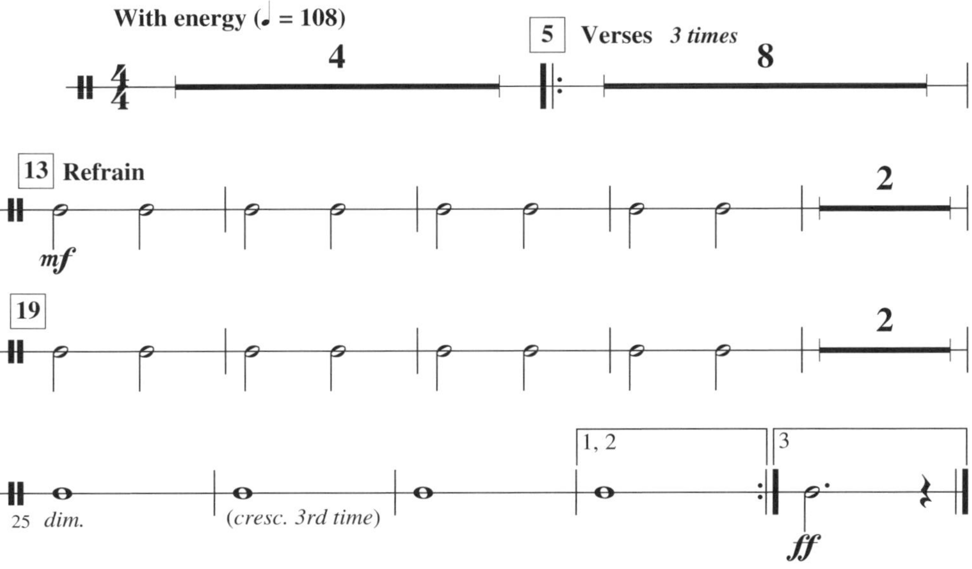

Angels We Have Heard on High

SUSPENDED CYMBAL

Traditional French Carol
Arranged by TOM ANDERSON

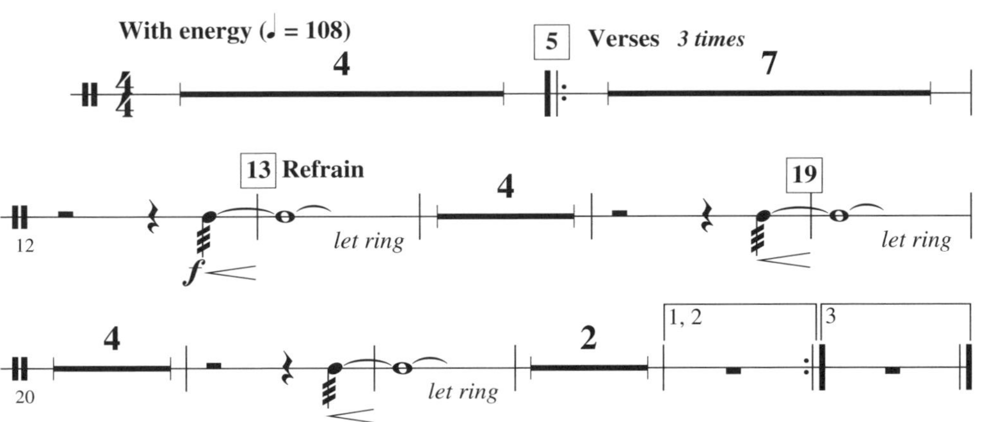

Angels We Have Heard on High

Away in a Manger

Music by JAMES R. MURRAY
Words, Stanza 1, 2, Anonymous
Stanza 3, JOHN THOMAS McFARLAND
Arranged by TOM ANDERSON

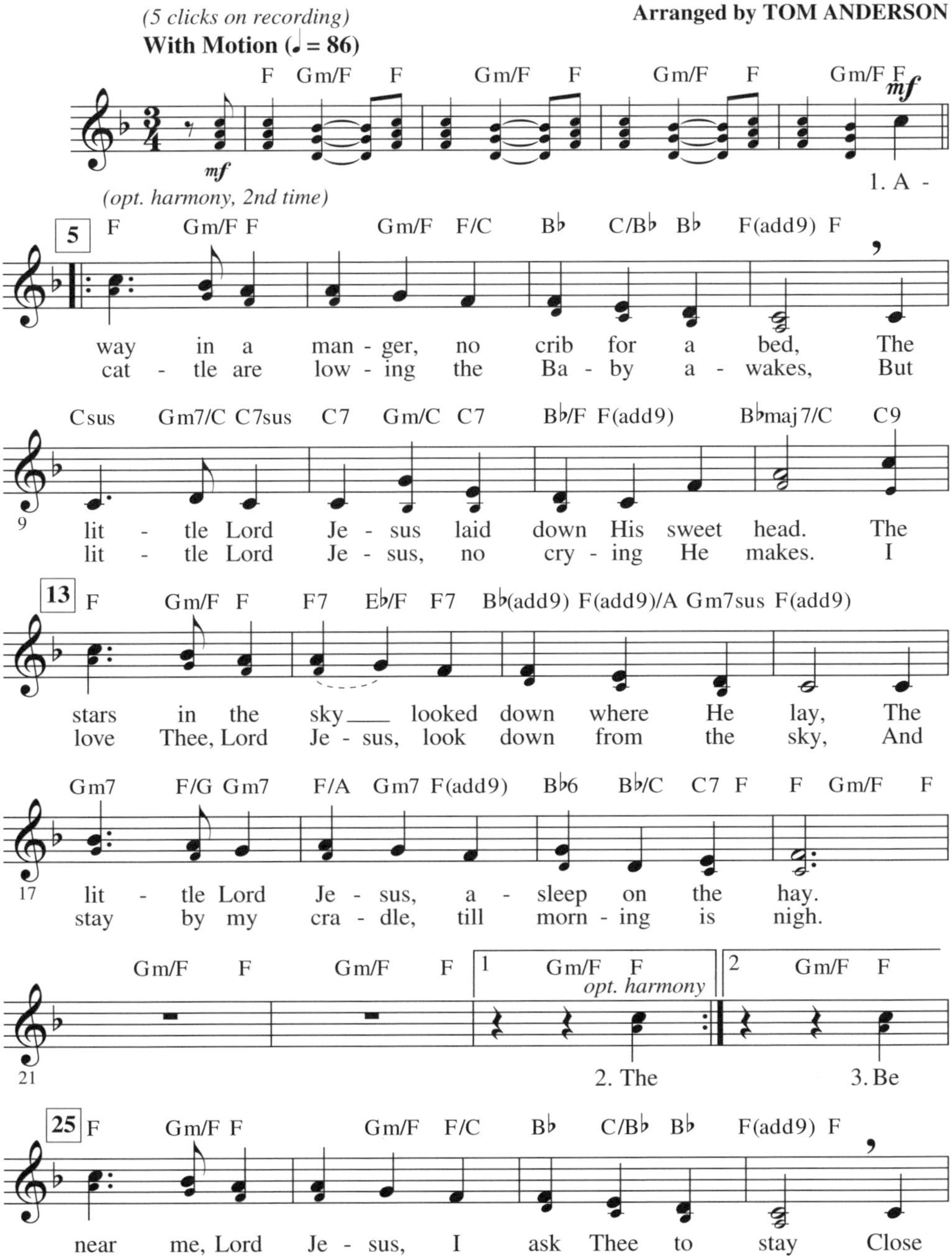

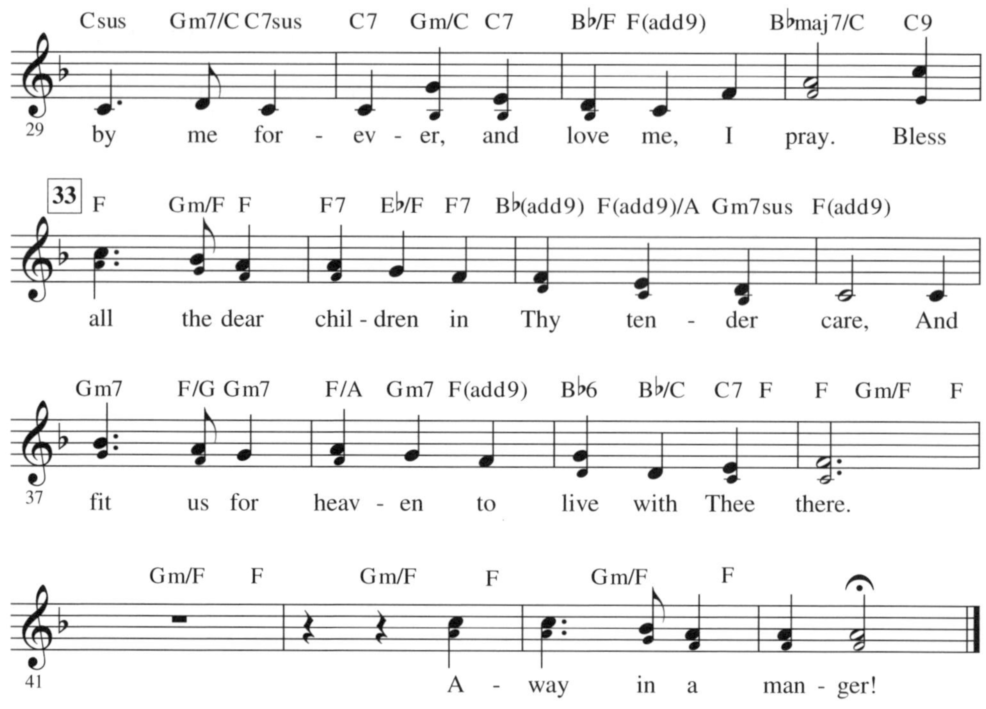

Csus   Gm7/C C7sus   C7   Gm/C C7   Bb/F F(add9)   Bbmaj7/C   C9
by   me   for - ev - er,   and   love   me,   I   pray.   Bless
33   F   Gm/F F   F7   Eb/F F7   Bb(add9) F(add9)/A Gm7sus   F(add9)
all   the dear   chil - dren   in   Thy   ten - der   care,   And
Gm7   F/G Gm7   F/A Gm7 F(add9)   Bb6   Bb/C   C7 F   F Gm/F   F
fit   us   for   heav - en   to   live   with   Thee   there.
Gm/F   F   Gm/F   F   Gm/F   F
A - way   in   a   man - ger!

Away in a Manger

25
let ring
cont. sim.
let ring
cont. sim.
let ring
cont. sim.
33
30
35
40
let ring
let ring
let ring

Away in a Manger

SUSPENDED CRASH CYMBAL

Music by JAMES R. MURRAY
Words, Stanza 1, 2, Anonymous
Stanza 3, JOHN THOMAS McFARLAND
Arranged by TOM ANDERSON

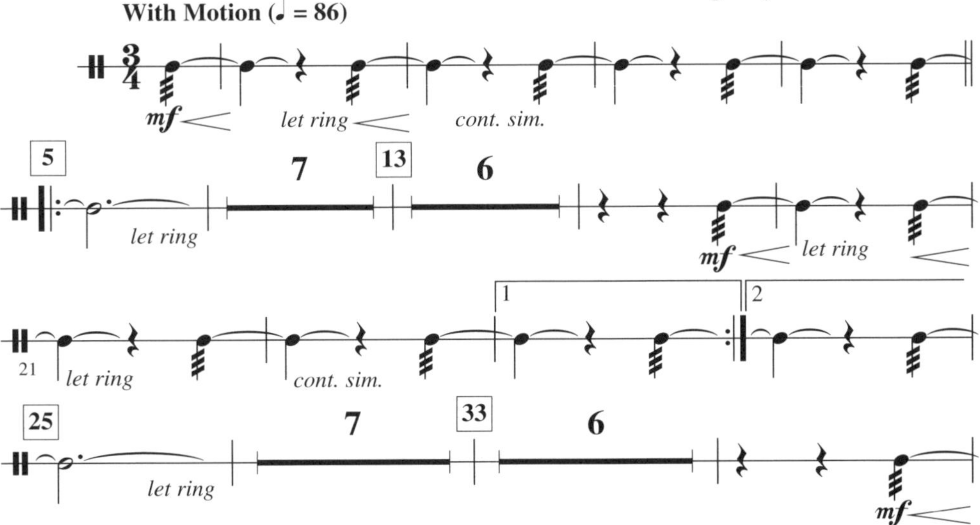

Away in a Manger

TIMPANI or TOM TOMS

Music by JAMES R. MURRAY
Words, Stanza 1, 2, Anonymous
Stanza 3, JOHN THOMAS McFARLAND
Arranged by TOM ANDERSON

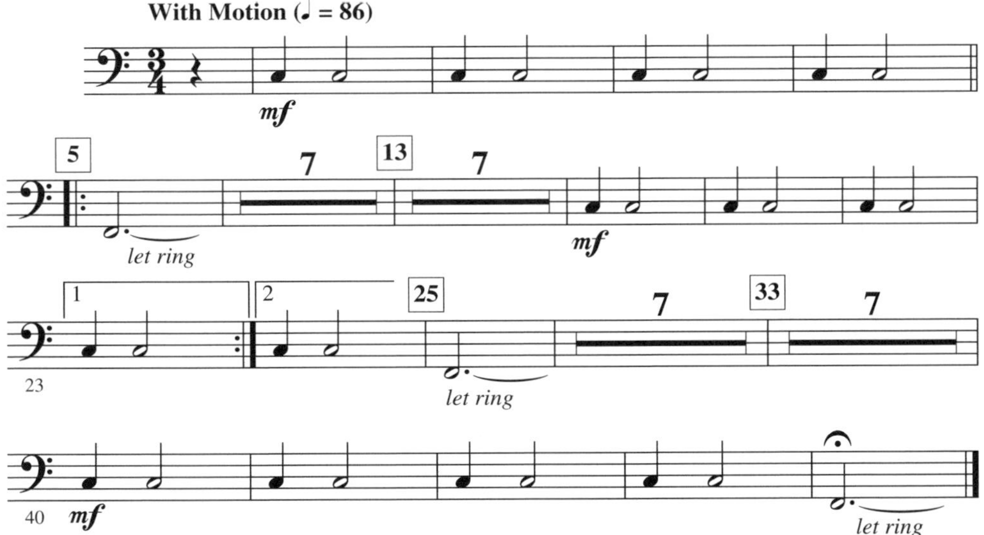

Deck the Halls

Traditional Welsh Carol
Arranged by TOM ANDERSON

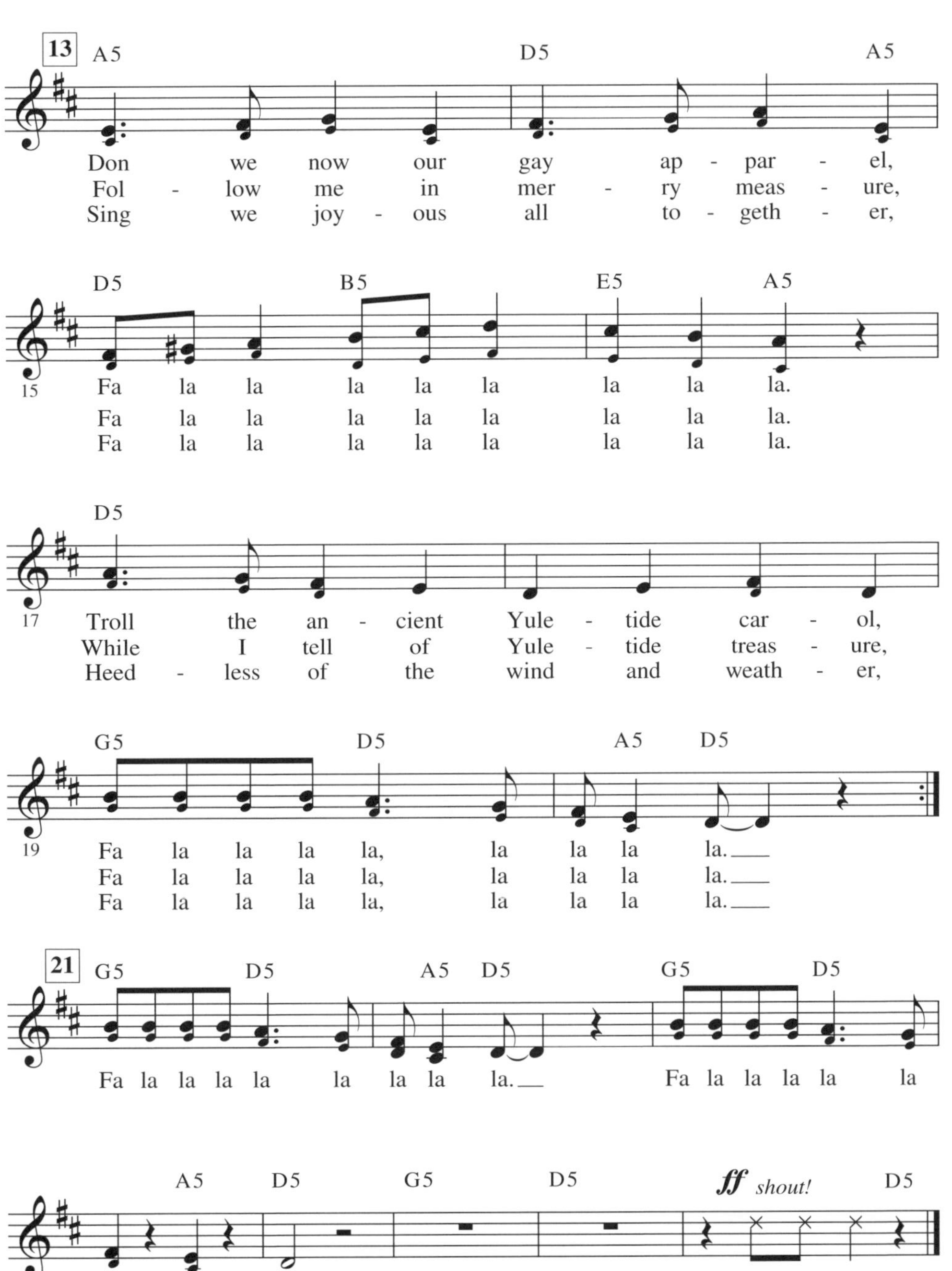

13
A5   D5   A5
Don we now our gay ap - par - el,
Fol - low me in mer - ry meas - ure,
Sing we joy - ous all to - geth - er,
D5   B5   E5   A5
15
Fa la la la la la la la la.
Fa la la la la la la la la.
Fa la la la la la la la la.
D5
17
Troll the an - cient Yule - tide car - ol,
While I tell of Yule - tide treas - ure,
Heed - less of the wind and weath - er,
G5   D5   A5   D5
19
Fa la la la la, la la la la.___
Fa la la la la, la la la la.___
Fa la la la la, la la la la.___
21
G5   D5   A5   D5   G5   D5
Fa la la la la la la la la.___   Fa la la la la la
A5   D5   G5   D5   ff shout!   D5
24
la la la.   Deck the halls!

Deck the Halls

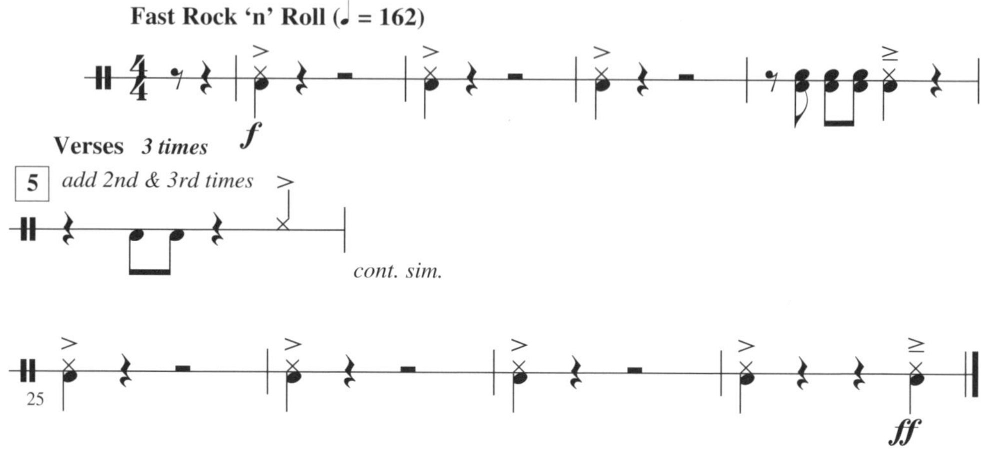

Deck the Halls

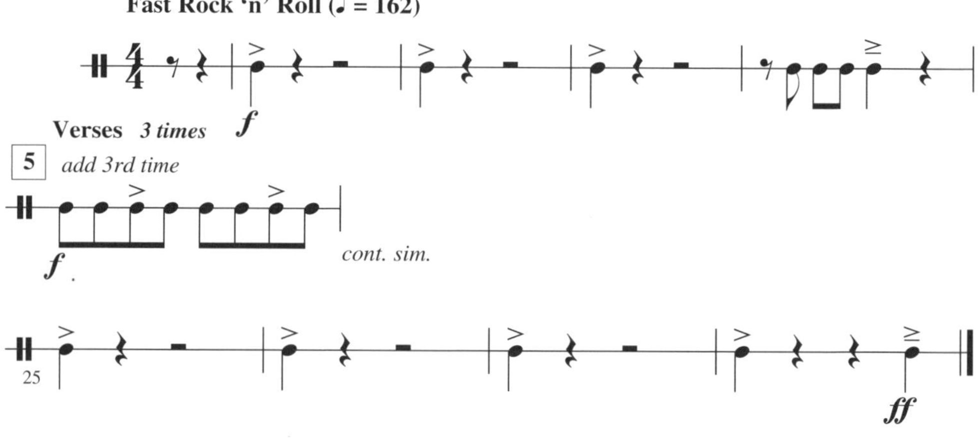

Here We Come A-Caroling

English Wassail Song
Arranged by TOM ANDERSON

Here We Come A-Caroling

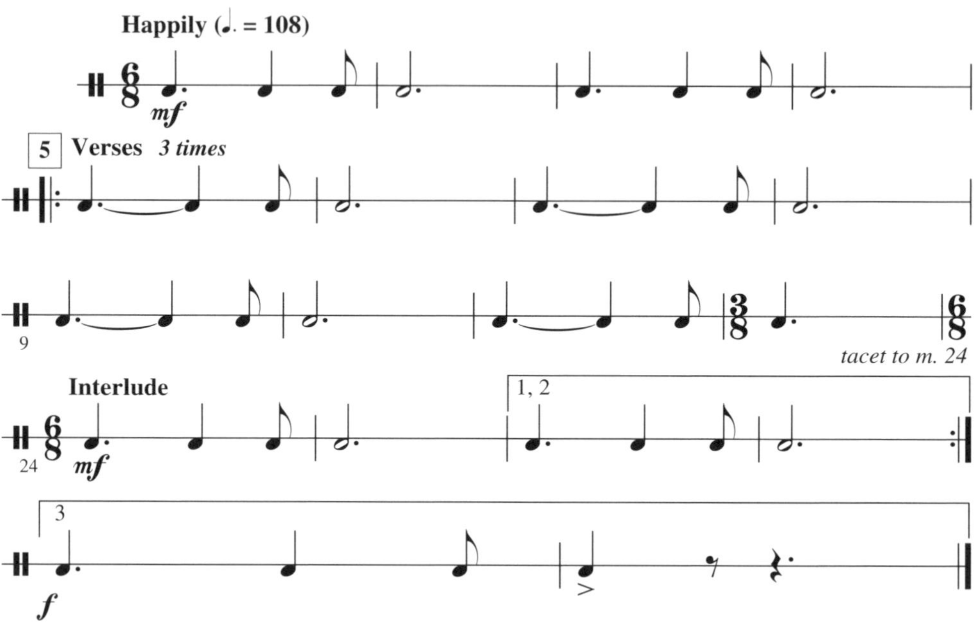

Here We Come A-Caroling

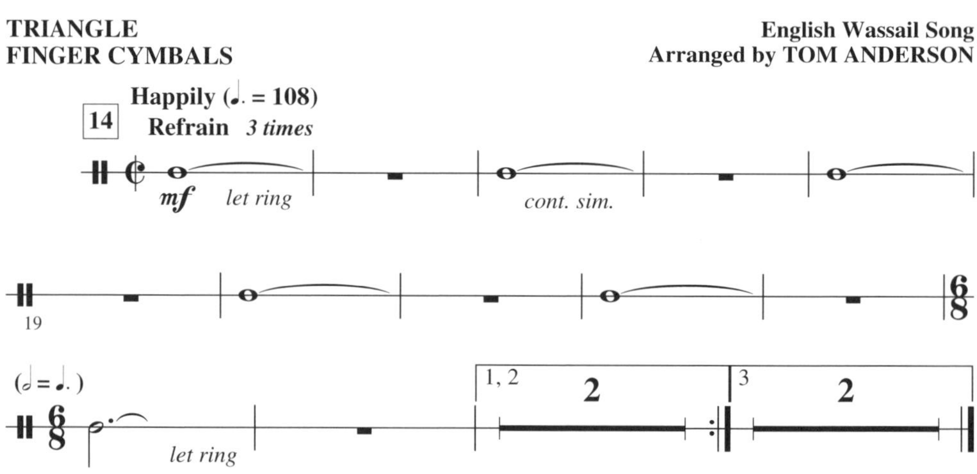

Jingle Bells

Words and Music by JAMES PIERPONT
Arranged by TOM ANDERSON

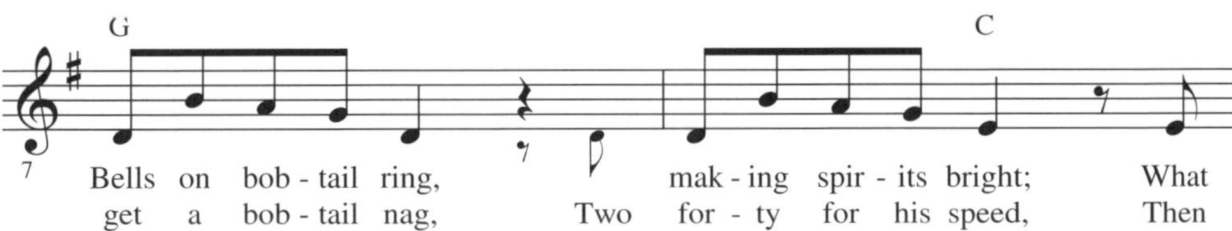

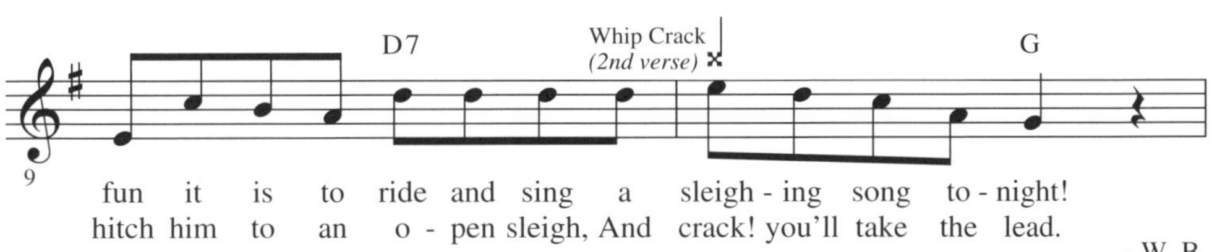

Refrain
11
G
opt. harmony
f
Jin - gle bells! Jin - gle bells! Jin - gle all the way!
+ Jingle Bells
C   G   A 7   A m7   D 7
13
Oh, what fun it is to ride in a one - horse o - pen sleigh!___
G
15
Jin - gle bells! Jin - gle bells! Jin - gle all the way!
1
C   G   D 7   G
17
Oh, what fun it is to ride in a one - horse o - pen sleigh!
- J. B.
2
D 7   G   Whip
shout!   N. C.
19
one - horse o - pen sleigh! Hey!

6/18

Jolly Old St. Nicholas

Traditional American Carol
Arranged by TOM ANDERSON

Straight Ahead Swing (♩ = 130)

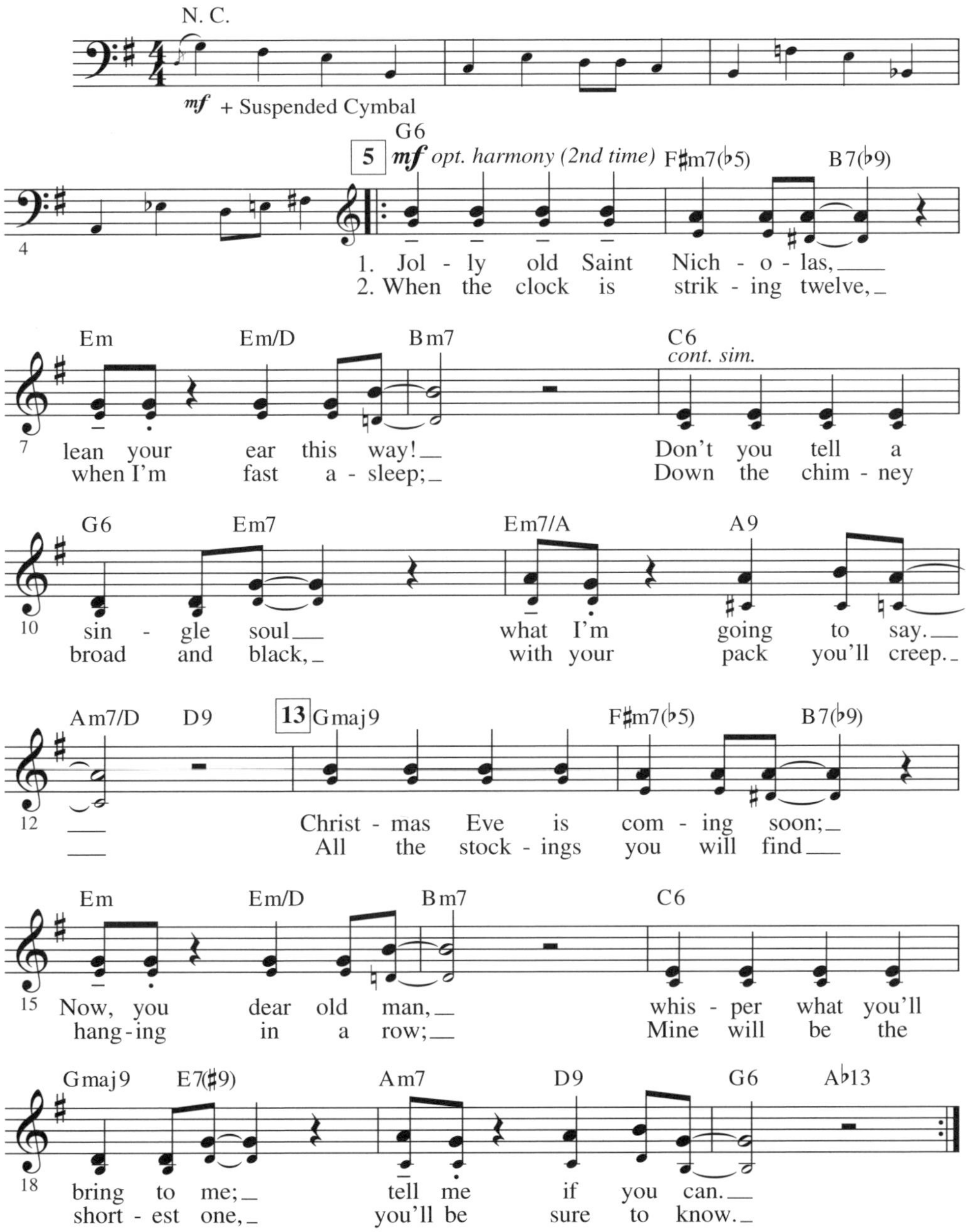

21 Recorder or Other Pitched Inst.
G6   F#m7(b5) B7(b9)   Em   Em/D   Bm7   C6   G6   Em7
mf
29
Em7/A   A9   Am7/D   D9   Gmaj9   F#m7(b5) B7(b9)   Em   Em/D
27
Bm7   C6   Gmaj9 E7(#9)   Am7   D9   G6   Ab13   - Recorder
32
37 G6   f   F#m7(b5)   B7(b9)   Em   Em/D   Bm7
3. John-ny wants a pair of skates,__ Su-sy wants a sled;__
+ Jingle Bells
C6   G6   Em7   Em7/A   A9
41
Nel-lie wants a pic-ture book;__ yel-low, blue and red.__
Am7/D   D9   45 Gmaj9   F#m7(b5)   B7(b9)
44   __   Now I think I'll leave to you__
Em   Em/D   Bm7   C6   Gmaj9 E7(#9)
47   what to give the rest;__ Choose for me, dear San-ta Claus,__
Am7   D9   G6   Bb13   53 Am7   D7(#9/#5)   cresc.   G6 E7(#9)
51   you will know the best.__ You will know the best.__
Am7   Am7/D D7(#9)   G6   2   N. C.
55   You will   know   the   best!______

Jolly Old St. Nicholas

Jolly Old St. Nicholas

Jolly Old St. Nicholas

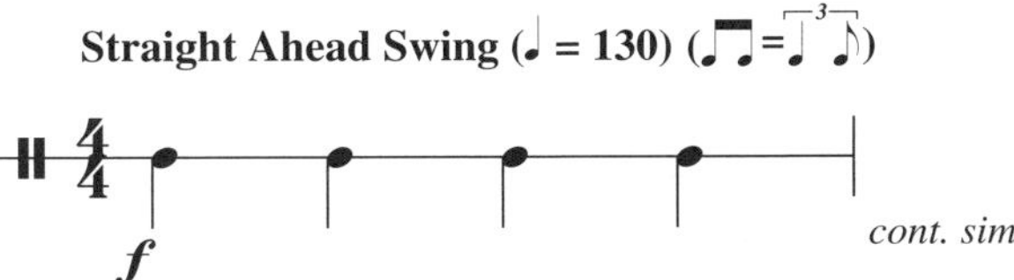

7/19

Joy to the World

Words by ISAAC WATTS
Music by GEORGE F. HANDEL
Arranged by TOM ANDERSON

(4-measure rhythm intro. on recording)

Mod. Gospel Shuffle (𝅗𝅥 = 86) (♫ = ♩♪ triplet)

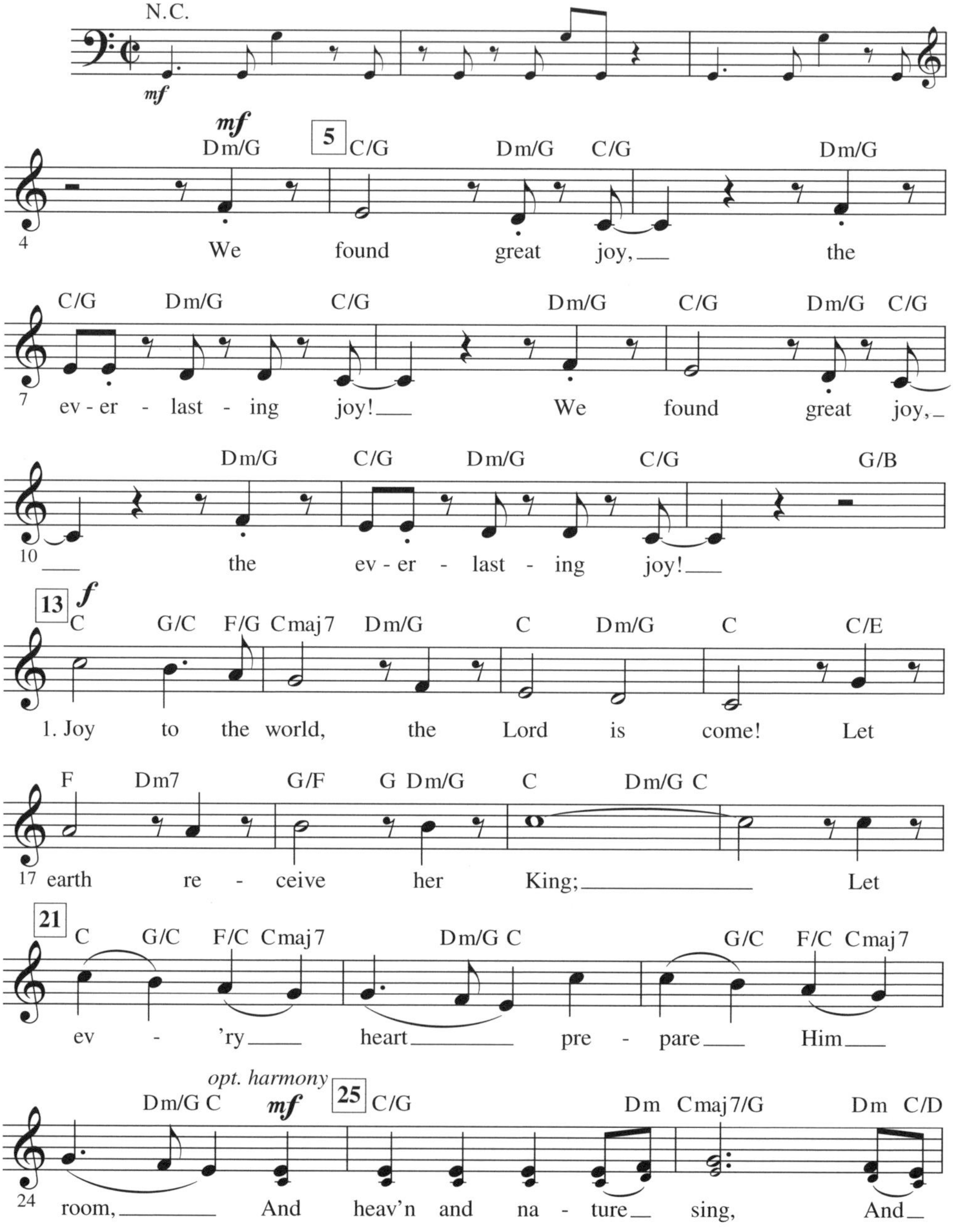

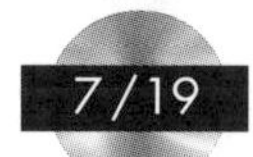

Dm7/G   C/D Dm7(♭5)/G Dm7(♭5)/A♭   Am7   Am7/G
27
heav'n   and   na - ture__   sing,   And__   heav'n__   and

F(add9)   C/E F2/A C/G   Dm/G   32 C   Dm/C   C   Dm/C
opt. small group We   found   great   joy, __
30
heav'n___   and   na - ture   sing.   the
mel.
+ Hand Claps on beat 2

C   Dm7(♭5)/C   C   Dm/C   C   Dm/C   C
34
ev - er - last - ing   joy!__   We   found   great   joy, _

Dm/C   C   Dm7(♭5)/C   C   G/B
37
__   the   ev - er - last - ing   joy!__
- Claps

40 f opt. harmony
C   G/C   F/G Cmaj7 Dm/G   C   Dm/G   C   C/E
2. He   rules   the   world   with   truth   and   grace,   And
mel.

F   Dm7   G/F   G Dm/G   C   Dm/G C
na - tions   prove_________
44 makes   the
We   found   great   joy!__   The

48 C   G/C   F/C Cmaj7   Dm/G C   G/C   F/C Cmaj7
glo - ries__   of ____   His   right - eous -

Dm/G C   mf 52 C/G   Dm Cmaj7/G   Dm C/D
51
ness,_______   And   won - ders   of   His__   love,   And__

Dm7/G
C/D Dm7(b5)/G Dm7(b5)/Ab
Am7
Am7/G
54
won - ders   of   His___ love,   And___ won - ders,

F(add9)   C/E F2/A
C/G
Dm/G
59 C
Dm/C   C
We   found   great   joy,___
57
won - ders   of   His   love.
mel.
+ Claps

Dm/C   C   Dm7(b5)/C   C   Dm/C
60
the   ev - er - last - ing   joy!___   We

C   Dm/C   C   Dm/C   C   Dm7(b5)/C   C
63 found   great   joy,___   the   ev - er - last - ing   joy!___

f Dm/C   67 C   Dm/C   C   Dm/C
build intensity
66 ___   We   found   great   joy,___   the
+ Tambourine on beat 2

C   Dm7(b5)/C   C   Dm/C   C   Dm/C   C
69 ev - er - last - ing   joy!___   We   found   great   joy,___

Dm/C   C   Dm7(b5)/C   C
72 ___   the   ev - er - last - ing   joy!___
ff

O Christmas Tree
(O Tannenbaum)

Traditional German Carol
Arranged by TOM ANDERSON

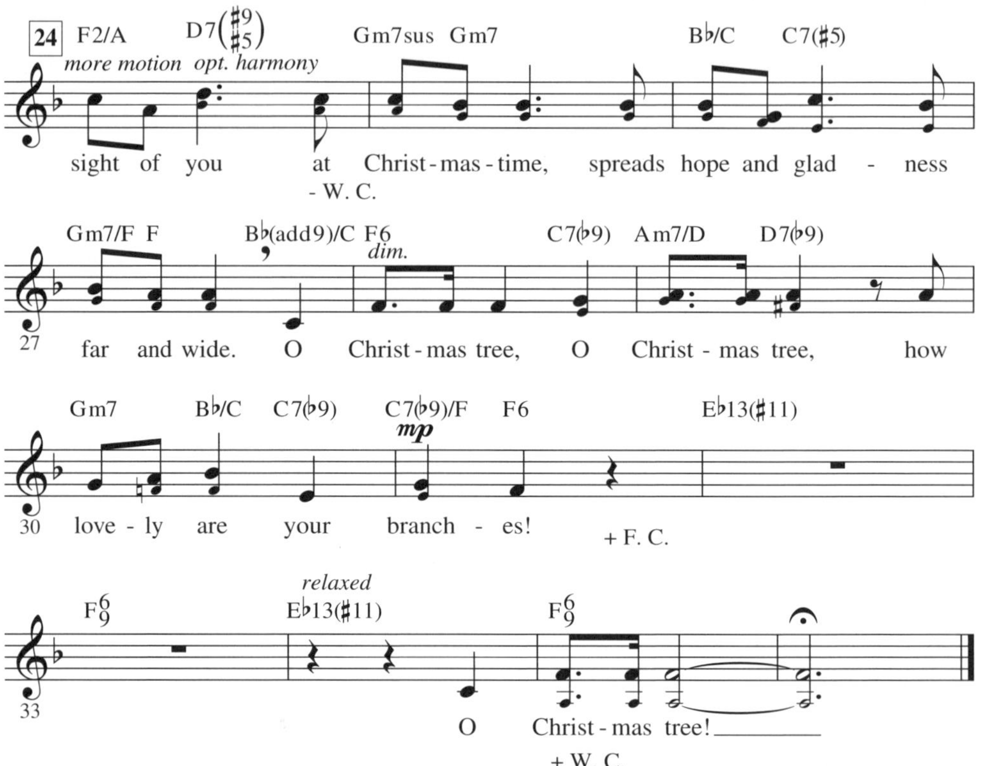

24 F2/A   D7(#9 #5)   Gm7sus Gm7   Bb/C   C7(#5)
more motion opt. harmony
sight of you   at Christ-mas-time,   spreads hope and glad - ness
- W. C.
Gm7/F F   Bb(add9)/C F6   C7(b9) Am7/D   D7(b9)
dim.
27 far and wide.   O   Christ-mas tree,   O   Christ - mas tree,   how
Gm7   Bb/C   C7(b9)   C7(b9)/F   F6   Eb13(#11)
mp
30 love - ly   are   your   branch - es!   + F. C.
relaxed
F6/9   Eb13(#11)   F6/9
33 O   Christ - mas tree!______
+ W. C.

Pat-a-Pan
(Willie, Take Your Little Drum)

Words and Music by
BERNARD de la MONNOYE
Arranged by TOM ANDERSON

mf
28 E5
27 3. God and man to - day be - come close-ly joined as
B5
30 flute and drum. Let the joy - ous tune play
E5 B5
33 on! Tu - re - lu - re - lu, pat - a - pat - a - pan. As the
E5 B5
36 in - stru - ments you play, we will sing, this Christ - mas
39 Ending
E5
6
Day.

Pat-a-Pan

(Willie, Take Your Little Drum)

Pat-a-Pan
(Willie, Take Your Little Drum)

ALTO METALLOPHONE

Pat-a-Pan
(Willie, Take Your Little Drum)

Pat-a-Pan
(Willie, Take Your Little Drum)

Silent Night

Words by JOSEPH MOHR
Music by FRANZ GRUBER
Arranged by TOM ANDERSON

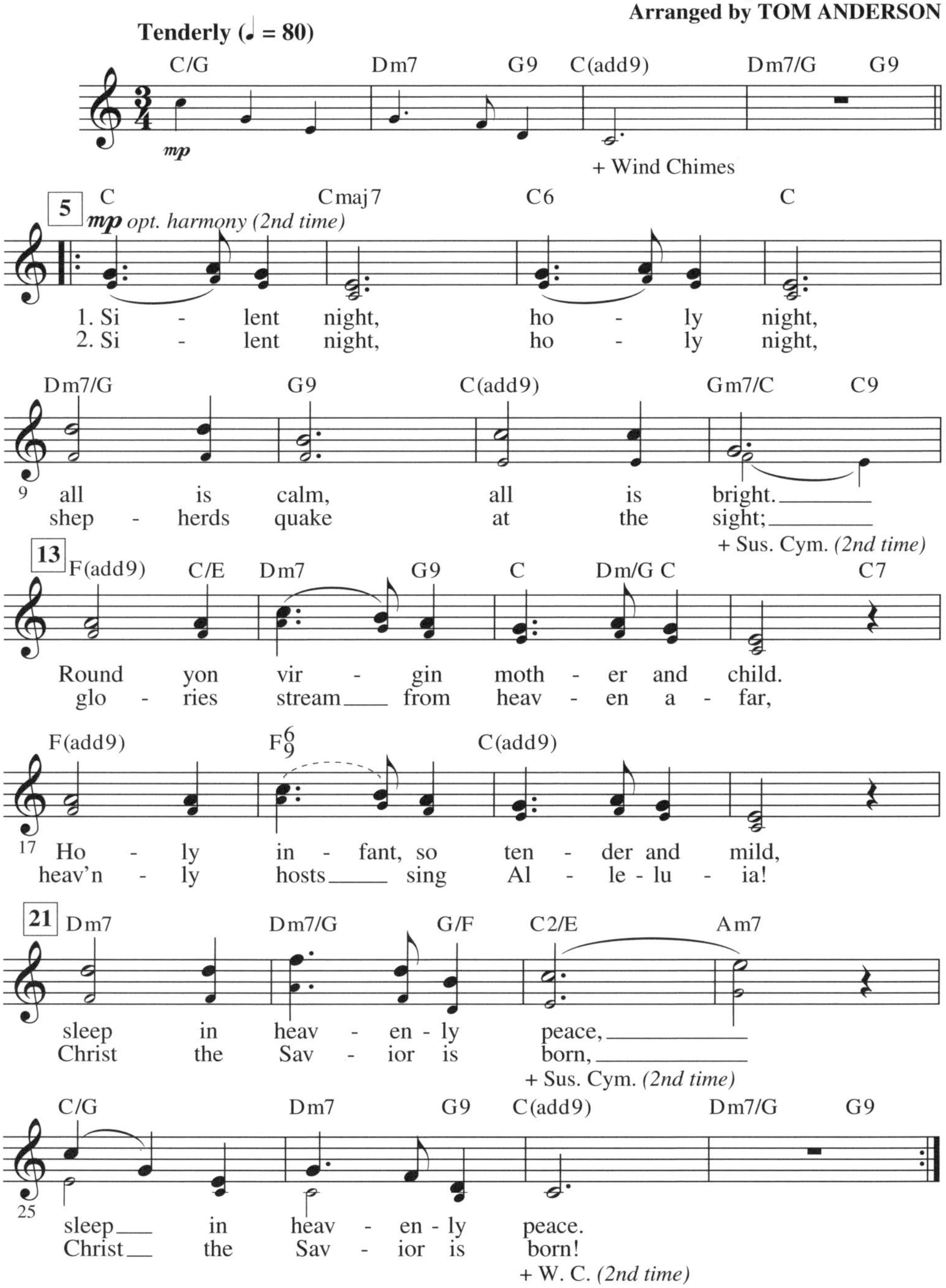

29 C more motion   Cmaj7   C6   C   Dm7/G
mf
3. Si - lent night,   ho - ly night,   Son of
+ Descant/Recorder
G9   C(add9)   Gm7/C   C9   37 F(add9)   C/E   Dm7   G9
34 God,   love's pure light;____   ra - diant beams__ from
+ Sus. Cym.
C   Dm/G   C   C7   F(add9)   F 6/9   C(add9)
39 Thy   ho - ly face,   with   the   dawn   of re - deem - ing
45 Dm7   Dm7/G   G/F   C2/E   Am7
44 grace,   Je - sus, Lord,   at Thy   birth,____
+ Sus. Cym.
C/G   Dm7   G9   C(add9)
dim.   slight rit.   mp
49 Je - sus,   Lord   at Thy   birth.
+ W. C.

Silent Night

11/23

Up on the Housetop

Words and Music by B. R. HANDY
Arranged by TOM ANDERSON

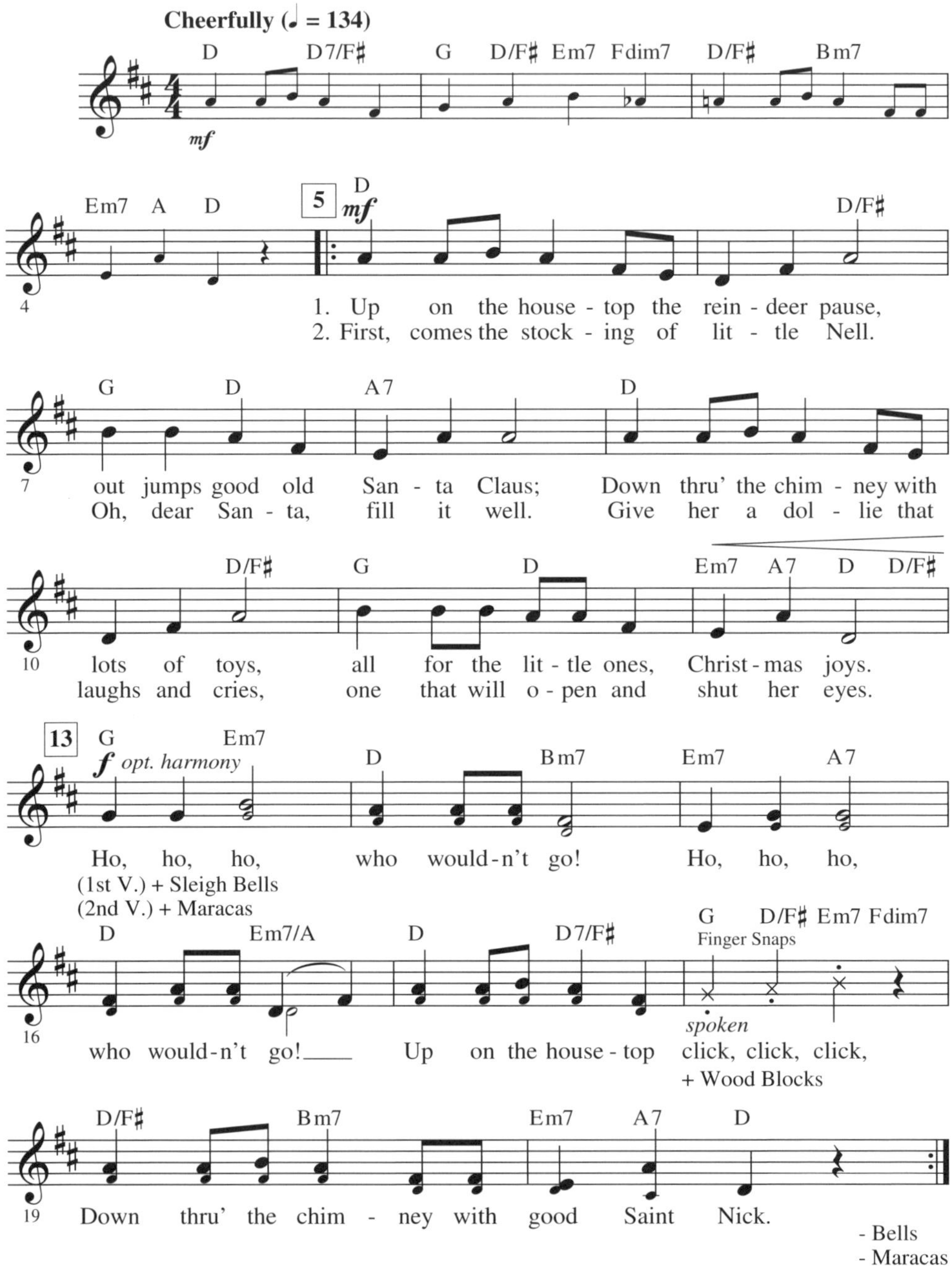

21
mf
D
D/F#
3. Next, comes the stock - ing of lit - tle Will;
G
D
A7
23
Oh, just see what a glo - rious fill!
D
D/F#
25
Here is a ham - mer and lots of tacks,
G
D
Em7
A7
D
Whip Crack
D/F#
27
al - so a ball and a whip that cracks.
29
f
G
Em7
D
Bm7
Ho, ho, ho, who would - n't go!
+ S. B. and Mar.
Em7
A7
D
Em7/A
31
Ho, ho, ho, who would - n't go!
Finger Snaps
D
D7/F#
G
D/F#
Em7
Fdim7
33
Up on the house - top click, click, click,
spoken
+ W. B.
D/F#
Bm7
Em7
A7
D
Whip Crack
N.C.
35
Down thru' the chim - ney with good Saint Nick.

We Wish You a Merry Christmas

Traditional English Carol
Arranged by TOM ANDERSON

wish you a mer - ry Christ - mas, We wish you a mer - ry
+ Tri./F. C., H. D., Tamb.
Christ - mas, We wish you a mer - ry Christ - mas, and a
- Tri./F. C.
- H. D.
- Tamb.
hap - py New
Year!
+ Tri./F. C., H. D., Tamb.

We Wish You a Merry Christmas

We Wish You a Merry Christmas

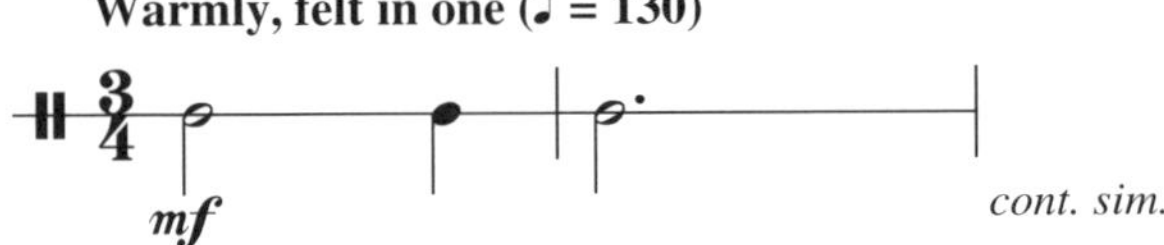

We Wish You a Merry Christmas

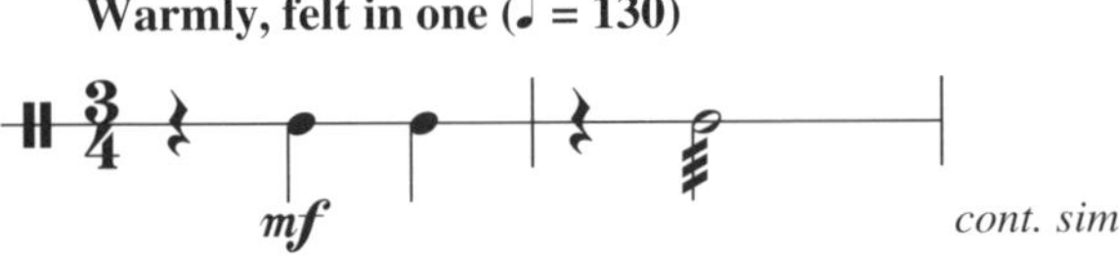

Disney Mickey's Caroling Book

HOLIDAY FUN WITH MICKEY AND HIS FRIENDS

Table of Contents

Visit Hal Leonard Online at
www.halleonard.com

1/13

Angels We Have Heard on High

Traditional French Carol
Arranged by TOM ANDERSON

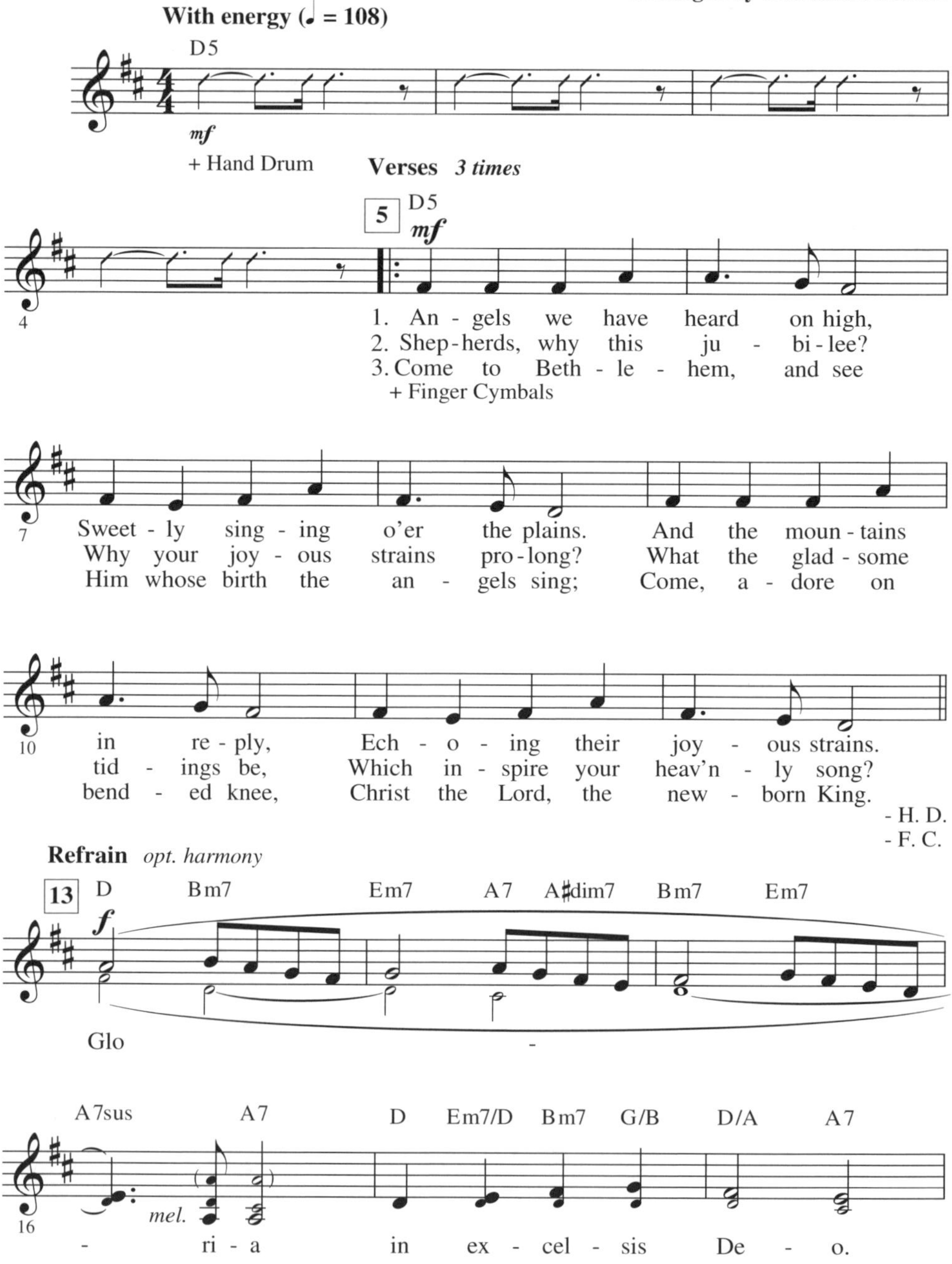

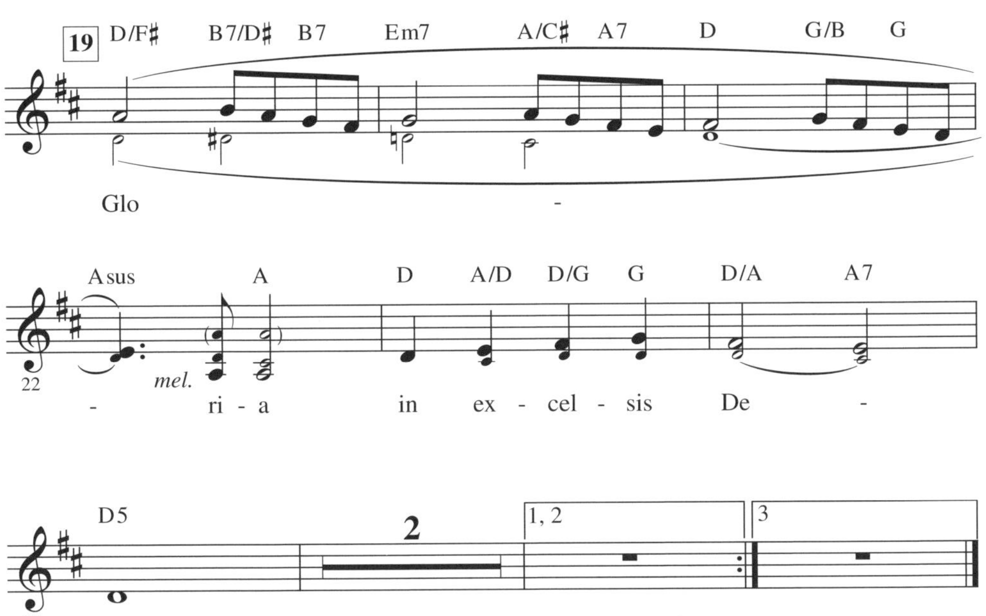

19
D/F♯   B7/D♯   B7   Em7   A/C♯   A7   D   G/B   G
Glo -

Asus   A   D   A/D   D/G   G   D/A   A7
mel.
- ri - a   in   ex - cel - sis   De -

D5
2   1, 2   3
o.

Angels We Have Heard on High

HAND DRUM

Traditional French Carol
Arranged by TOM ANDERSON

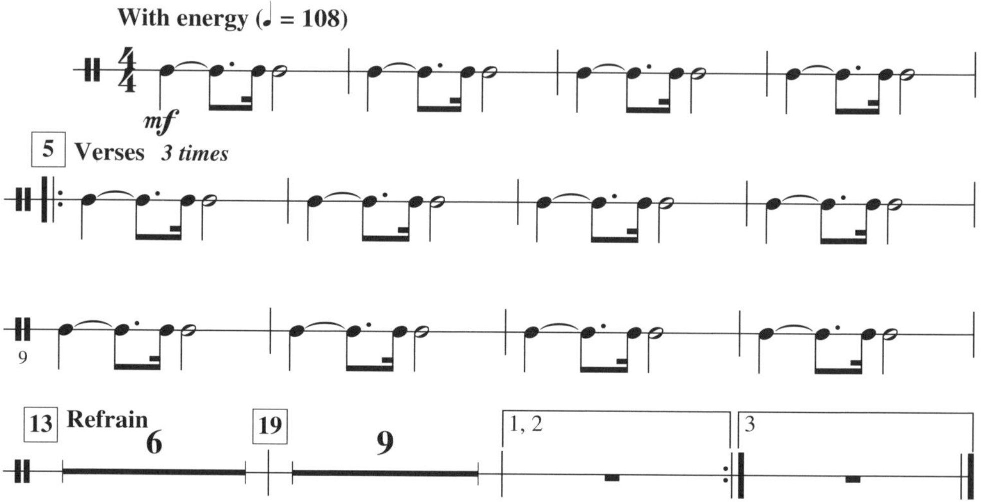

Angels We Have Heard on High

FINGER CYMBALS

Traditional French Carol
Arranged by TOM ANDERSON

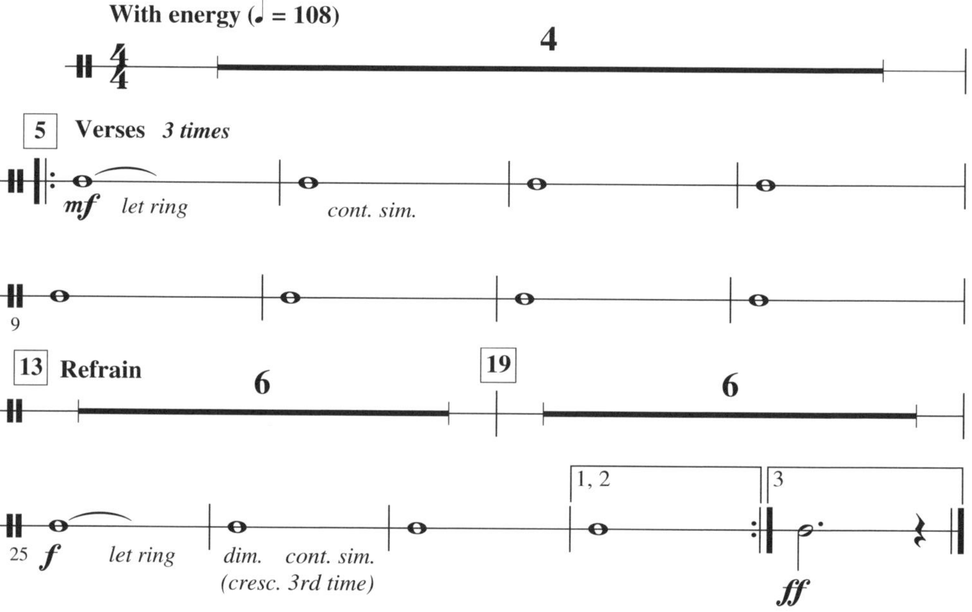

Angels We Have Heard on High

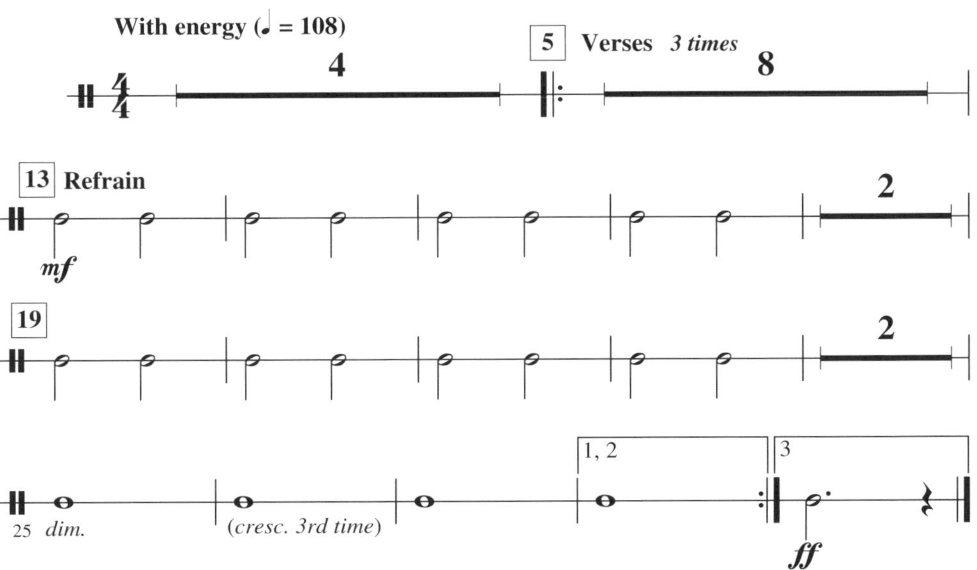

Angels We Have Heard on High

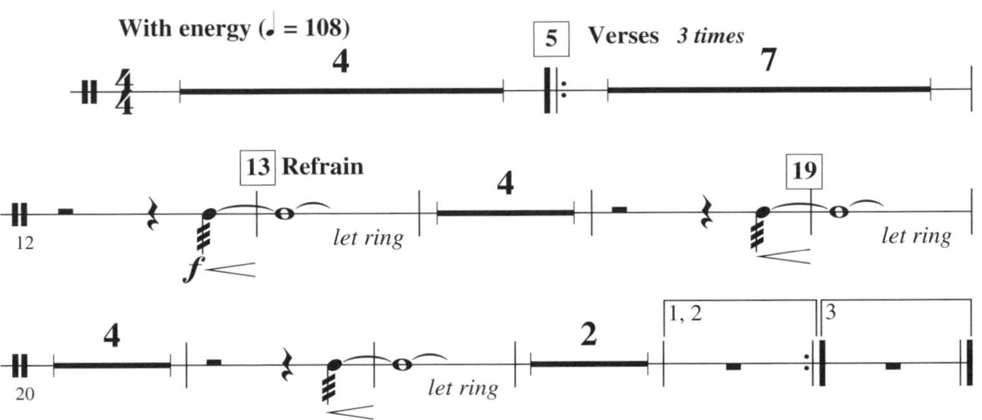

Angels We Have Heard on High

ORFF INSTRUMENTS

Traditional French Carol
Arranged by TOM ANDERSON

With energy ($\quarternote$ = 108)

Away in a Manger

Music by JAMES R. MURRAY
Words, Stanza 1, 2, Anonymous
Stanza 3, JOHN THOMAS McFARLAND
Arranged by TOM ANDERSON

Copyright © 2012 by HAL LEONARD CORPORATION
International Copyright Secured   All Rights Reserved

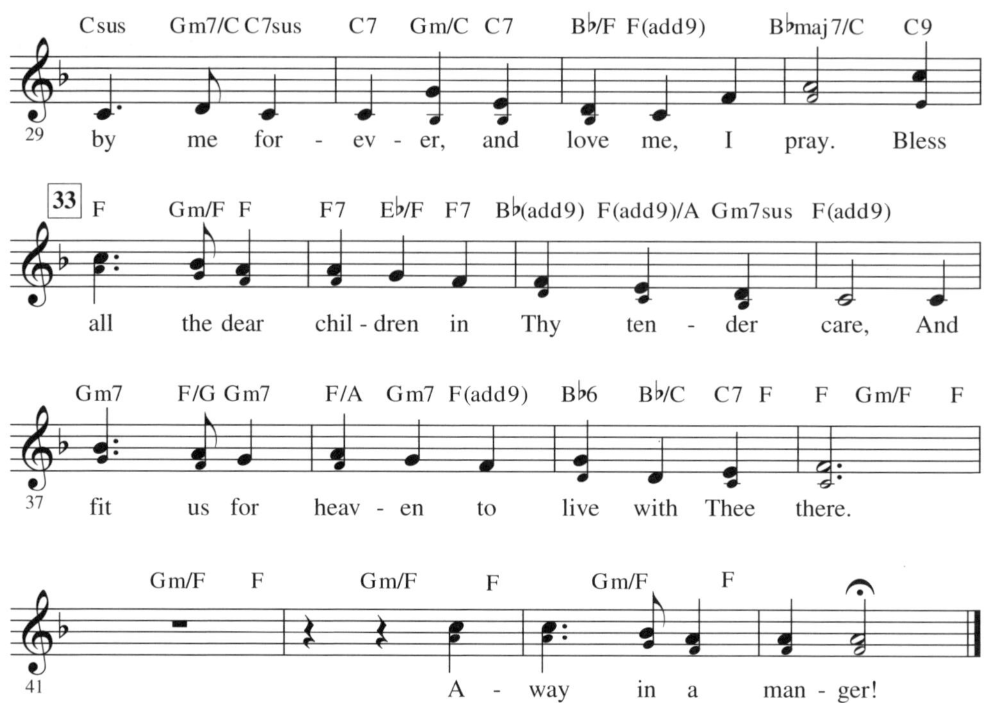

Csus   Gm7/C C7sus   C7   Gm/C C7   Bb/F F(add9)   Bbmaj7/C   C9
by   me   for - ev - er,   and   love   me,   I   pray.   Bless
33 F   Gm/F F   F7   Eb/F F7   Bb(add9) F(add9)/A Gm7sus   F(add9)
all   the dear   chil - dren   in   Thy   ten - der   care,   And
Gm7   F/G Gm7   F/A Gm7 F(add9)   Bb6   Bb/C   C7 F   F Gm/F   F
fit   us   for   heav - en   to   live   with   Thee   there.
Gm/F   F   Gm/F   F   Gm/F   F
A - way   in   a   man - ger!

Away in a Manger

25
let ring
cont. sim.
let ring
cont. sim.
let ring
cont. sim.
33
30
35
40
let ring
let ring
let ring

Away in a Manger

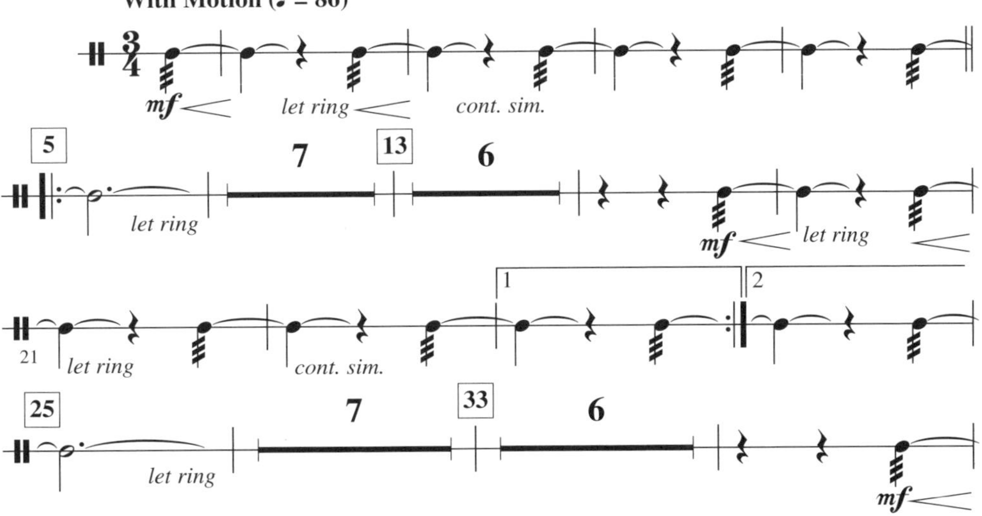

Away in a Manger

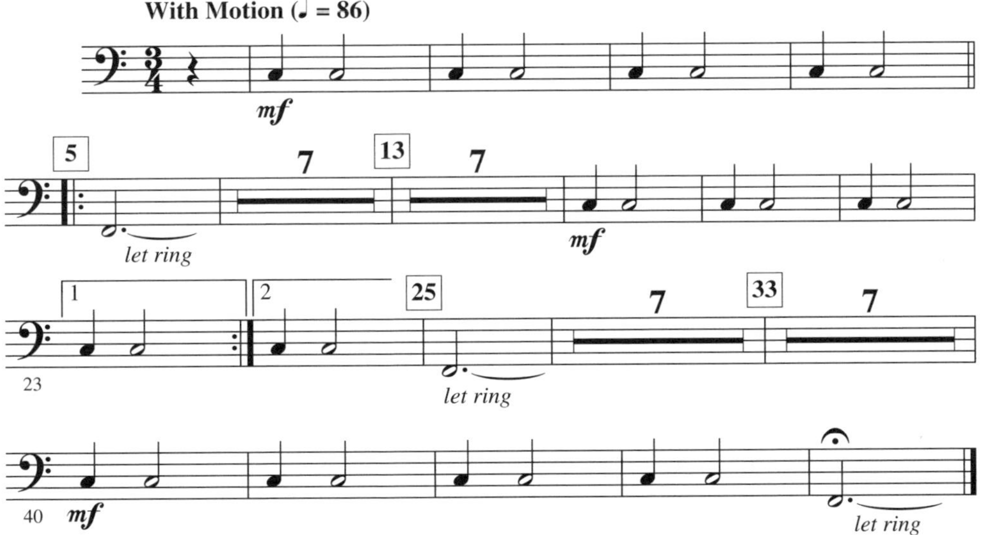

Deck the Halls

Traditional Welsh Carol
Arranged by TOM ANDERSON

Don we now our gay ap - par - el,
Fol - low me in mer - ry meas - ure,
Sing we joy - ous all to - geth - er,

Fa la la la la la la la la.
Fa la la la la la la la la.
Fa la la la la la la la la.

Troll the an - cient Yule - tide car - ol,
While I tell of Yule - tide treas - ure,
Heed - less of the wind and weath - er,

Fa la la la la, la la la la.
Fa la la la la, la la la la.
Fa la la la la, la la la la.

Fa la la la la la la la la.

Fa la la la la la

la la la.

Deck the halls!

Deck the Halls

BONGO/CONGA DRUMS

Traditional Welsh Carol
Arranged by TOM ANDERSON

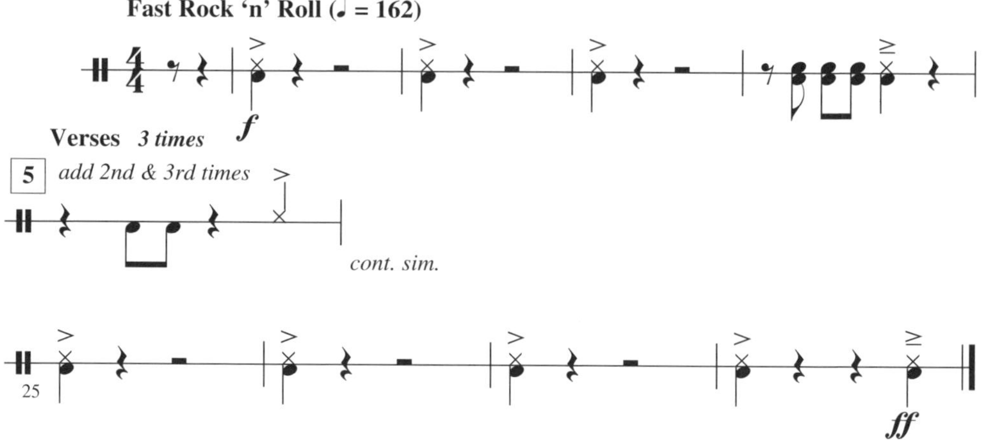

Deck the Halls

TAMBOURINE

Traditional Welsh Carol
Arranged by TOM ANDERSON

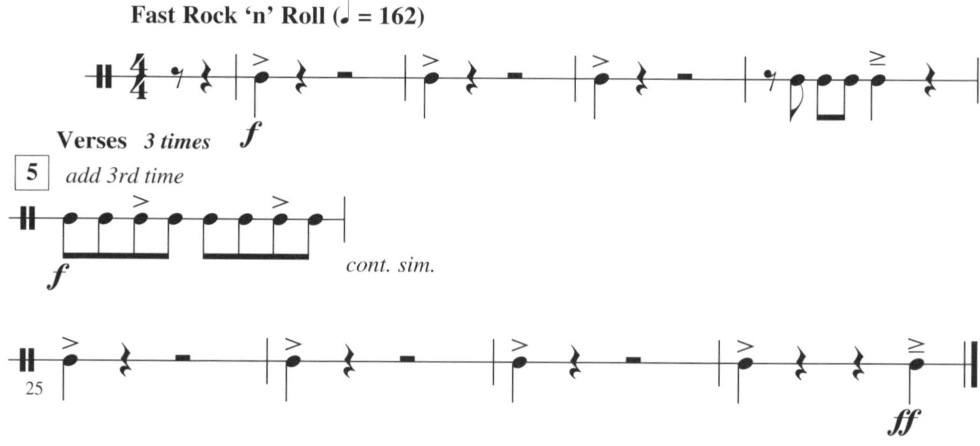

Here We Come A-Caroling

English Wassail Song
Arranged by TOM ANDERSON

Here We Come A-Caroling

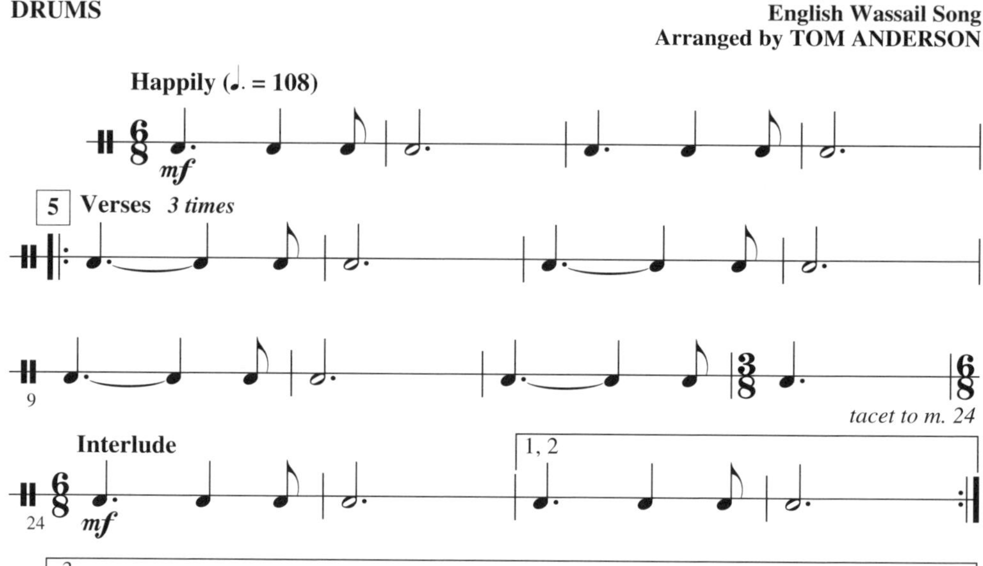

Here We Come A-Caroling

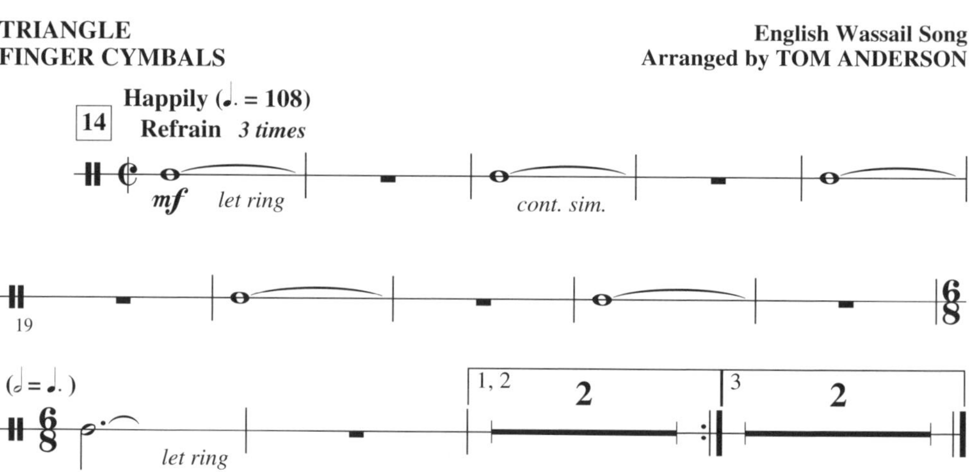

Jingle Bells

Words and Music by JAMES PIERPONT
Arranged by TOM ANDERSON

Verses

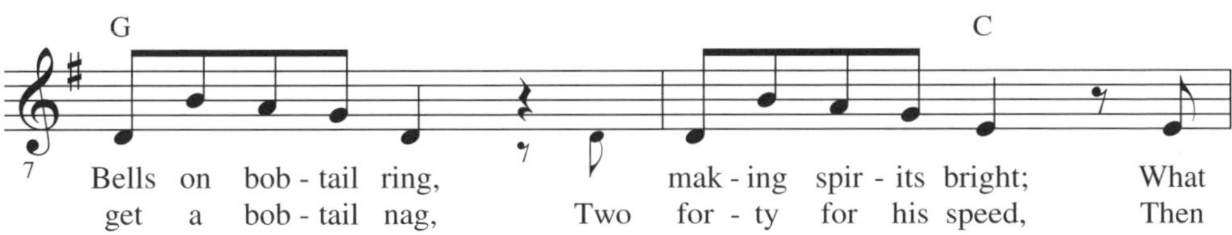

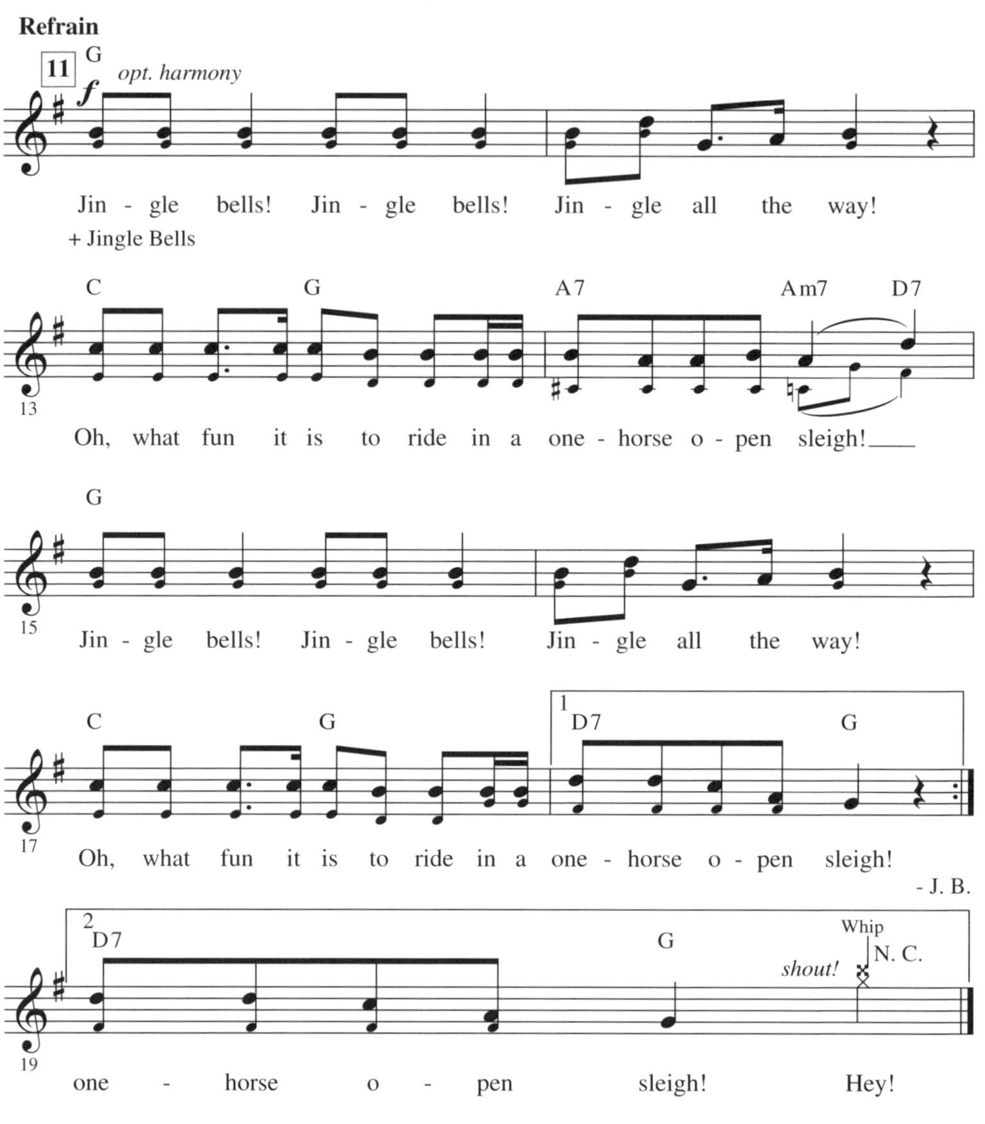
11   G   opt. harmony
Jin - gle   bells!   Jin - gle   bells!   Jin - gle   all   the   way!
+ Jingle Bells
C   G   A7   Am7   D7
13
Oh,   what   fun   it   is   to   ride   in   a   one - horse   o - pen   sleigh!___
G
15
Jin - gle   bells!   Jin - gle   bells!   Jin - gle   all   the   way!
C   G   1 D7   G
17
Oh,   what   fun   it   is   to   ride   in   a   one - horse   o - pen   sleigh!
- J. B.
2 D7   G   Whip   N. C.   shout!
19
one - horse   o - pen   sleigh!   Hey!

Jolly Old St. Nicholas

Traditional American Carol
Arranged by TOM ANDERSON

21 Recorder or Other Pitched Inst.
mf
29
27
- Recorder
32
37 f
3. John-ny wants a pair of skates,_ Su-sy wants a sled;_
+ Jingle Bells
41 Nel-lie wants a pic-ture book;_ yel-low, blue and red._
45
44 ___ Now I think I'll leave to you_
47 what to give the rest;_ Choose for me, dear San-ta Claus,_
cresc.
53
51 you will know the best._ You will know the best._
2
55 You will know the best!_______

Jolly Old St. Nicholas

Jolly Old St. Nicholas

Jolly Old St. Nicholas

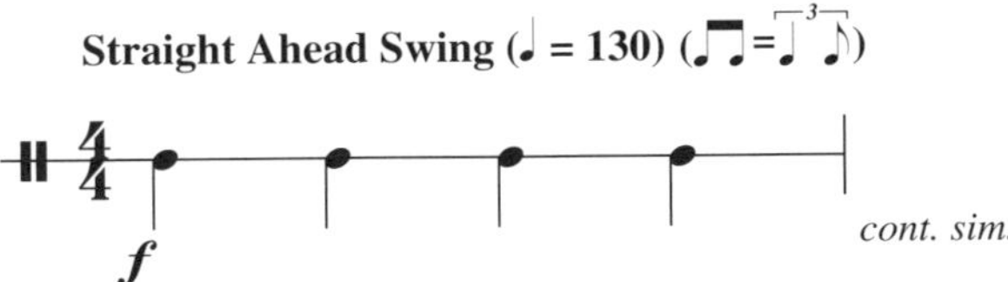

Joy to the World

Dm7/G   C/D Dm7(b5)/G Dm7(b5)/Ab   Am7   Am7/G
27
heav'n and na - ture sing,   And heav'n and

F(add9)   C/E F2/A C/G Dm/G   32 C   Dm/C C   Dm/C
opt. small group We found great joy,
30
heav'n and na - ture sing.   the
+ Hand Claps on beat 2

C   Dm7(b5)/C   C   Dm/C   C   Dm/C C
34 ev - er - last - ing joy!   We found great joy,

Dm/C   C   Dm7(b5)/C   C   G/B
37   the ev - er - last - ing joy!   - Claps

40 f opt. harmony
C   G/C F/G Cmaj7 Dm/G   C   Dm/G   C   C/E
2. He rules the world with truth and grace,   And

F   Dm7   G/F G Dm/G   C   Dm/G C
na - tions prove
44 makes the   We found great joy!   The

48 C   G/C F/C Cmaj7   Dm/G C   G/C F/C Cmaj7
glo - ries of   His right - eous -

Dm/G C   mf   52 C/G   Dm Cmaj7/G   Dm C/D
51 ness,   And won - ders of His love,   And

24   **Mickey's Caroling Book – Singer**

O Christmas Tree
(O Tannenbaum)

Traditional German Carol
Arranged by TOM ANDERSON

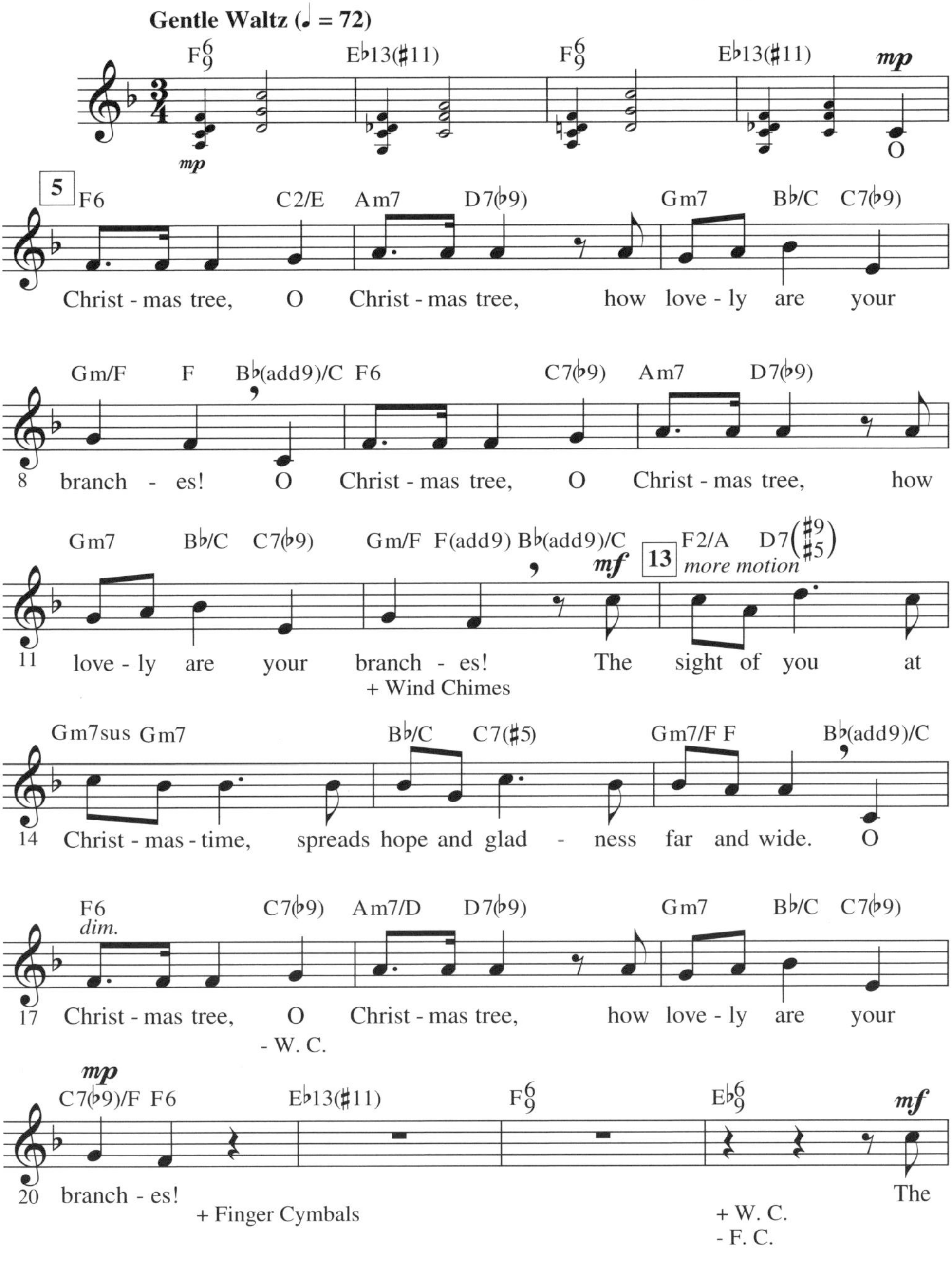

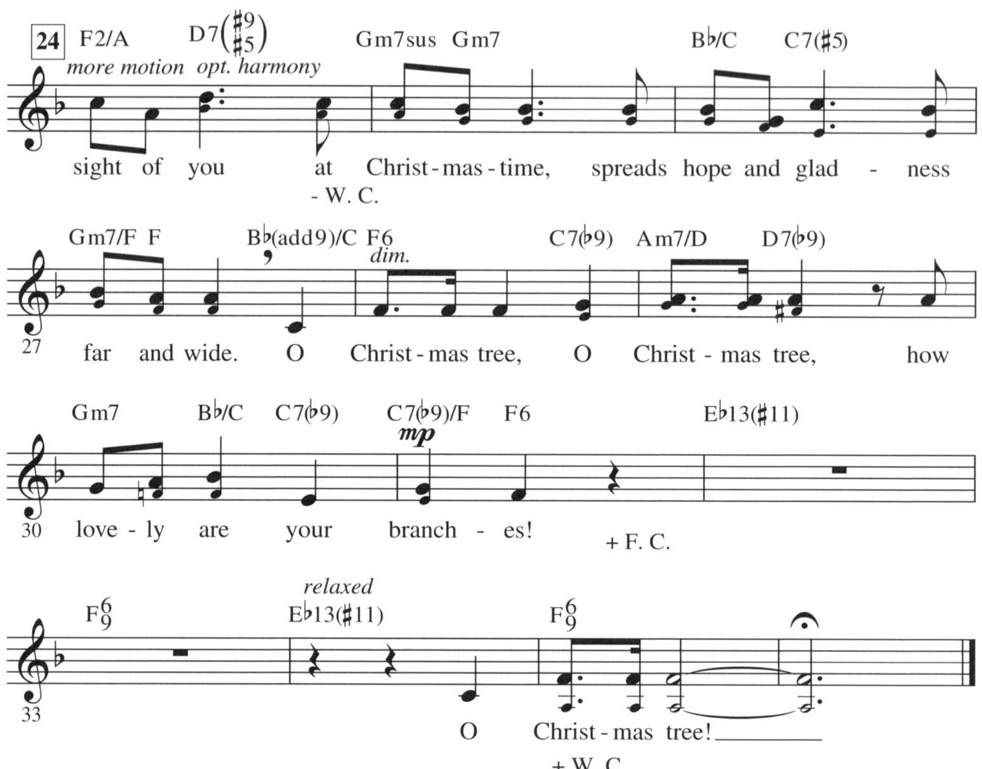

more motion opt. harmony
sight of you at Christ-mas-time, spreads hope and glad - ness
- W. C.
dim.
far and wide. O Christ-mas tree, O Christ - mas tree, how
love - ly are your branch - es!
+ F. C.
relaxed
O Christ - mas tree!
+ W. C.

Pat-a-Pan
(Willie, Take Your Little Drum)

Words and Music by
BERNARD de la MONNOYE
Arranged by **TOM ANDERSON**

mf
28 E5
27 3. God and man to - day be - come close-ly joined as
B5
30 flute and drum. Let the joy - ous tune play
E5 B5
33 on! Tu - re - lu - re - lu, pat - a - pat - a - pan. As the
E5 B5
36 in - stru - ments you play, we will sing, this Christ - mas
39 Ending
E5
6
Day.

Pat-a-Pan
(Willie, Take Your Little Drum)

Pat-a-Pan
(Willie, Take Your Little Drum)

Pat-a-Pan
(Willie, Take Your Little Drum)

Pat-a-Pan
(Willie, Take Your Little Drum)

Silent Night

Words by JOSEPH MOHR
Music by FRANZ GRUBER
Arranged by TOM ANDERSON

Mickey's Caroling Book – Singer   33

more motion
29 C Cmaj7 C6 C Dm7/G
mf
3. Si - lent night, ho - ly night, Son of
+ Descant/Recorder
G9 C(add9) Gm7/C C9 37 F(add9) C/E Dm7 G9
34 God, love's pure light; ra - diant beams from
+ Sus. Cym.
C Dm/G C C7 F(add9) F6/9 C(add9)
39 Thy ho - ly face, with the dawn of re - deem - ing
45 Dm7 Dm7/G G/F C2/E Am7
44 grace, Je - sus, Lord, at Thy birth,
+ Sus. Cym.
C/G Dm7 G9 C(add9)
dim. slight rit. mp
49 Je - sus, Lord at Thy birth.
+ W. C.

Silent Night

Up on the Housetop

Words and Music by B. R. HANDY
Arranged by TOM ANDERSON

21
mf
D
D/F#
3. Next, comes the stock - ing of lit - tle Will;
G
D
A7
23
Oh, just see what a glo - rious fill!
D
D/F#
25
Here is a ham - mer and lots of tacks,
G
D
Em7
A7
D
Whip Crack
D/F#
27
al - so a ball and a whip that cracks.
29
f
G
Em7
D
Bm7
Ho, ho, ho, who would - n't go!
+ S. B. and Mar.
Em7
A7
D
Em7/A
31
Ho, ho, ho, who would - n't go!
Finger Snaps
D
D7/F#
G
D/F#
Em7
Fdim7
spoken
33
Up on the house - top click, click, click,
+ W. B.
N.C.
D/F#
Bm7
Em7
A7
D
Whip Crack
35
Down thru' the chim - ney with good Saint Nick.

We Wish You a Merry Christmas

Traditional English Carol
Arranged by TOM ANDERSON

22
G   G/B   C   C/B   A7sus   A7
wish   you   a   mer - ry   Christ - mas,   We   wish   you   a   mer - ry
+ Tri./F. C., H. D., Tamb.
D   D/C   B7sus   B7   Em   G/B
25   Christ - mas,   We   wish   you   a   mer - ry   Christ - mas,   and   a
- Tri./F. C.
- H. D.
- Tamb.
C6   Am7   cresc.   Am7/D   D9
28   hap   -   py   New
ff   G   G2/B   C   Am7   D9   G6/9
32   Year!
+ Tri./F. C., H. D., Tamb.

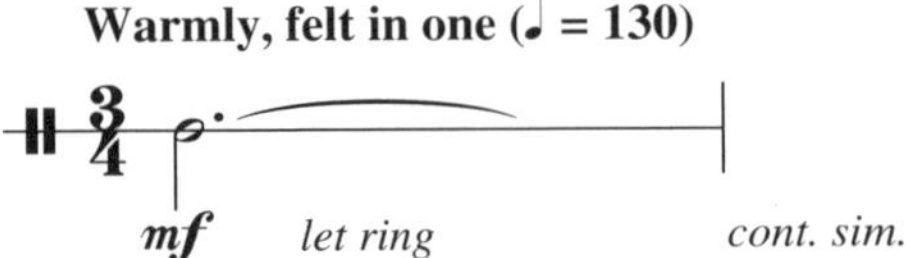

We Wish You a Merry Christmas

We Wish You a Merry Christmas

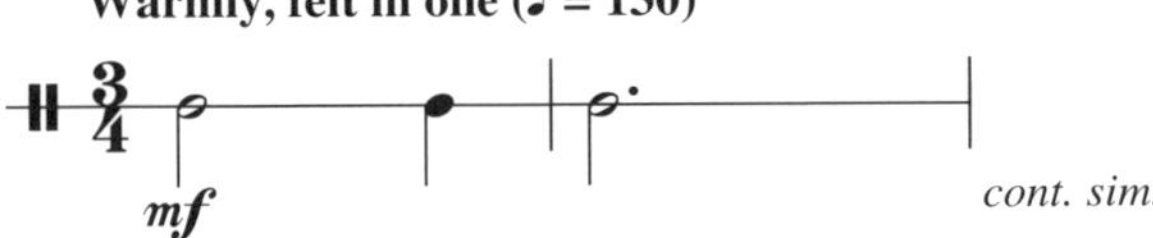

We Wish You a Merry Christmas

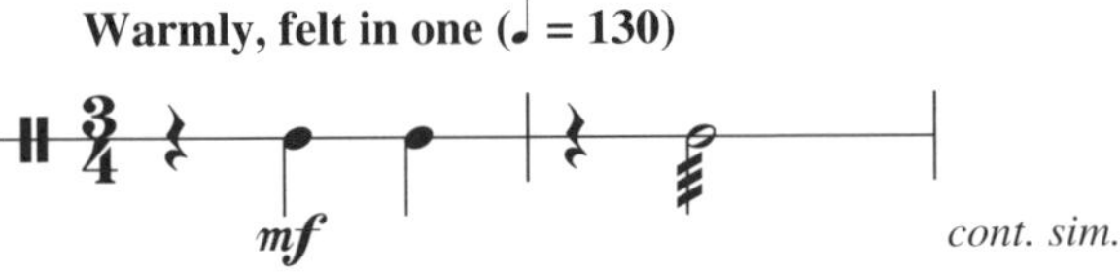

Disney
Mickey's Caroling Book

HOLIDAY FUN WITH MICKEY AND HIS FRIENDS

Table of Contents

HAL•LEONARD® CORPORATION

7777 W. BLUEMOUND RD. P.O. BOX 13819 MILWAUKEE, WI 53213

Visit Hal Leonard Online at
www.halleonard.com

Angels We Have Heard on High

Traditional French Carol
Arranged by TOM ANDERSON

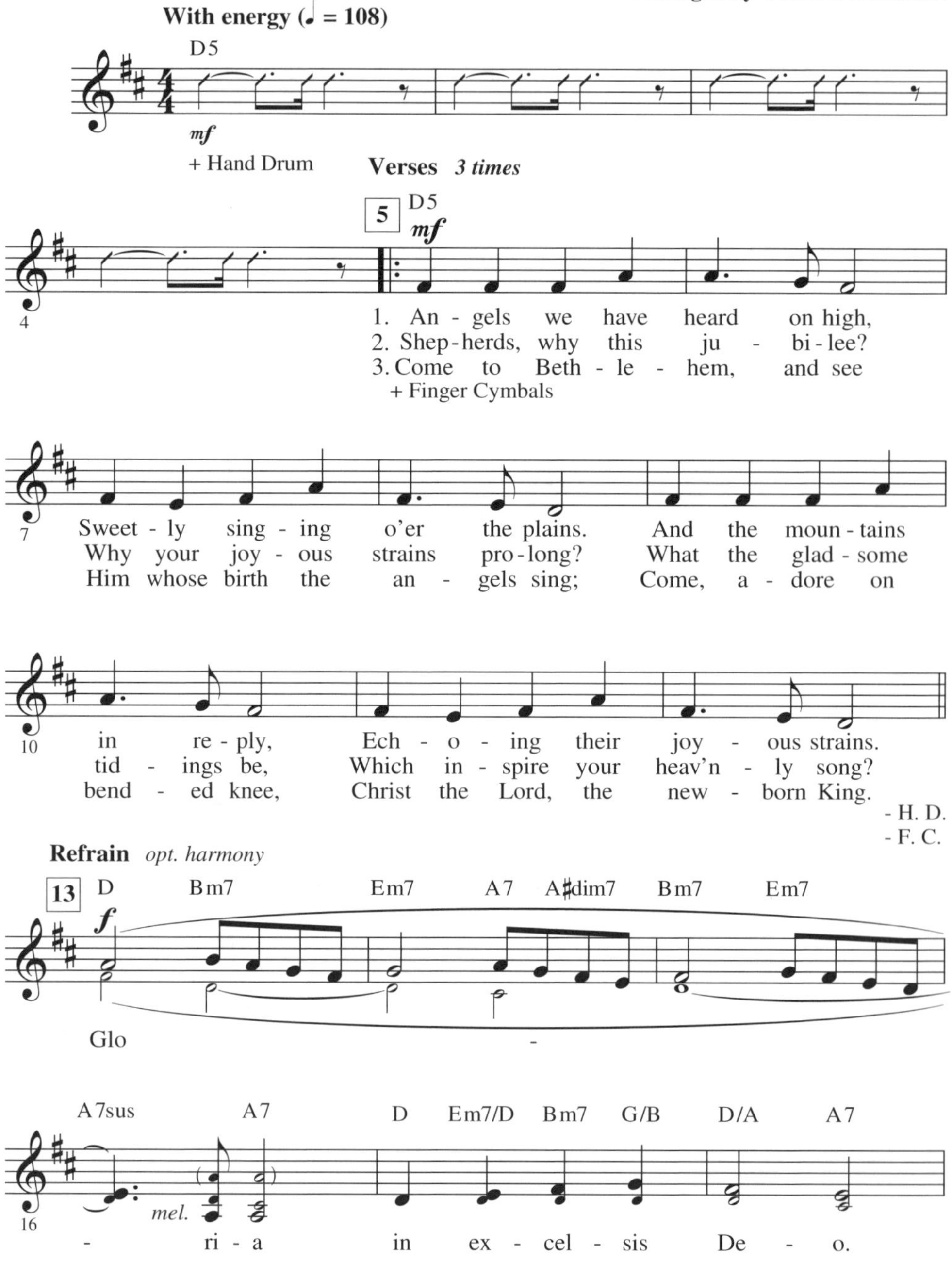

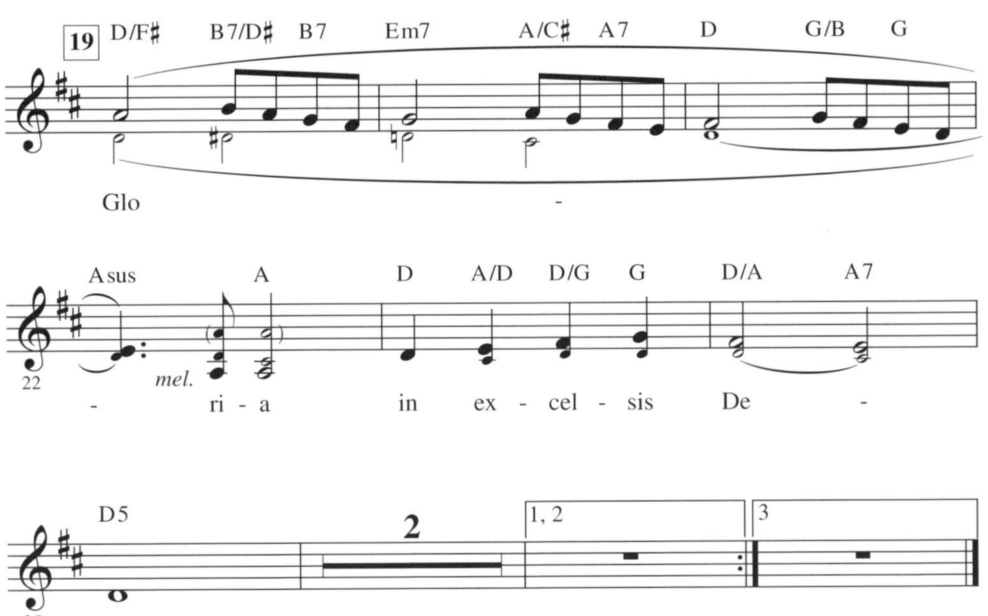
19
D/F♯   B7/D♯   B7   Em7   A/C♯   A7   D   G/B   G
Glo -
A sus   A   D   A/D   D/G   G   D/A   A7
mel.
- ri - a   in   ex - cel - sis   De -
D5
2
1, 2
3
o.

Angels We Have Heard on High

HAND DRUM

Traditional French Carol
Arranged by TOM ANDERSON

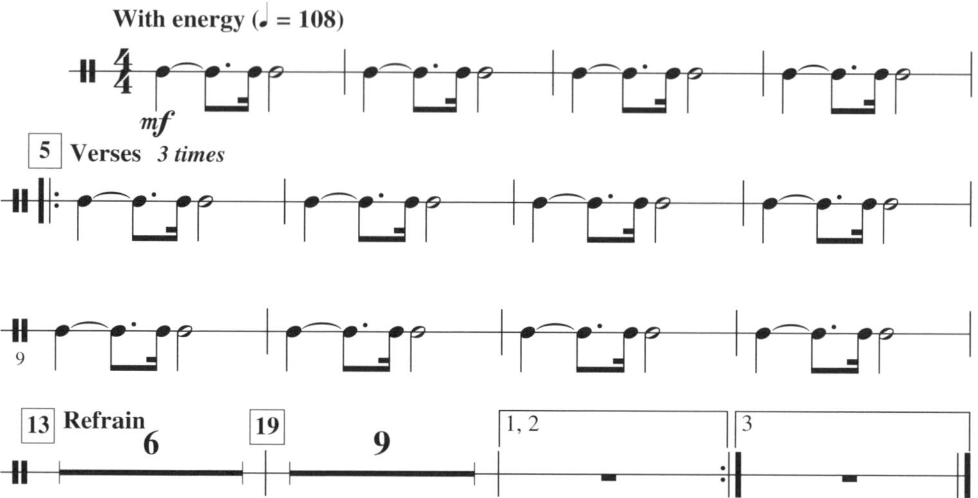

Angels We Have Heard on High

FINGER CYMBALS

Traditional French Carol
Arranged by TOM ANDERSON

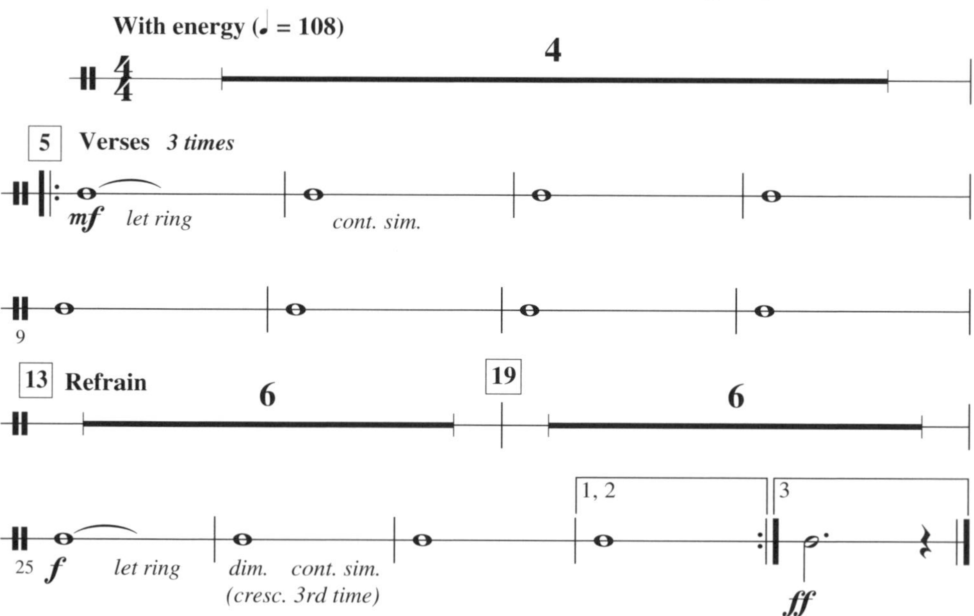

Angels We Have Heard on High

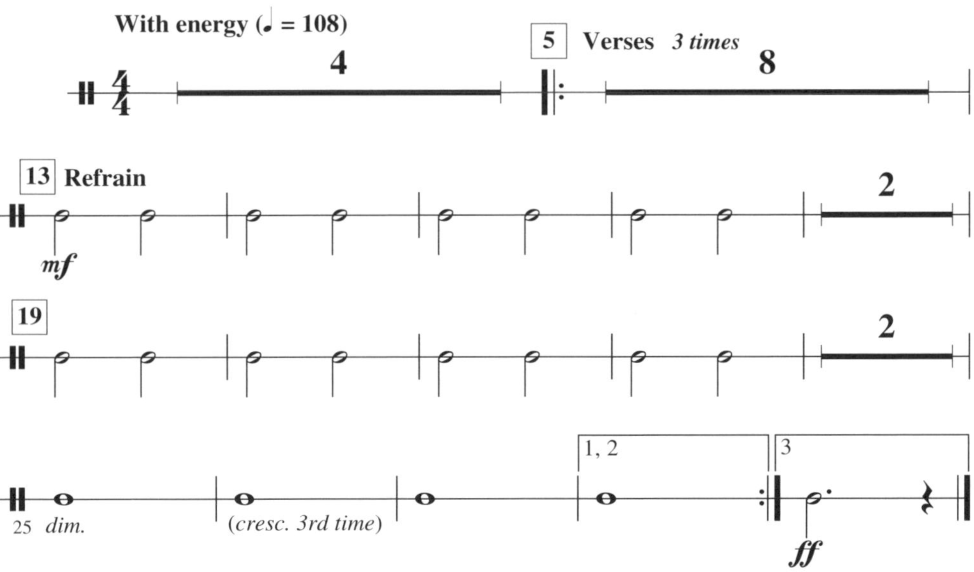

Angels We Have Heard on High

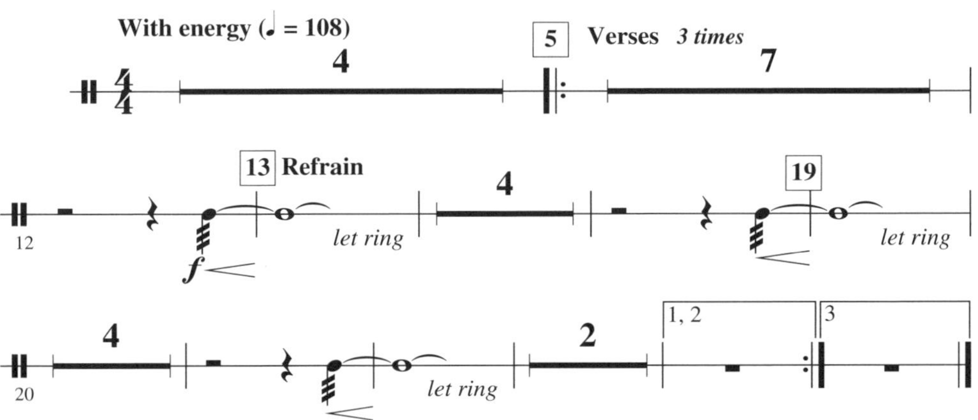

Angels We Have Heard on High

Copyright © 2012 by HAL LEONARD CORPORATION
International Copyright Secured   All Rights Reserved

Away in a Manger

Music by JAMES R. MURRAY
Words, Stanza 1, 2, Anonymous
Stanza 3, JOHN THOMAS McFARLAND
Arranged by TOM ANDERSON

(5 clicks on recording)
With Motion (♩ = 86)

(opt. harmony, 2nd time)

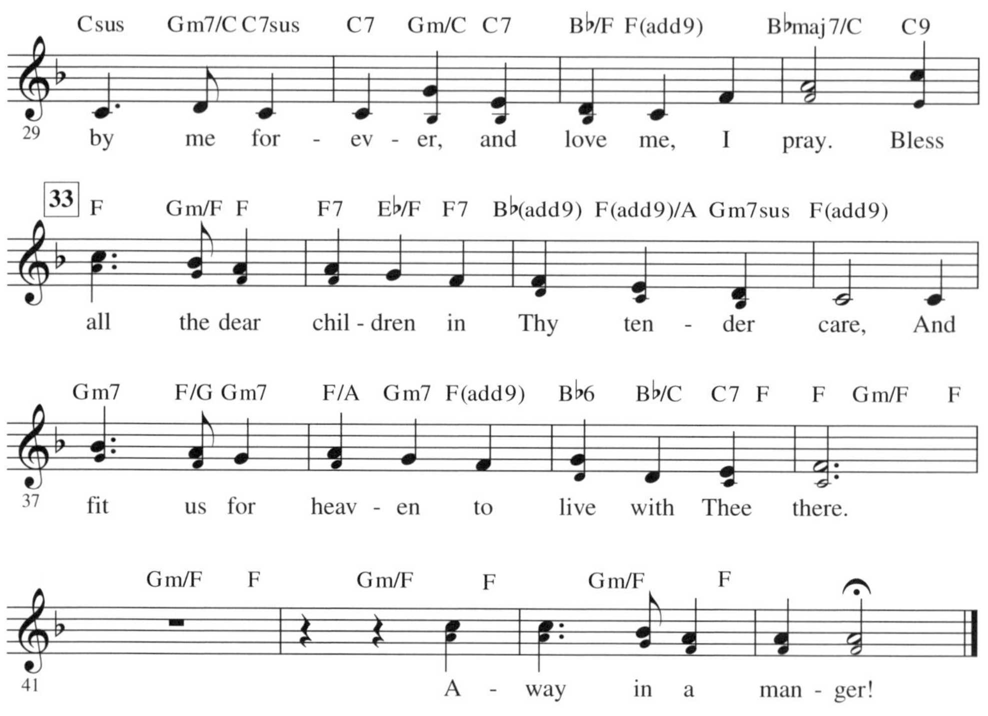

Csus   Gm7/C C7sus   C7   Gm/C C7   Bb/F F(add9)   Bbmaj7/C   C9
29
by   me   for - ev - er,   and   love   me,   I   pray.   Bless

33   F   Gm/F F   F7   Eb/F F7   Bb(add9)   F(add9)/A   Gm7sus   F(add9)
all   the dear   chil - dren   in   Thy   ten - der   care,   And

Gm7   F/G Gm7   F/A Gm7 F(add9)   Bb6   Bb/C C7 F   F Gm/F   F
37
fit   us   for   heav - en   to   live   with   Thee   there.

Gm/F   F   Gm/F   F   Gm/F   F
41
A - way   in   a   man - ger!

Away in a Manger

Music by JAMES R. MURRAY
Words, Stanza 1, 2, Anonymous
Stanza 3, JOHN THOMAS McFARLAND
Arranged by TOM ANDERSON

25
let ring
cont. sim.
let ring
cont. sim.
let ring
cont. sim.
33
30
35
40
let ring
let ring
let ring
let ring

Away in a Manger

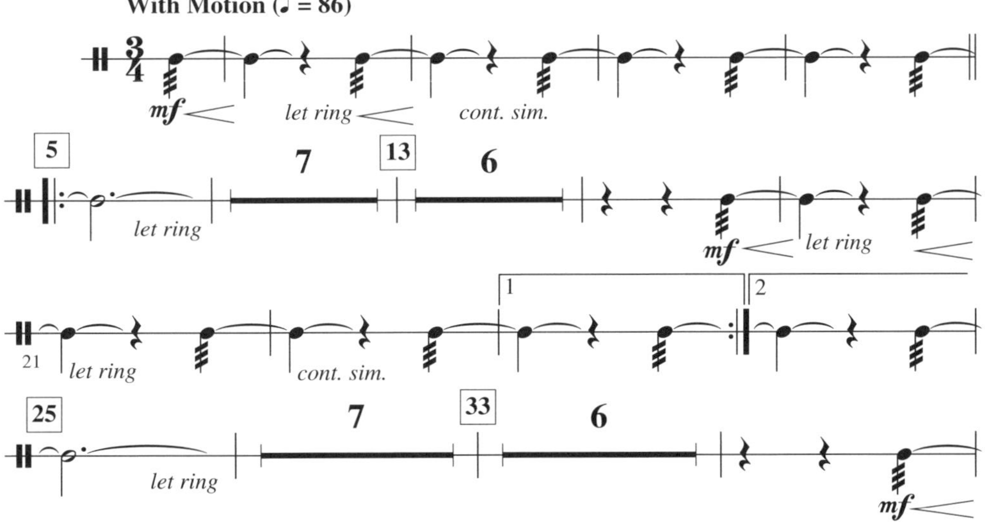

Away in a Manger

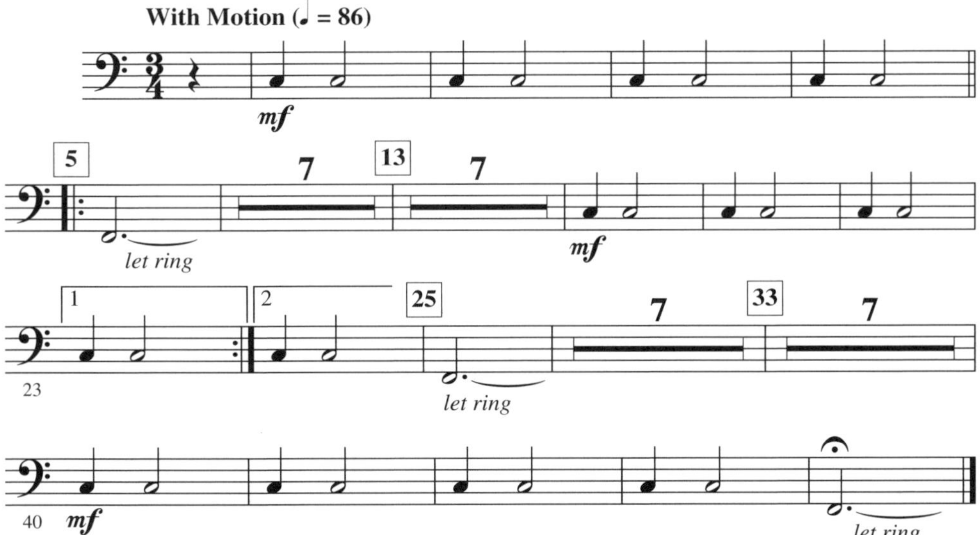

Deck the Halls

Traditional Welsh Carol
Arranged by TOM ANDERSON

Don we now our gay ap - par - el,
Fol - low me in mer - ry meas - ure,
Sing we joy - ous all to - geth - er,
Fa la la la la la la la la.
Fa la la la la la la la la.
Fa la la la la la la la la.
Troll the an - cient Yule - tide car - ol,
While I tell of Yule - tide treas - ure,
Heed - less of the wind and weath - er,
Fa la la la la, la la la la.
Fa la la la la, la la la la.
Fa la la la la, la la la la.
Fa la la la la la la la la.
Fa la la la la la la
la la la.
Deck the halls!

Deck the Halls

BONGO/CONGA DRUMS

Traditional Welsh Carol
Arranged by TOM ANDERSON

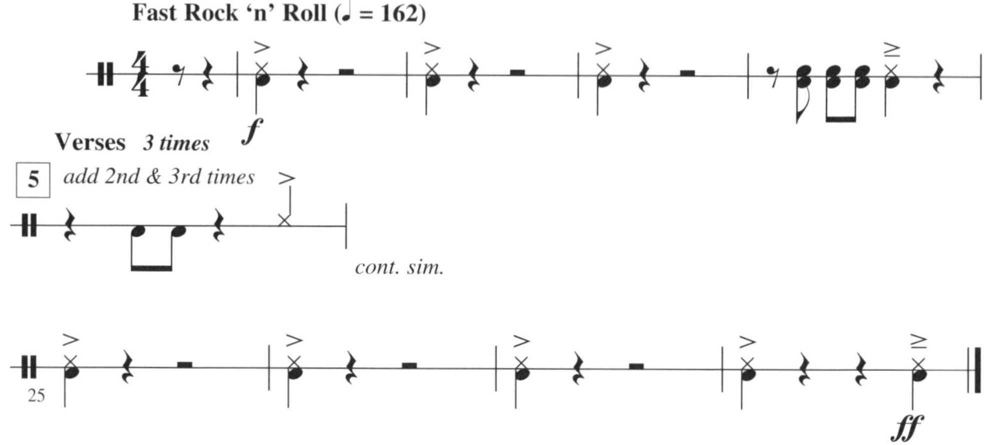

Deck the Halls

TAMBOURINE

Traditional Welsh Carol
Arranged by TOM ANDERSON

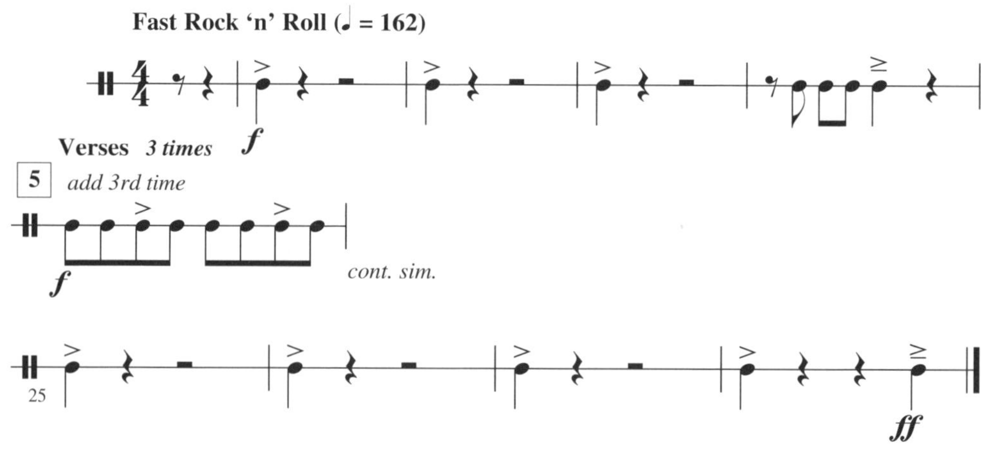

Here We Come A-Caroling

English Wassail Song
Arranged by TOM ANDERSON

Here We Come A-Caroling

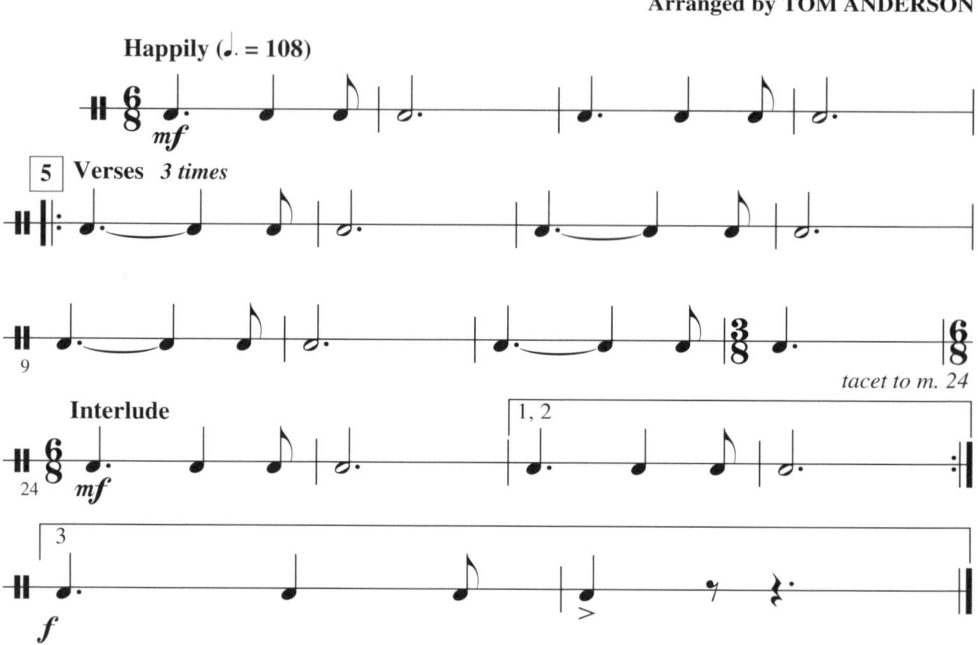

Here We Come A-Caroling

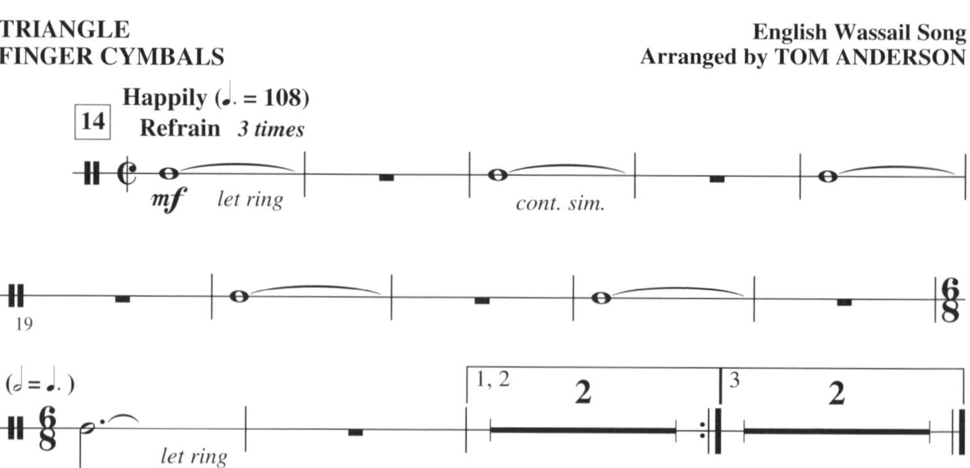

Copyright © 2012 by HAL LEONARD CORPORATION
International Copyright Secured   All Rights Reserved

Jingle Bells

Words and Music by JAMES PIERPONT
Arranged by TOM ANDERSON

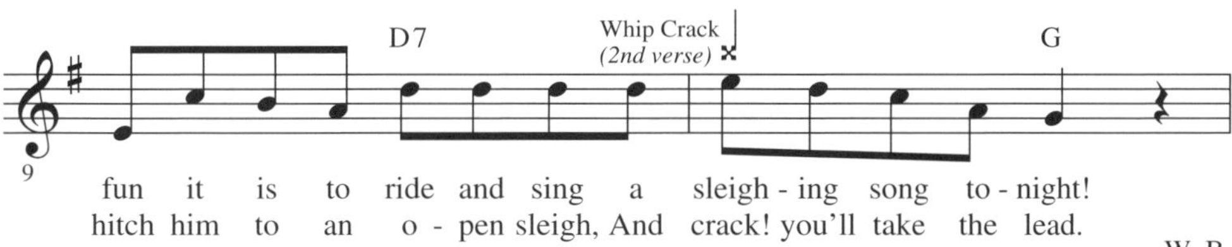

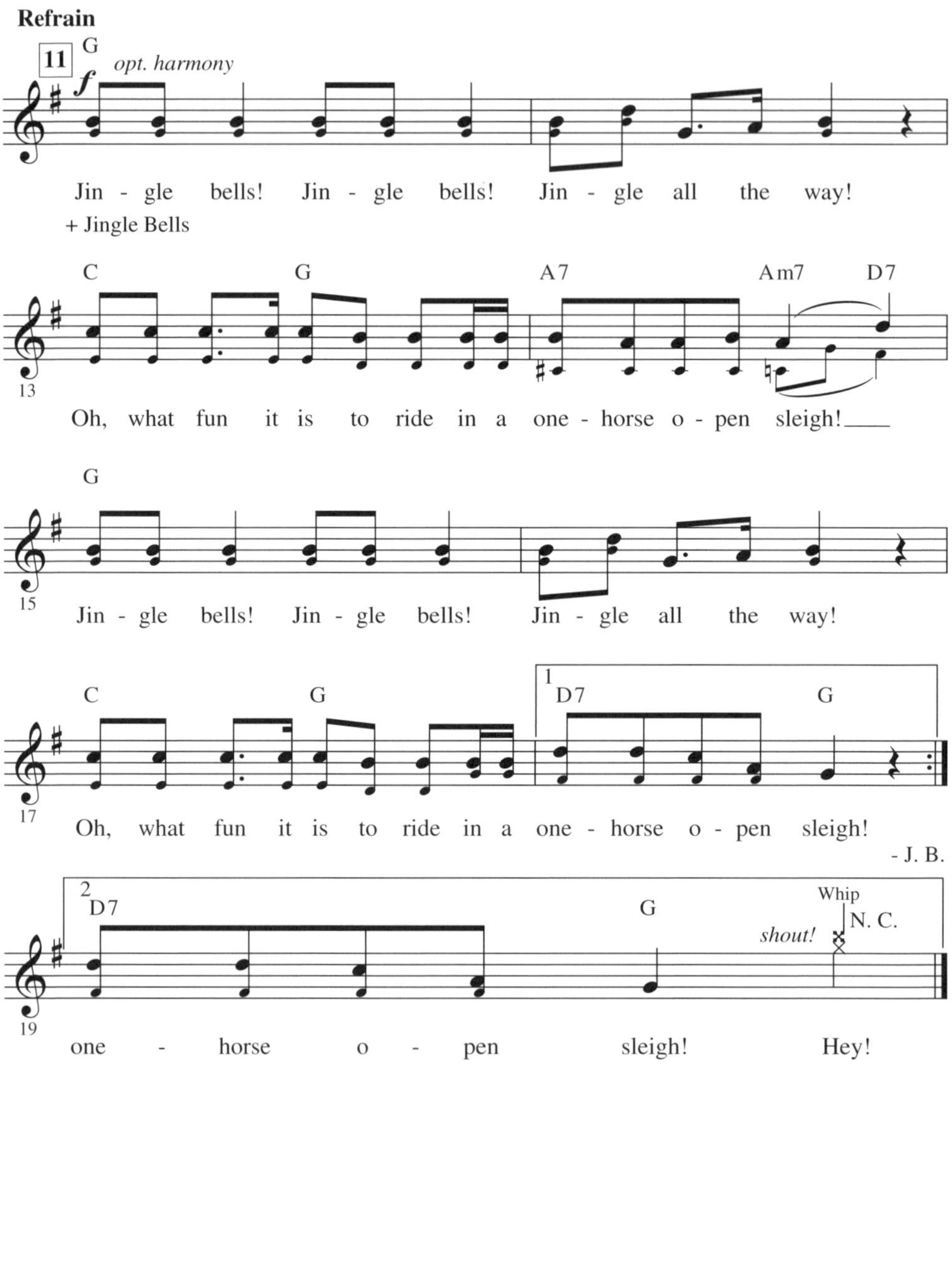

Refrain
11
G
opt. harmony
f
Jin - gle bells! Jin - gle bells! Jin - gle all the way!
+ Jingle Bells
C G A7 Am7 D7
Oh, what fun it is to ride in a one - horse o - pen sleigh!___
G
Jin - gle bells! Jin - gle bells! Jin - gle all the way!
C G 1 D7 G
Oh, what fun it is to ride in a one - horse o - pen sleigh!
- J. B.
2 D7 G Whip N. C. shout!
one - horse o - pen sleigh! Hey!

6/18

Jolly Old St. Nicholas

Traditional American Carol
Arranged by TOM ANDERSON

Straight Ahead Swing (♩ = 130)

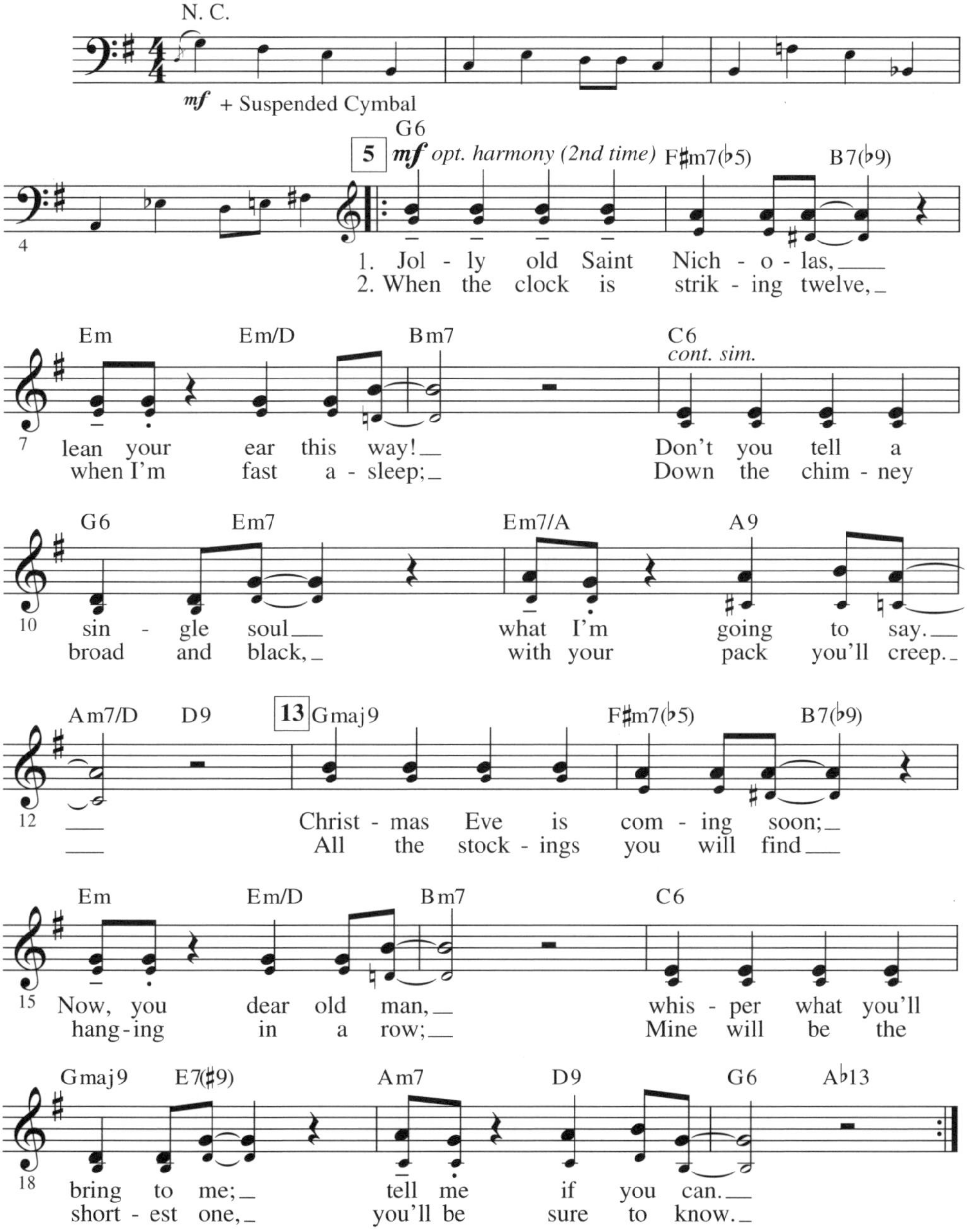

21 Recorder or Other Pitched Inst.
29
27
- Recorder
32
37
3. John-ny wants a pair of skates,__ Su-sy wants a sled;__
+ Jingle Bells
Nel-lie wants a pic-ture book;__ yel-low, blue and red.__
45
44 __ Now I think I'll leave to you__
47 what to give the rest;__ Choose for me, dear San-ta Claus,__
53 cresc.
51 you will know the best.__ You will know the best.__
2
55 You will know the best!____

Jolly Old St. Nicholas

Jolly Old St. Nicholas

Jolly Old St. Nicholas

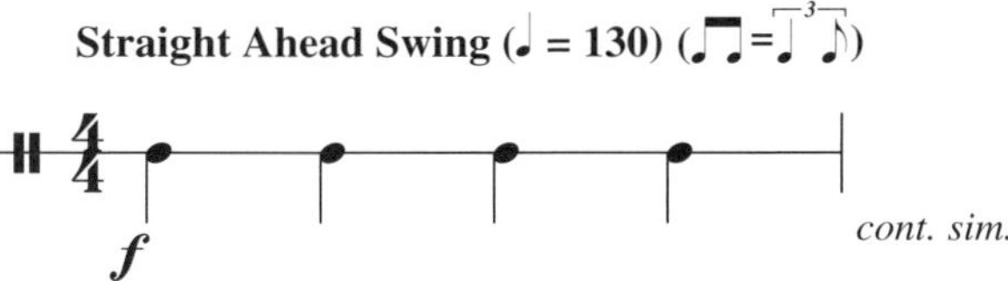

Joy to the World

Dm7/G   C/D Dm7(b5)/G Dm7(b5)/Ab   Am7   Am7/G
27
heav'n and na - ture sing,   And heav'n and

F(add9) C/E F2/A C/G Dm/G   32 C   Dm/C C   Dm/C
opt. small group We found great joy,
30
heav'n and na - ture sing.   the
+ Hand Claps on beat 2

C   Dm7(b5)/C   C   Dm/C   C   Dm/C C
34 ev - er - last - ing joy!   We found great joy,

Dm/C   C   Dm7(b5)/C   C   G/B
37   the ev - er - last - ing joy!   - Claps

40 f opt. harmony
C   G/C   F/G Cmaj7 Dm/G   C   Dm/G   C   C/E
mel.
2. He rules the world with truth and grace, And

F   Dm7   G/F   G Dm/G   C   Dm/G C
na - tions prove
44 makes the   We found great joy!   The

48 C   G/C   F/C Cmaj7   Dm/G C   G/C   F/C Cmaj7
glo - ries of His right - eous -

Dm/G C   mf   52 C/G   Dm Cmaj7/G   Dm C/D
51 ness, And won - ders of His love, And

Dm7/G
C/D Dm7(b5)/G Dm7(b5)/Ab
Am7
Am7/G
54
won - ders of His love, And won - ders,
F(add9) C/E F2/A
C/G Dm/G
59 C
Dm/C C
We found great joy,
57
mel.
won - ders of His love.
+ Claps
Dm/C C Dm7(b5)/C C Dm/C
60
the ev - er - last - ing joy! We
C Dm/C C Dm/C C Dm7(b5)/C C
63 found great joy, the ev - er - last - ing joy!
build intensity
f Dm/C 67 C Dm/C C Dm/C
66 We found great joy, the
+ Tambourine on beat 2
C Dm7(b5)/C C Dm/C C Dm/C C
69 ev - er - last - ing joy! We found great joy,
Dm/C C Dm7(b5)/C C
72 the ev - er - last - ing joy!
ff

O Christmas Tree
(O Tannenbaum)

Traditional German Carol
Arranged by TOM ANDERSON

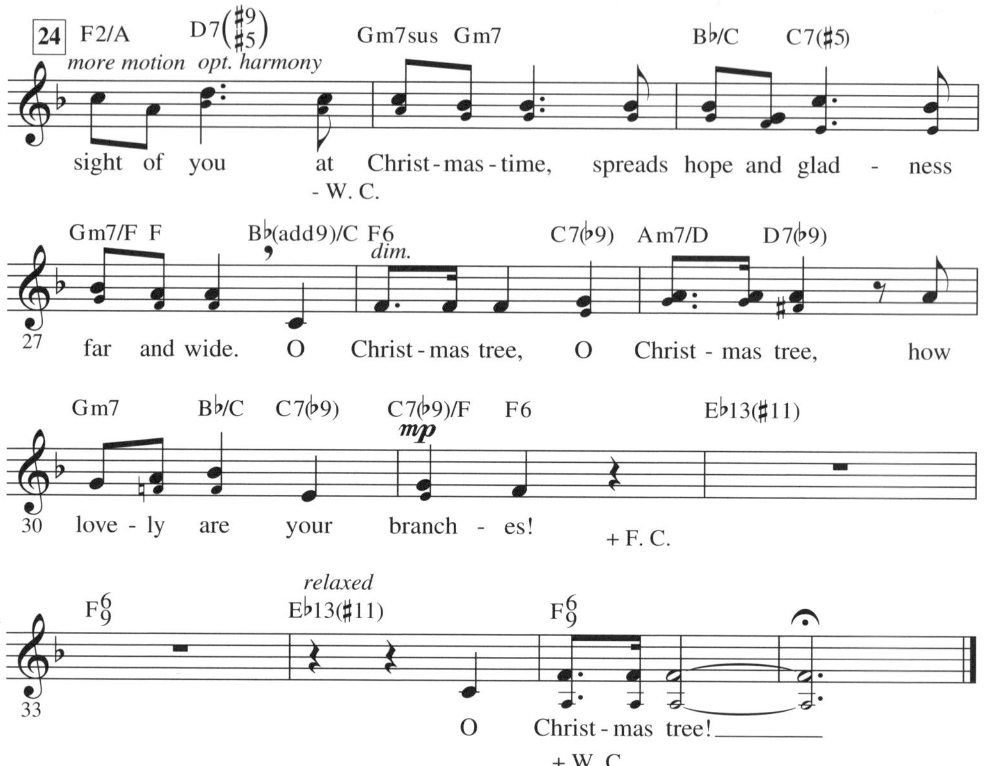

24 F2/A D7(#9 #5) Gm7sus Gm7 Bb/C C7(#5)
more motion opt. harmony
sight of you   at Christ-mas-time,   spreads hope and glad - ness
- W. C.
Gm7/F F Bb(add9)/C F6 C7(b9) Am7/D D7(b9)
dim.
far and wide.   O Christ-mas tree,   O Christ - mas tree,   how
Gm7 Bb/C C7(b9) C7(b9)/F F6 Eb13(#11)
mp
love - ly are your branch - es!   + F. C.
relaxed
F6/9 Eb13(#11) F6/9
O Christ - mas tree!
+ W. C.

Pat-a-Pan
(Willie, Take Your Little Drum)

Words and Music by
BERNARD de la MONNOYE
Arranged by TOM ANDERSON

mf
28 E5
27 3. God and man to - day be - come close-ly joined as
B5
30 flute and drum. Let the joy - ous tune play
E5   B5
33 on! Tu - re - lu - re - lu, pat - a - pat - a - pan. As the
E5   B5
36 in - stru - ments you play, we will sing, this Christ - mas
39 Ending
E5   6
Day.

Pat-a-Pan
(Willie, Take Your Little Drum)

Pat-a-Pan
(Willie, Take Your Little Drum)

Pat-a-Pan
(Willie, Take Your Little Drum)

Mickey's Caroling Book – Singer   31

Pat-a-Pan
(Willie, Take Your Little Drum)

10/22

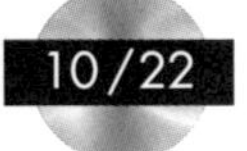

Silent Night

Words by JOSEPH MOHR
Music by FRANZ GRUBER
Arranged by TOM ANDERSON

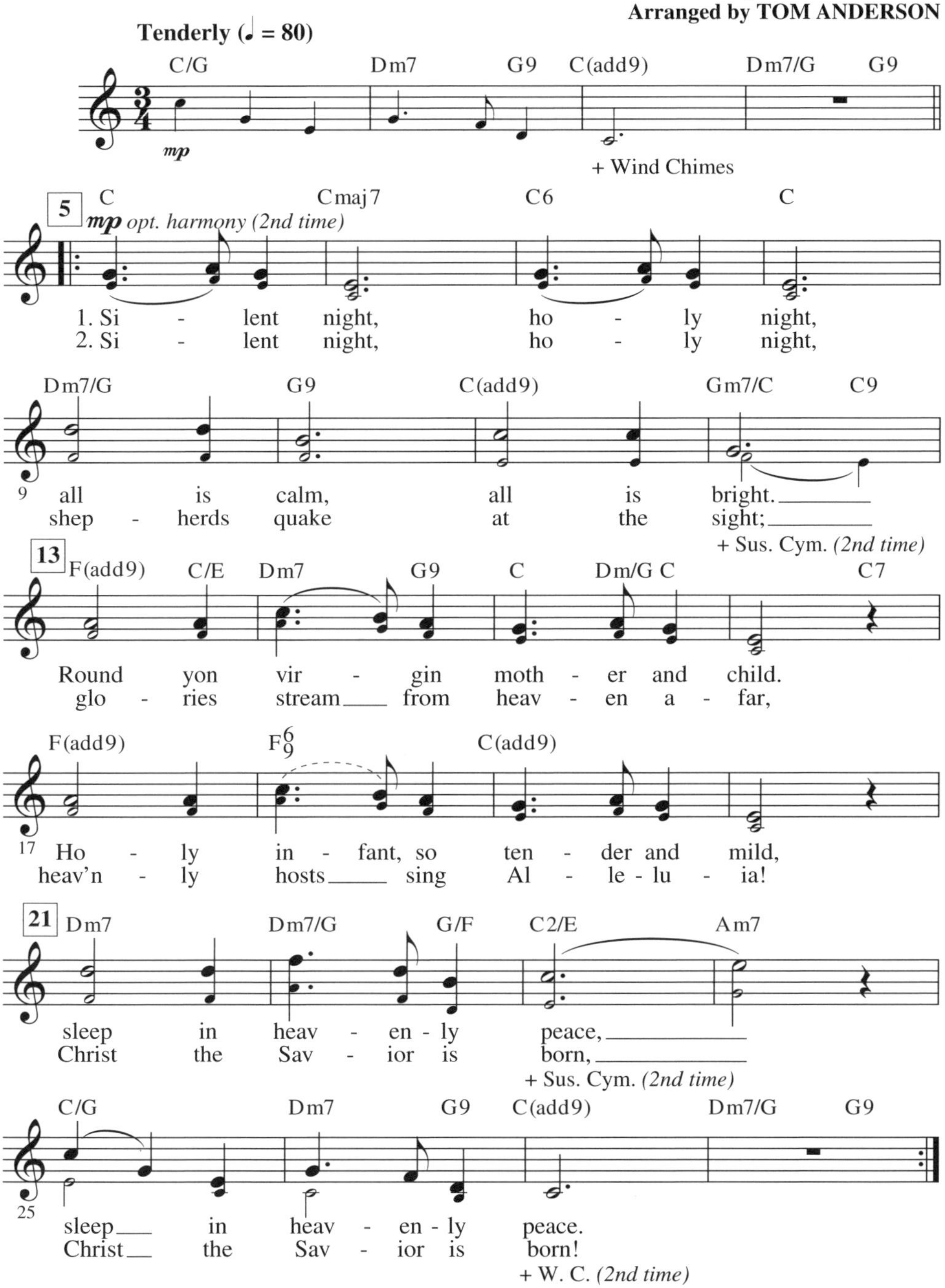

29 C more motion Cmaj7 C6 C Dm7/G
mf
3. Si - lent night, ho - ly night, Son of
+ Descant/Recorder
G9 C(add9) Gm7/C C9 37 F(add9) C/E Dm7 G9
34 God, love's pure light; ra - diant beams from
+ Sus. Cym.
C Dm/G C C7 F(add9) F6/9 C(add9)
39 Thy ho - ly face, with the dawn of re - deem - ing
45 Dm7 Dm7/G G/F C2/E Am7
44 grace, Je - sus, Lord, at Thy birth,
+ Sus. Cym.
C/G Dm7 G9 C(add9)
dim. slight rit. mp
49 Je - sus, Lord at Thy birth.
+ W. C.

Silent Night

Up on the Housetop

Words and Music by B. R. HANDY
Arranged by TOM ANDERSON

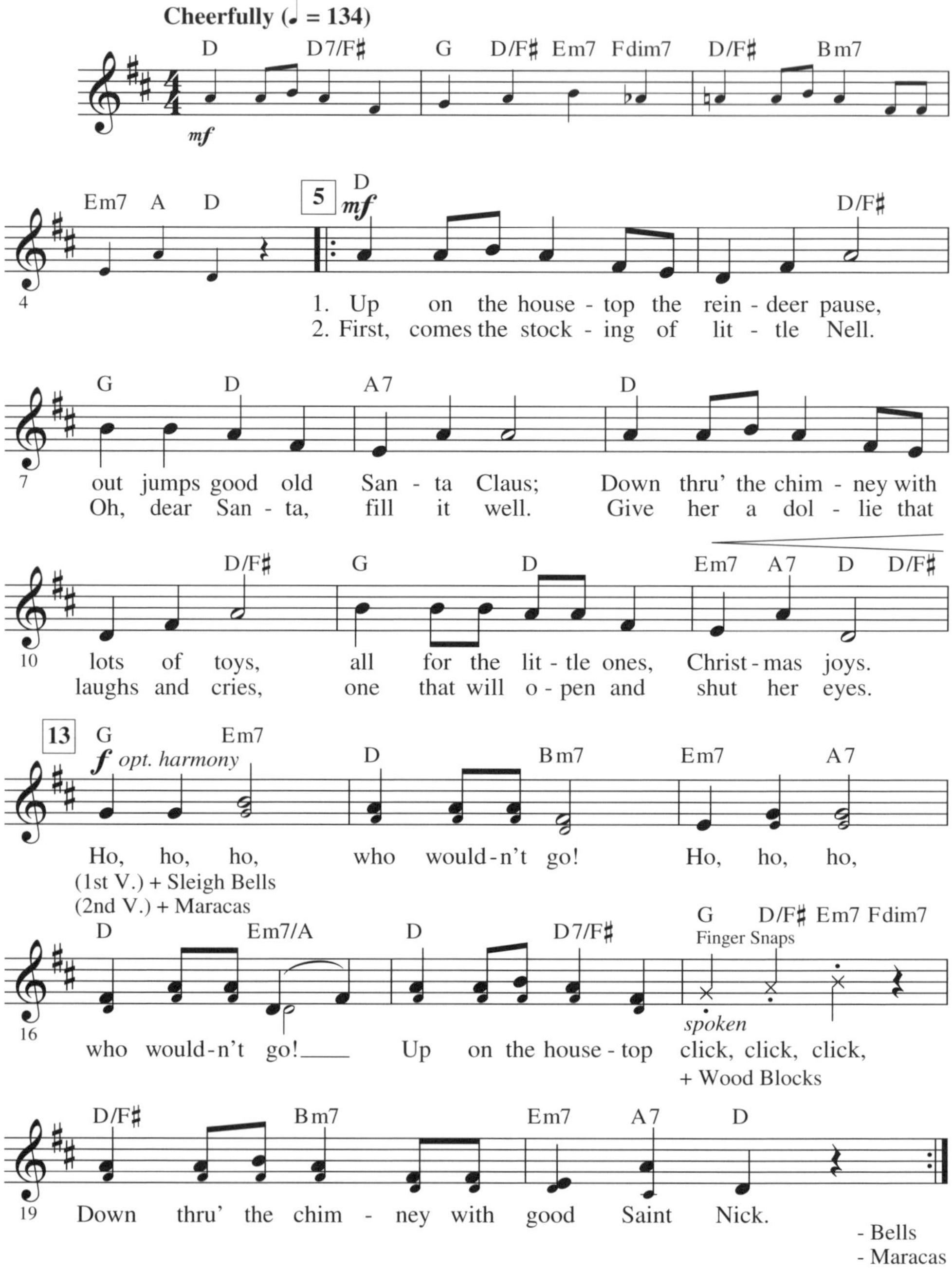

21
mf
D
D/F#
3. Next, comes the stock - ing of lit - tle Will;
G
D
A7
23
Oh, just see what a glo - rious fill!
D
D/F#
25
Here is a ham - mer and lots of tacks,
G
D
Em7
A7
D
Whip
Crack
D/F#
27
al - so a ball and a whip that cracks.
29
f
G
Em7
D
Bm7
Ho, ho, ho, who would - n't go!
+ S. B. and Mar.
Em7
A7
D
Em7/A
31
Ho, ho, ho, who would - n't go!
Finger Snaps
D
D7/F#
G
D/F#
Em7
Fdim7
spoken
33
Up on the house - top click, click, click,
+ W. B.
D/F#
Bm7
Em7
A7
D
Whip
Crack
N.C.
35
Down thru' the chim - ney with good Saint Nick.

We Wish You a Merry Christmas

Traditional English Carol
Arranged by TOM ANDERSON

22
G   G/B   C   C/B   A7sus   A7
wish you a mer-ry Christ-mas, We wish you a mer-ry
+ Tri./F. C., H. D., Tamb.
D   D/C   B7sus   B7   Em   G/B
Christ-mas, We wish you a mer-ry Christ-mas, and a
- Tri./F. C.
- H. D.
- Tamb.
C6   Am7 cresc.   Am7/D   D9
hap - py New
ff G   G2/B   C   Am7   D9   G6/9
Year!
+ Tri./F. C., H. D., Tamb.

We Wish You a Merry Christmas

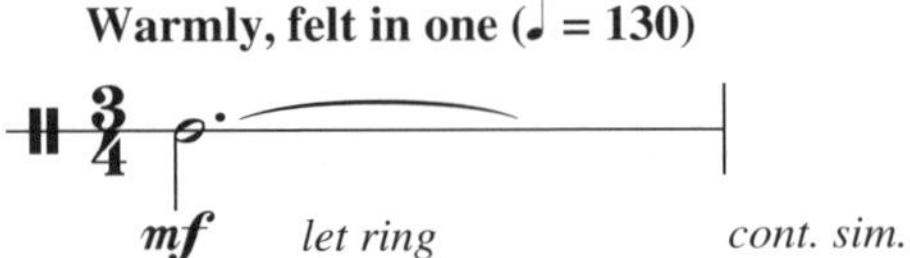

TRIANGLE/FINGER CYMBALS

Traditional English Carol
Arranged by TOM ANDERSON

We Wish You a Merry Christmas

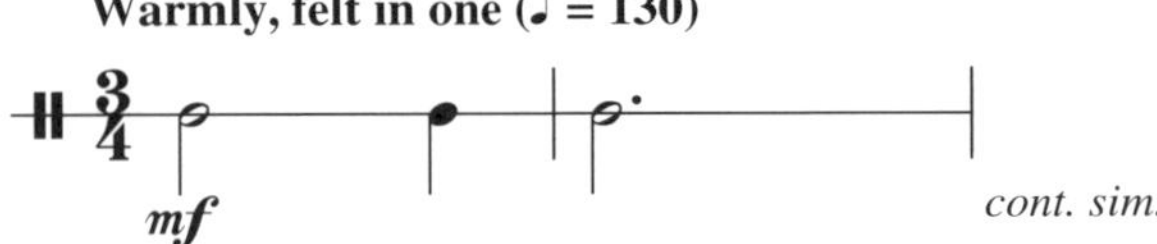

HAND DRUM

Traditional English Carol
Arranged by TOM ANDERSON

We Wish You a Merry Christmas

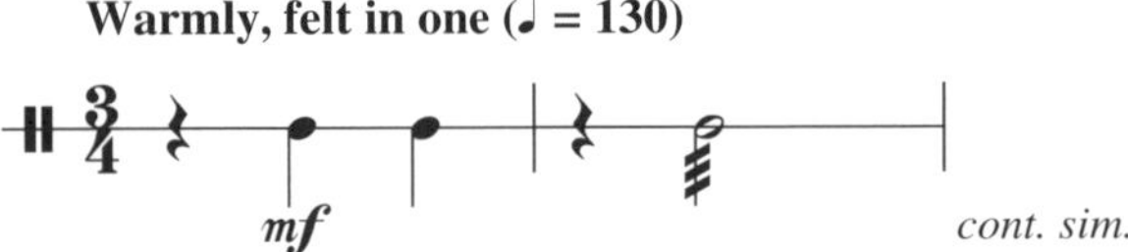

TAMBOURINE

Traditional English Carol
Arranged by TOM ANDERSON

Disney
Mickey's Caroling Book
HOLIDAY FUN WITH MICKEY AND HIS FRIENDS

Table of Contents

HAL•LEONARD® CORPORATION
7777 W. BLUEMOUND RD. P.O. BOX 13819 MILWAUKEE, WI 53213

Visit Hal Leonard Online at
www.halleonard.com

Angels We Have Heard on High

Traditional French Carol
Arranged by TOM ANDERSON

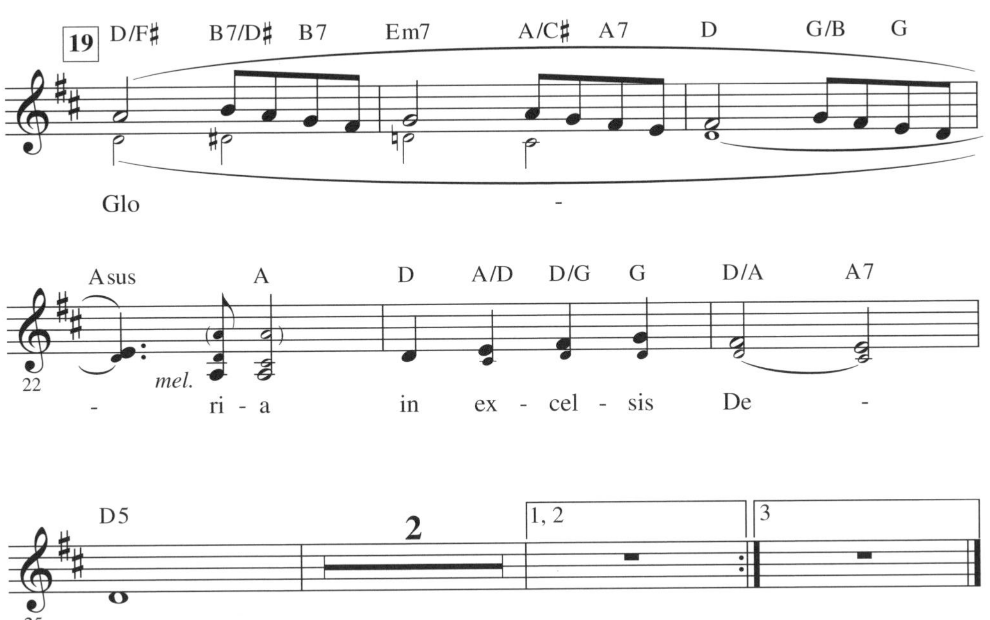
19 D/F#   B7/D# B7   Em7   A/C# A7   D   G/B   G
Glo -
22 Asus   A   D   A/D D/G G   D/A   A7
mel.
- ri - a   in   ex - cel - sis   De -
25 D5   2   1, 2   3
o.

Angels We Have Heard on High

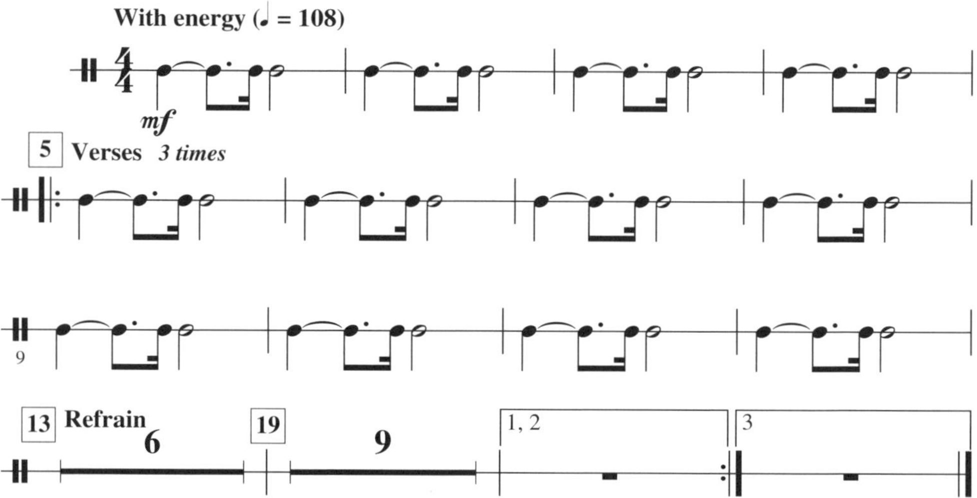

Angels We Have Heard on High

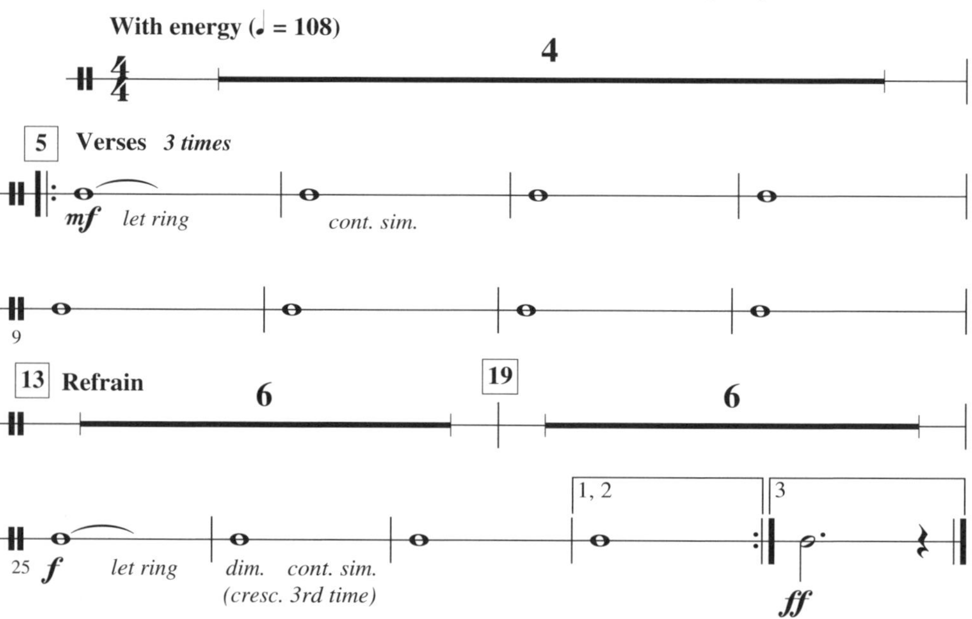

Angels We Have Heard on High

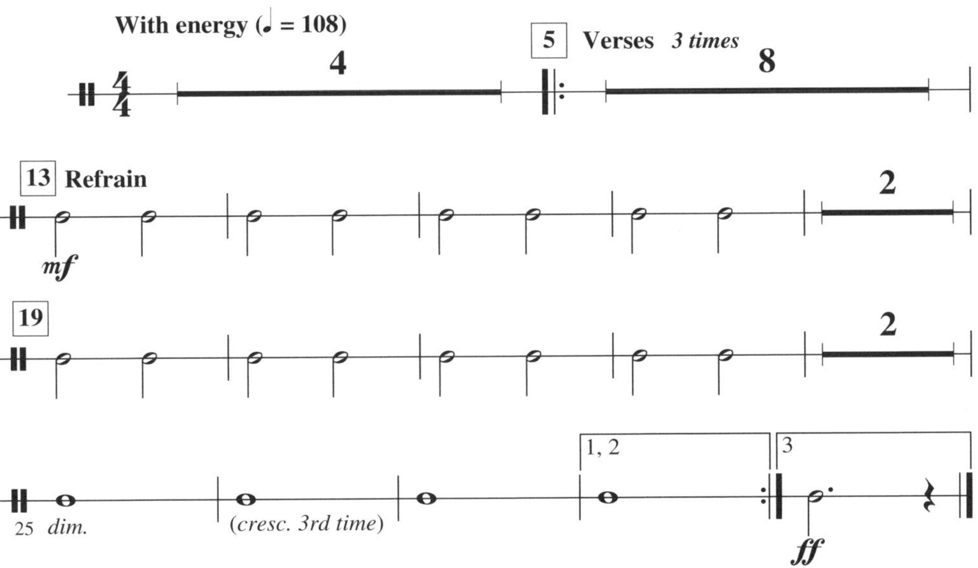

Angels We Have Heard on High

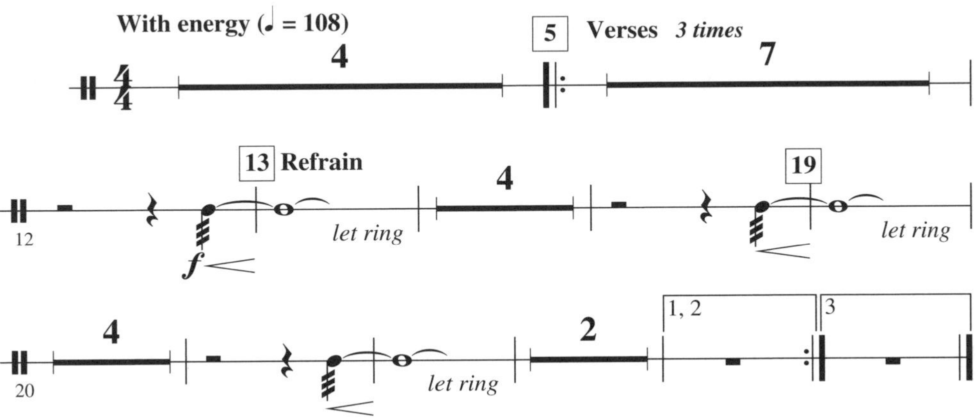

Angels We Have Heard on High

Away in a Manger

Music by JAMES R. MURRAY
Words, Stanza 1, 2, Anonymous
Stanza 3, JOHN THOMAS McFARLAND
Arranged by TOM ANDERSON

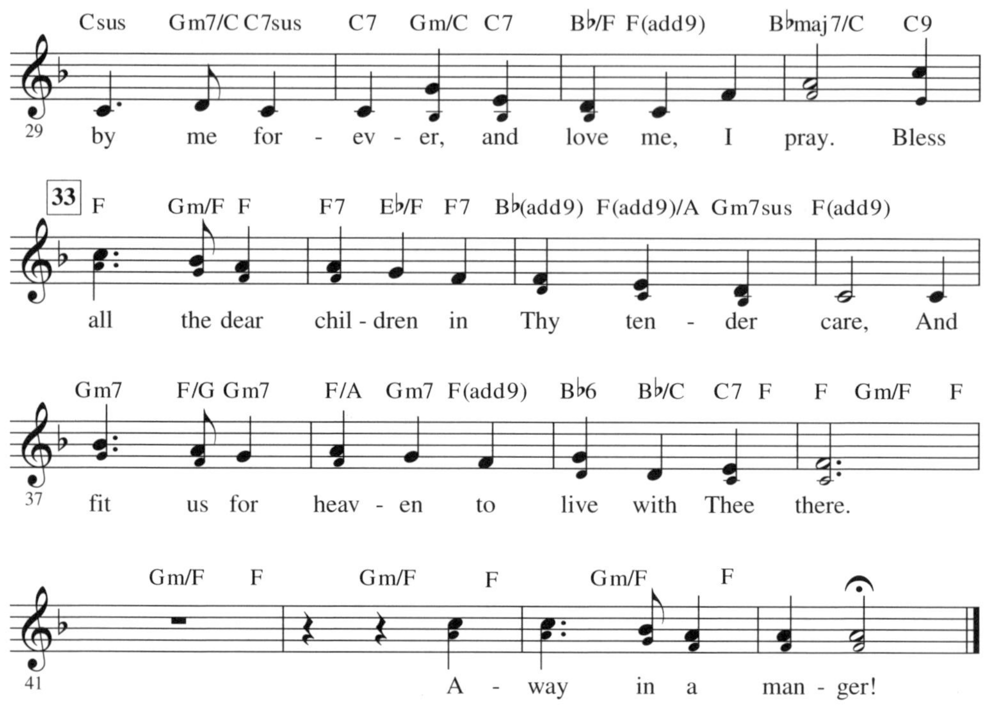

Csus   Gm7/C C7sus   C7   Gm/C C7   B♭/F F(add9)   B♭maj7/C   C9
29
by   me   for - ev - er,   and   love   me,   I   pray.   Bless
33 F   Gm/F F   F7 E♭/F F7 B♭(add9) F(add9)/A Gm7sus F(add9)
all   the   dear   chil - dren   in   Thy   ten - der   care,   And
Gm7   F/G Gm7   F/A Gm7 F(add9)   B♭6   B♭/C C7 F   F Gm/F F
37
fit   us   for   heav - en   to   live   with   Thee   there.
Gm/F   F   Gm/F   F   Gm/F   F
41
A - way   in   a   man - ger!

Away in a Manger

ORFF INSTRUMENTS

Music by JAMES R. MURRAY
Words, Stanza 1, 2, Anonymous
Stanza 3, JOHN THOMAS McFARLAND
Arranged by TOM ANDERSON

let ring
cont. sim.
let ring
cont. sim.
let ring
cont. sim.
let ring
let ring
let ring
let ring

Away in a Manger

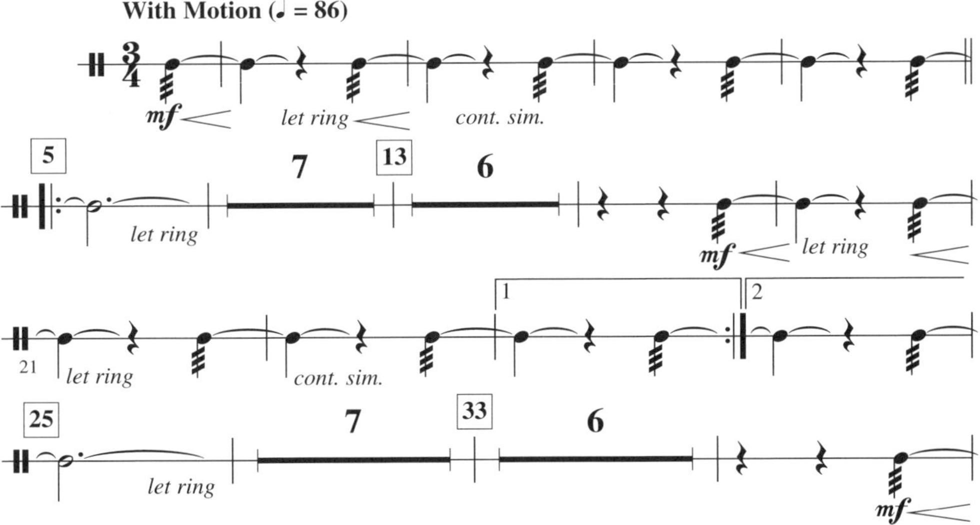

Away in a Manger

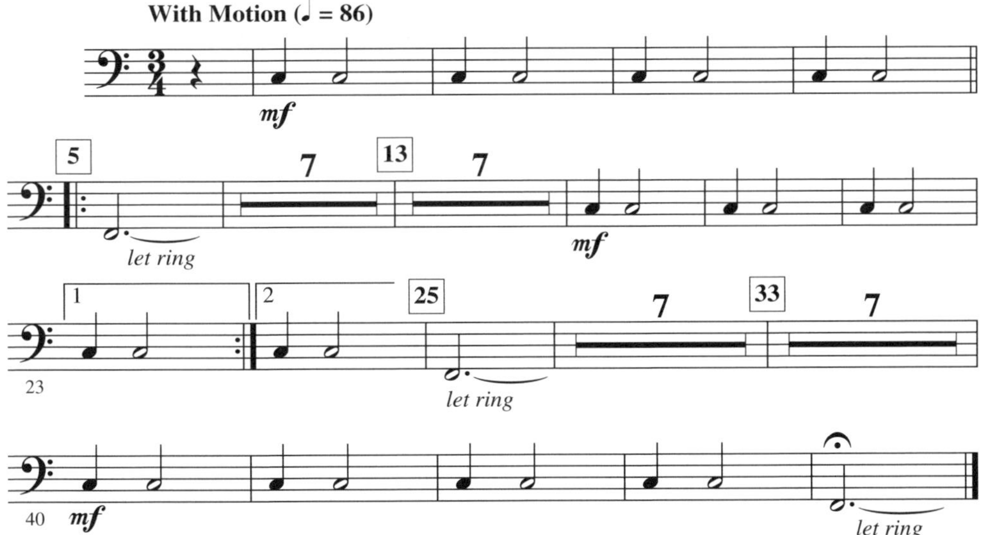

3/15

Deck the Halls

Traditional Welsh Carol
Arranged by TOM ANDERSON

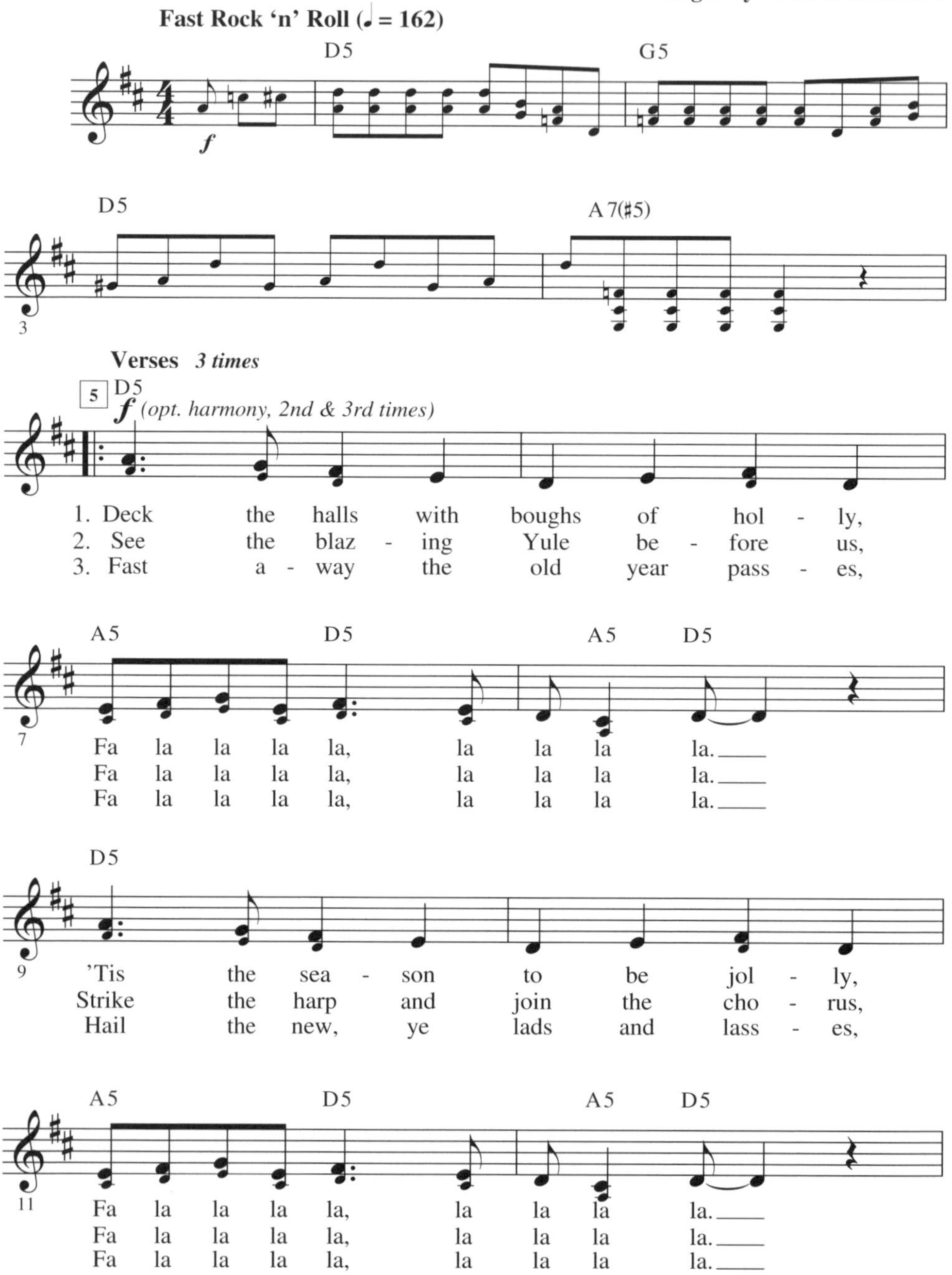

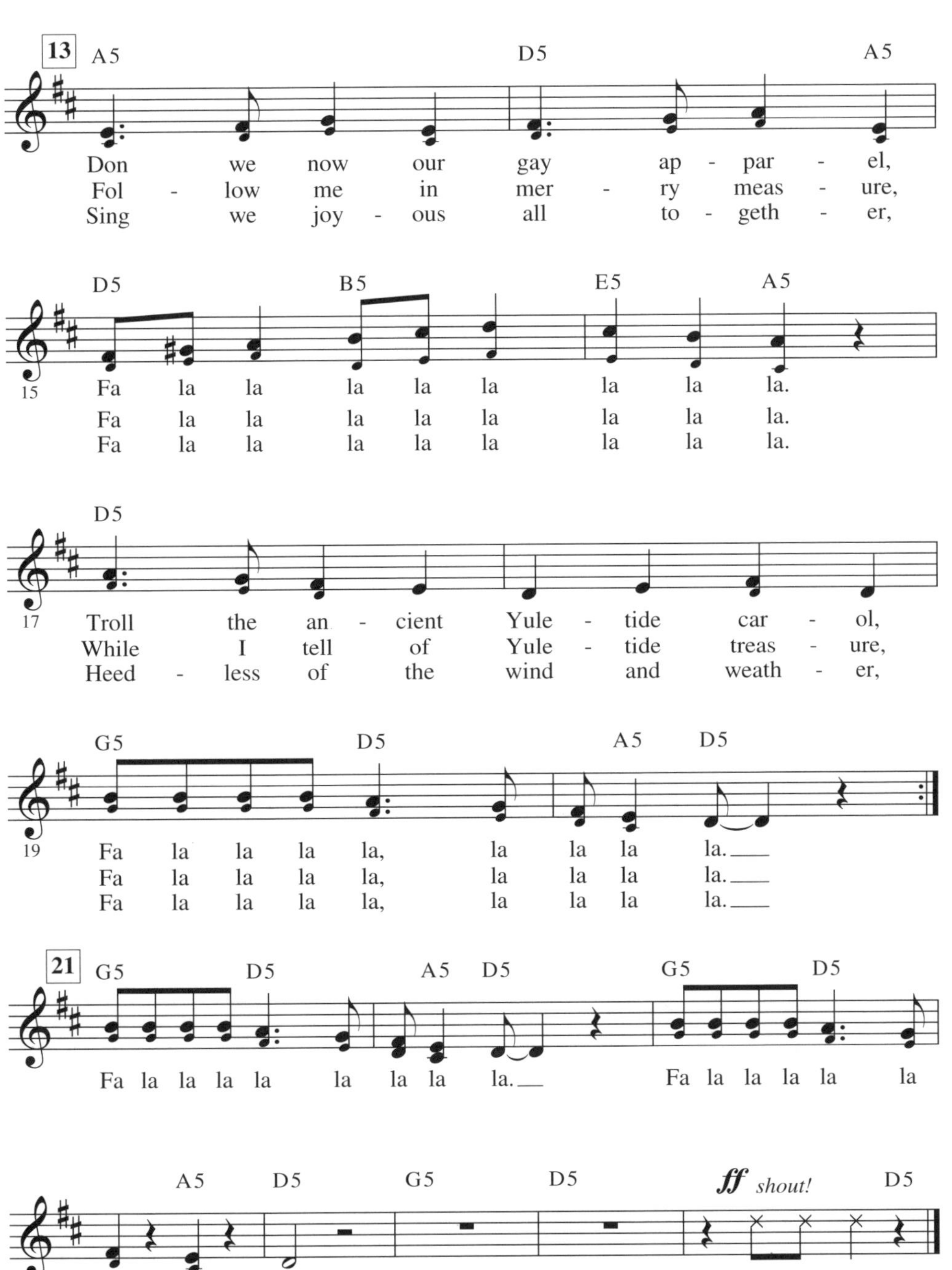

13
A5   D5   A5
Don we now our gay ap - par - el,
Fol - low me in mer - ry meas - ure,
Sing we joy - ous all to - geth - er,

D5   B5   E5   A5
15 Fa la la la la la la la la.
Fa la la la la la la la la.
Fa la la la la la la la la.

D5
17 Troll the an - cient Yule - tide car - ol,
While I tell of Yule - tide treas - ure,
Heed - less of the wind and weath - er,

G5   D5   A5   D5
19 Fa la la la la, la la la la.___
Fa la la la la, la la la la.___
Fa la la la la, la la la la.___

21 G5   D5   A5 D5   G5   D5
Fa la la la la la la la la.___ Fa la la la la la

A5 D5   G5   D5   ff shout!   D5
24 la la la. Deck the halls!

Deck the Halls

BONGO/CONGA DRUMS

Traditional Welsh Carol
Arranged by TOM ANDERSON

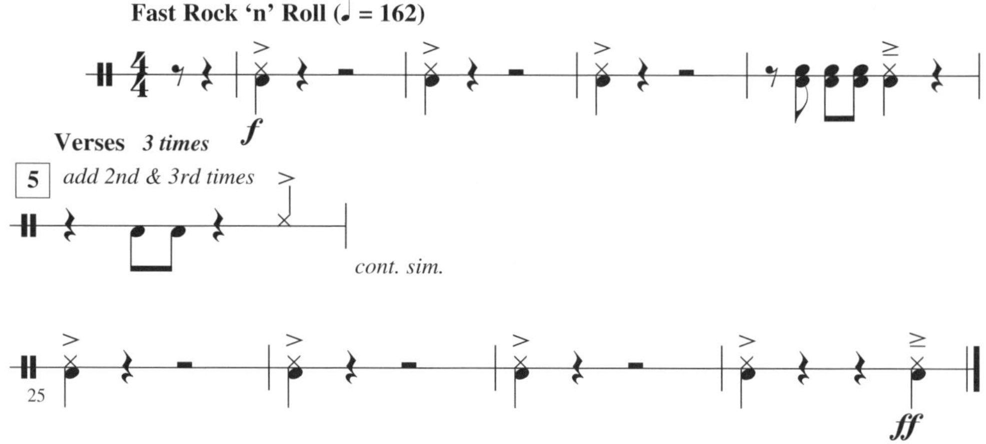

Deck the Halls

TAMBOURINE

Traditional Welsh Carol
Arranged by TOM ANDERSON

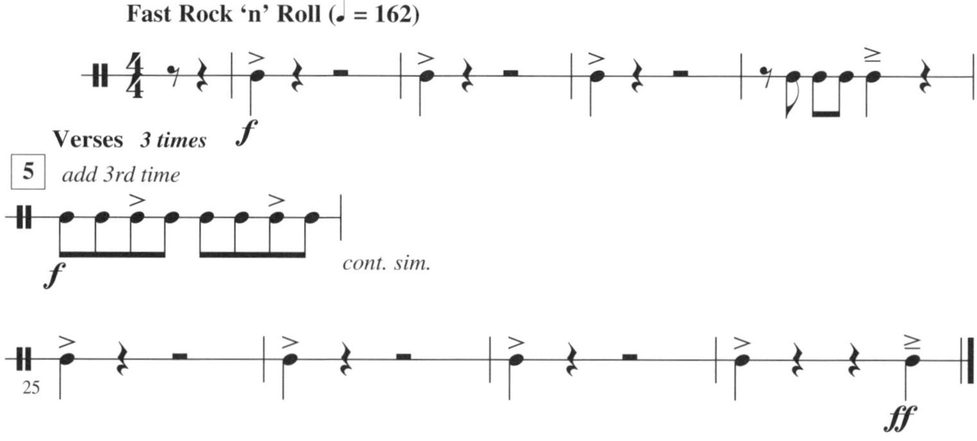

Here We Come A-Caroling

English Wassail Song
Arranged by TOM ANDERSON

Here We Come A-Caroling

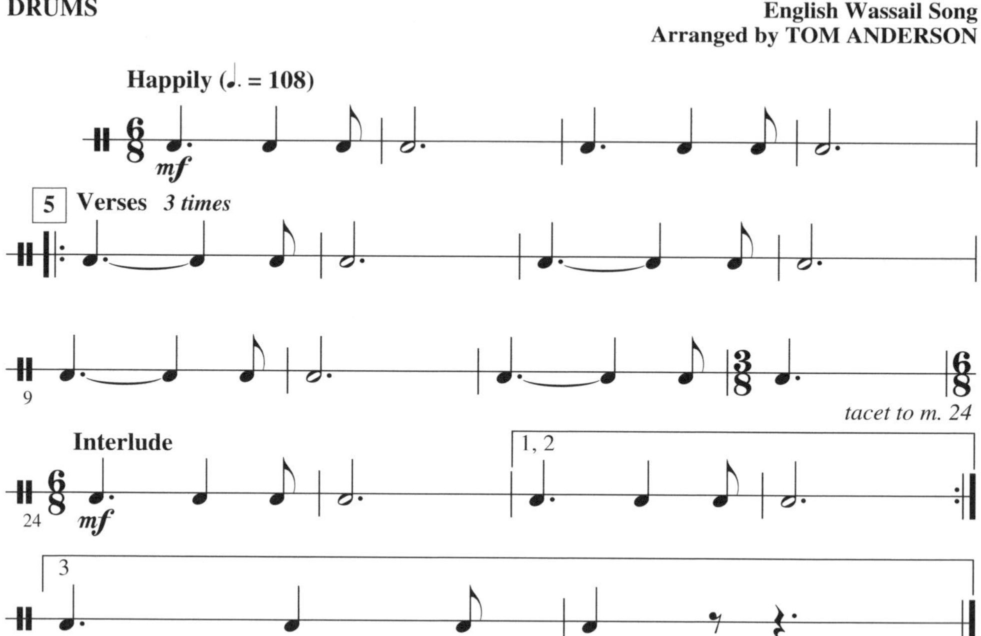

Here We Come A-Caroling

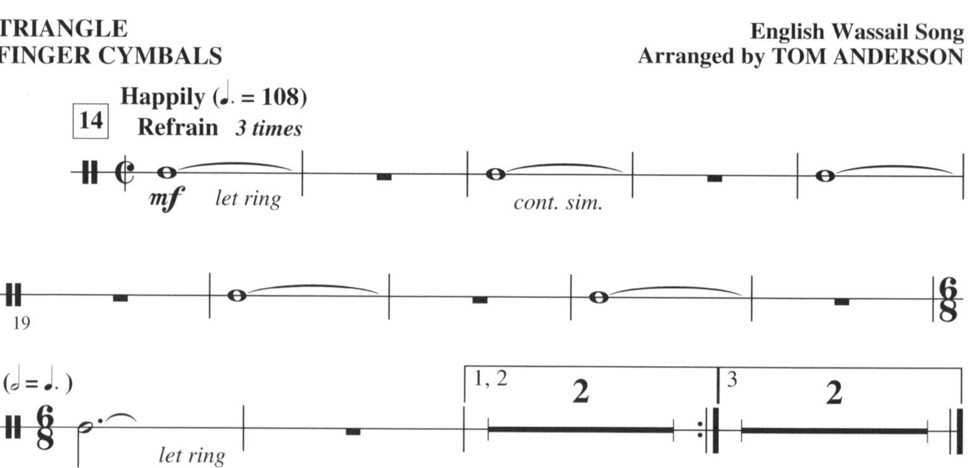

Jingle Bells

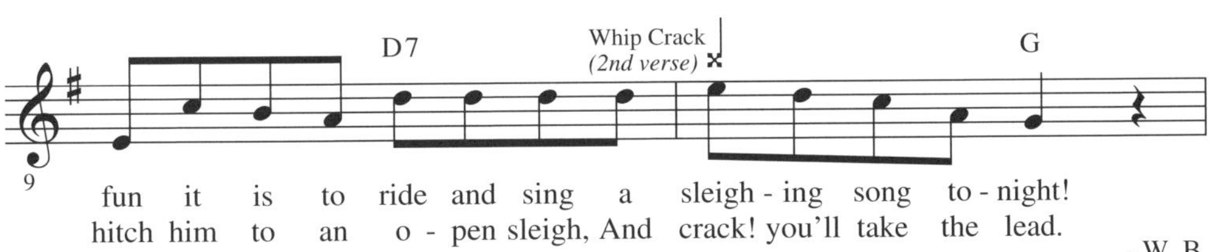

Refrain
11
G
opt. harmony
f
Jin - gle bells! Jin - gle bells! Jin - gle all the way!
+ Jingle Bells
C G A7 Am7 D7
13
Oh, what fun it is to ride in a one - horse o - pen sleigh!___
G
15
Jin - gle bells! Jin - gle bells! Jin - gle all the way!
C G 1 D7 G
17
Oh, what fun it is to ride in a one - horse o - pen sleigh!
- J. B.
2 D7 G Whip N. C.
shout!
19
one - horse o - pen sleigh! Hey!

6/18

Jolly Old St. Nicholas

Traditional American Carol
Arranged by TOM ANDERSON

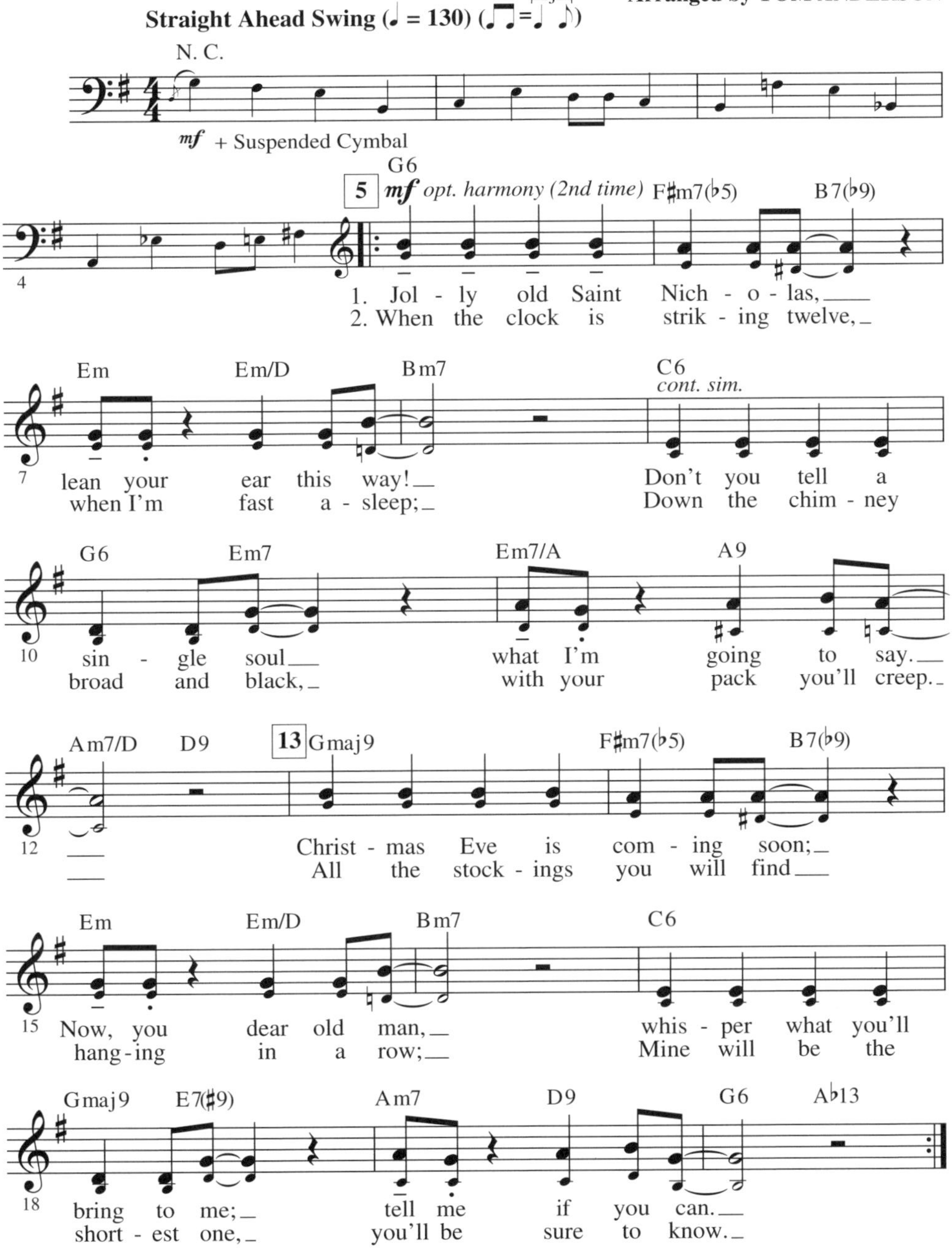

Recorder or Other Pitched Inst.
3. John-ny wants a pair of skates,__ Su-sy wants a sled;__
+ Jingle Bells
Nel-lie wants a pic-ture book;__ yel-low, blue and red..__
Now I think I'll leave to you__
what to give the rest;__ Choose for me, dear San-ta Claus,__
you will know the best.__ You will know the best.__
You will know the best!______
- Recorder

Jolly Old St. Nicholas

Jolly Old St. Nicholas

Jolly Old St. Nicholas

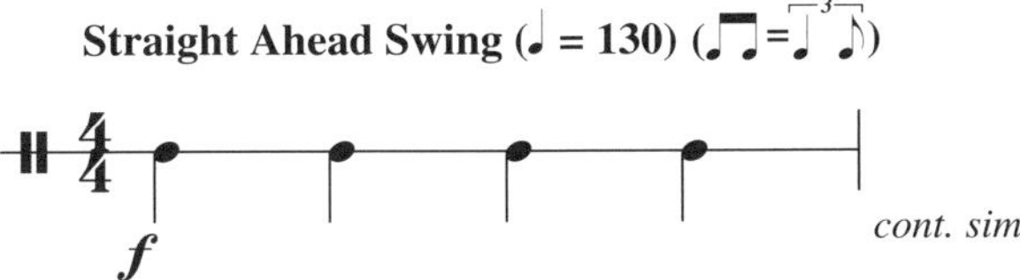

7/19

Joy to the World

Words by ISAAC WATTS
Music by GEORGE F. HANDEL
Arranged by TOM ANDERSON

(4-measure rhythm intro. on recording)

Mod. Gospel Shuffle (𝅗𝅥 = 86)

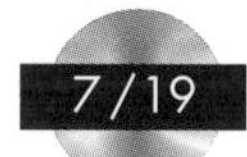

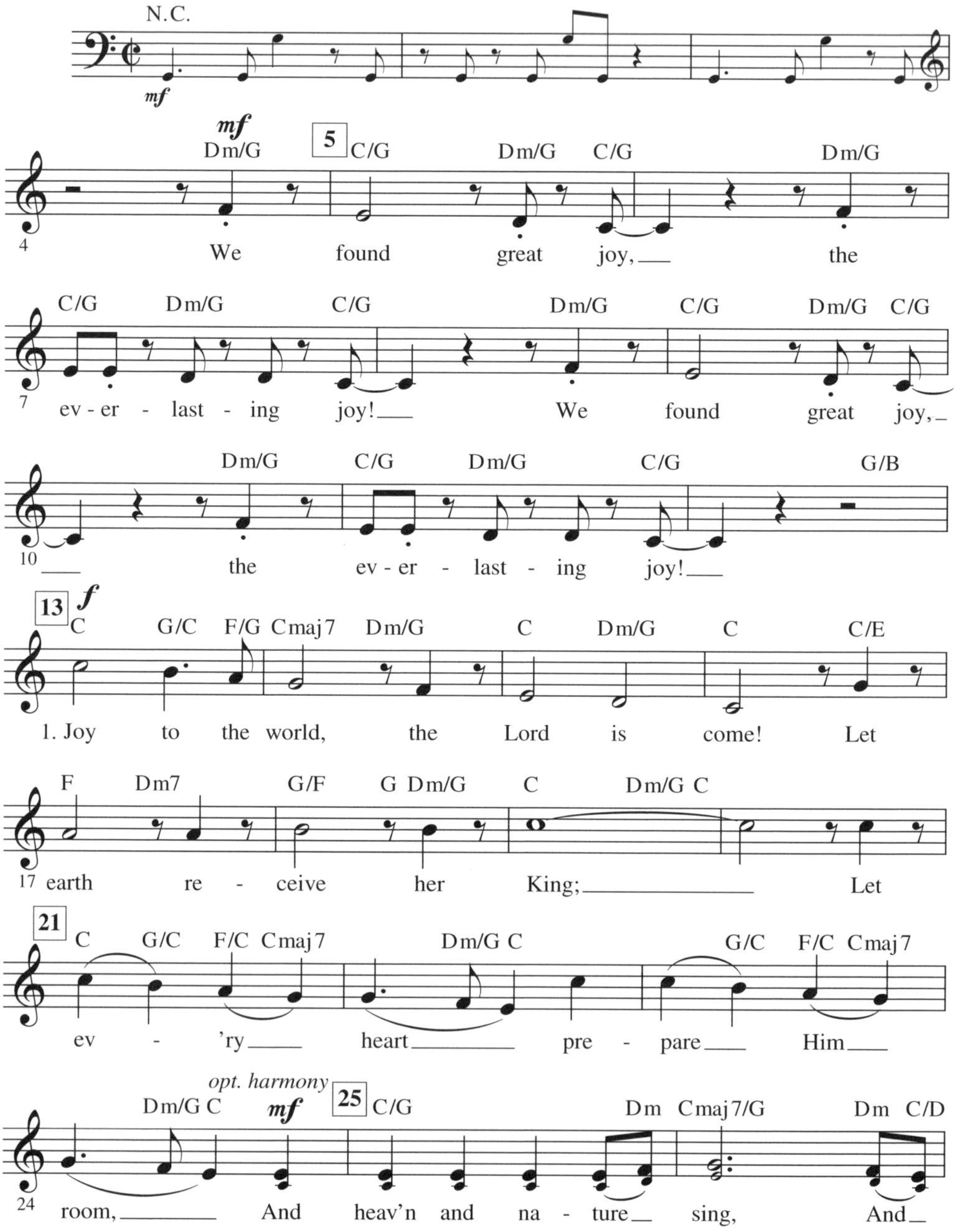

Dm7/G   C/D Dm7(b5)/G Dm7(b5)/Ab   Am7   Am7/G
27 heav'n and na - ture sing,   And heav'n and
F(add9)   C/E F2/A C/G Dm/G   32 C   Dm/C C   Dm/C
opt. small group We found great joy, ___
30 heav'n and na - ture sing.   the
mel.
+ Hand Claps on beat 2
C   Dm7(b5)/C   C   Dm/C   C   Dm/C C
34 ev - er - last - ing joy!___ We found great joy, _
Dm/C   C   Dm7(b5)/C   C   G/B
37 ___ the ev - er - last - ing joy!___ - Claps
40 f opt. harmony
C   G/C   F/G Cmaj7 Dm/G   C   Dm/G   C   C/E
2. He rules the world with truth and grace, And
mel.
F   Dm7   G/F   G Dm/G   C   Dm/G C
na - tions prove___
44 makes the   We found great joy!___ The
48 C   G/C F/C Cmaj7   Dm/G C   G/C F/C Cmaj7
glo - ries___ of___ His right - eous -
Dm/G C   mf   52 C/G   Dm Cmaj7/G   Dm C/D
51 ness,___ And won - ders of His__ love, And__

Dm7/G
C/D Dm7(b5)/G Dm7(b5)/Ab
Am7
Am7/G
54
won - ders   of   His___ love,   And___   won - ders,

F(add9)   C/E F2/A   C/G   Dm/G   59 C   Dm/C   C
We   found   great   joy,___
57
won   -   ders   of   His   love.
mel.
+ Claps

Dm/C   C   Dm7(b5)/C   C   Dm/C
60
the   ev - er - last - ing   joy!___   We

C   Dm/C   C   Dm/C   C   Dm7(b5)/C   C
63 found   great   joy,___   the   ev - er - last - ing   joy!_

build intensity
f Dm/C   67 C   Dm/C   C   Dm/C
66 ___   We   found   great   joy,___   the
+ Tambourine on beat 2

C   Dm7(b5)/C   C   Dm/C   C   Dm/C   C
69 ev - er - last - ing   joy!___   We   found   great   joy,_

Dm/C   C   Dm7(b5)/C   C
72 ___   the   ev - er - last - ing   joy!___
ff

O Christmas Tree
(O Tannenbaum)

Traditional German Carol
Arranged by TOM ANDERSON

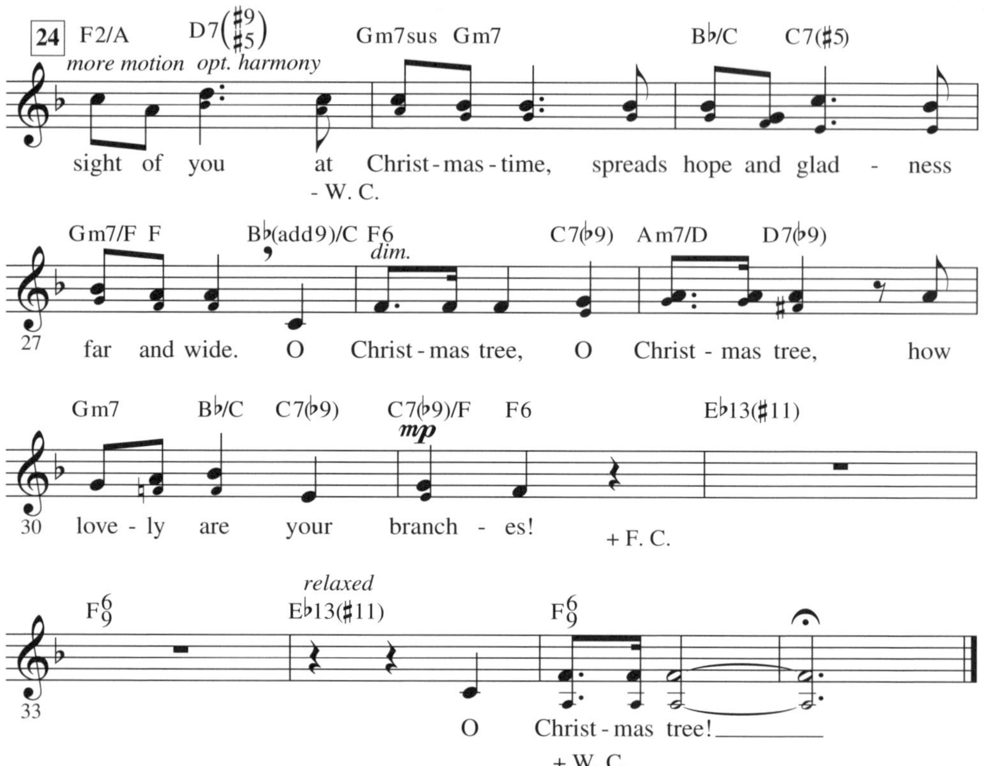

more motion   opt. harmony
sight of you   at Christ-mas-time,   spreads hope and glad - ness
- W. C.
far and wide.   O   Christ-mas tree,   O   Christ - mas tree,   how
love - ly   are   your   branch - es!   + F. C.
O   Christ - mas tree!
+ W. C.

Pat-a-Pan
(Willie, Take Your Little Drum)

Words and Music by
BERNARD de la MONNOYE
Arranged by TOM ANDERSON

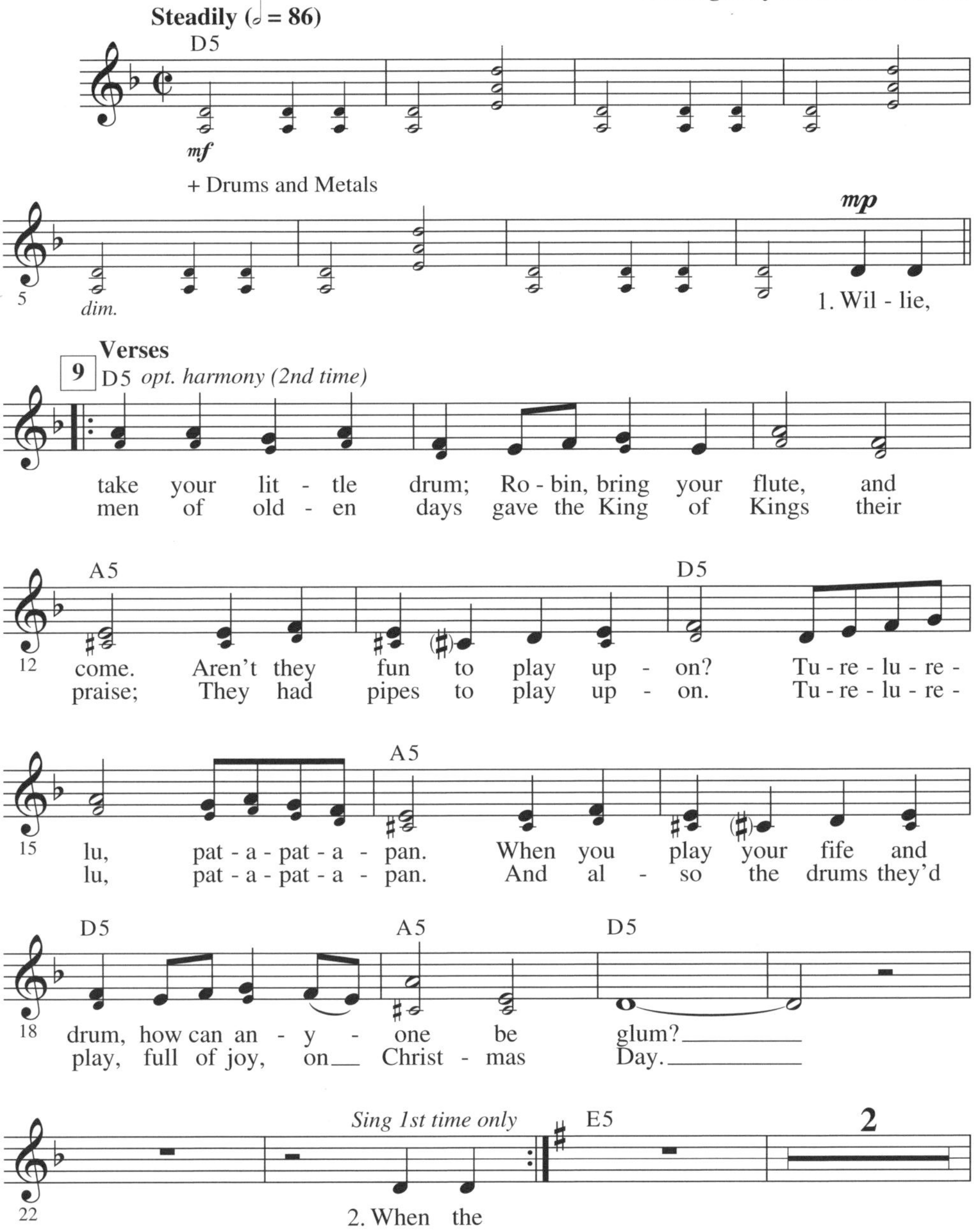

mf
28 E5
27 3. God and man to - day be - come close-ly joined as
B5
30 flute and drum. Let the joy - ous tune play
E5
B5
33 on! Tu - re - lu - re - lu, pat - a - pat - a - pan. As the
E5
B5
36 in - stru - ments you play, we will sing, this Christ - mas
39 Ending
E5
6
Day.

Pat-a-Pan
(Willie, Take Your Little Drum)

Pat-a-Pan
(Willie, Take Your Little Drum)

Pat-a-Pan
(Willie, Take Your Little Drum)

Pat-a-Pan
(Willie, Take Your Little Drum)

10/22

Silent Night

Words by JOSEPH MOHR
Music by FRANZ GRUBER
Arranged by TOM ANDERSON

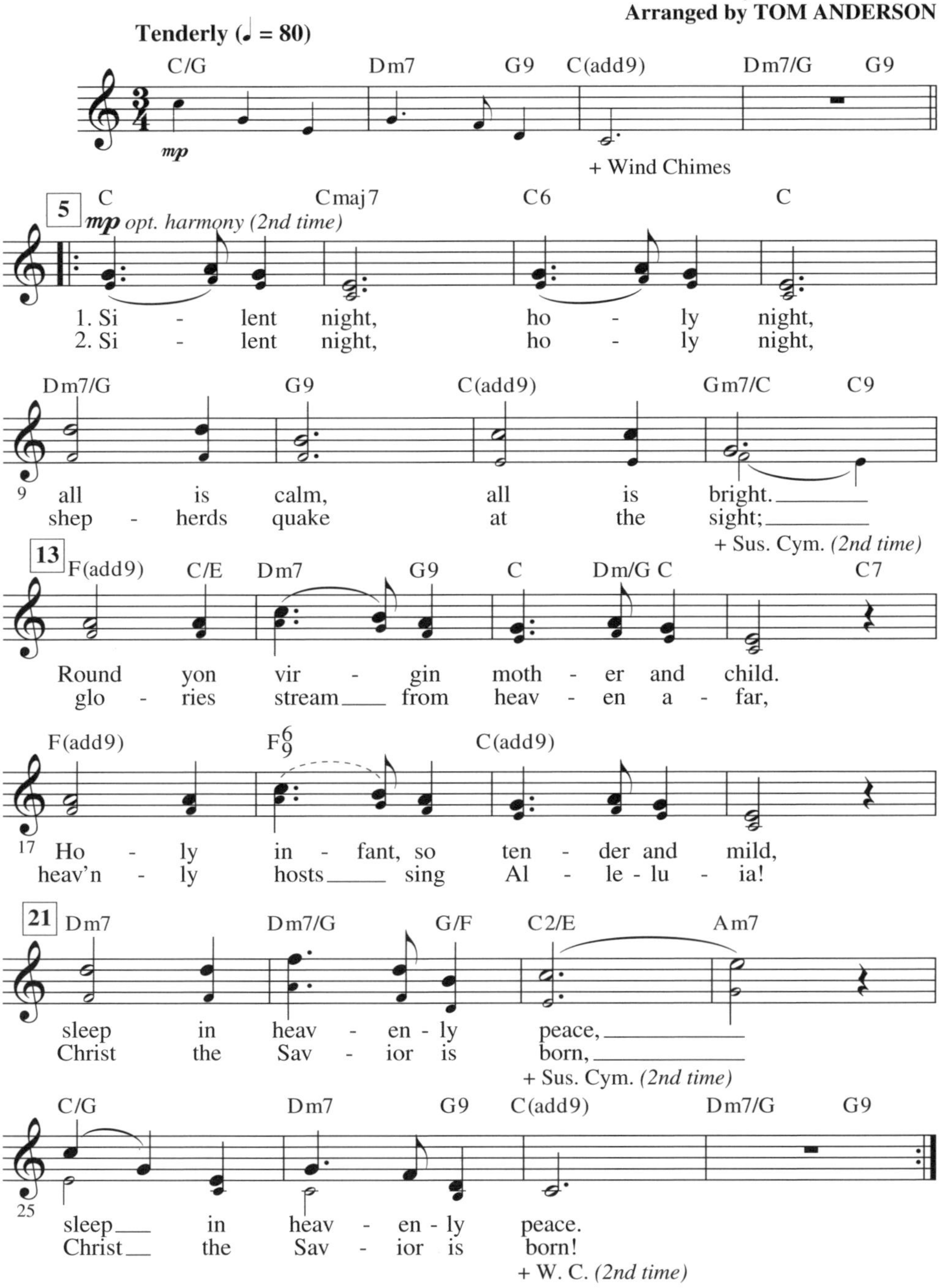

more motion
29 C   Cmaj7   C6   C   Dm7/G
mf
3. Si - lent night,   ho - ly night,   Son of
+ Descant/Recorder
G9   C(add9)   Gm7/C   C9   37 F(add9)   C/E Dm7   G9
34 God,   love's   pure light;____   ra - diant beams__ from
+ Sus. Cym.
C   Dm/G C   C7   F(add9)   F6/9   C(add9)
39 Thy   ho - ly   face,   with   the   dawn   of re - deem - ing
45 Dm7   Dm7/G   G/F   C2/E   Am7
44 grace,   Je - sus, Lord,   at Thy   birth,____
+ Sus. Cym.
C/G   Dm7   G9   C(add9)
dim.   slight rit.   mp
49 Je - sus,   Lord   at Thy   birth.
+ W. C.

Silent Night

Up on the Housetop

Words and Music by B. R. HANDY
Arranged by TOM ANDERSON

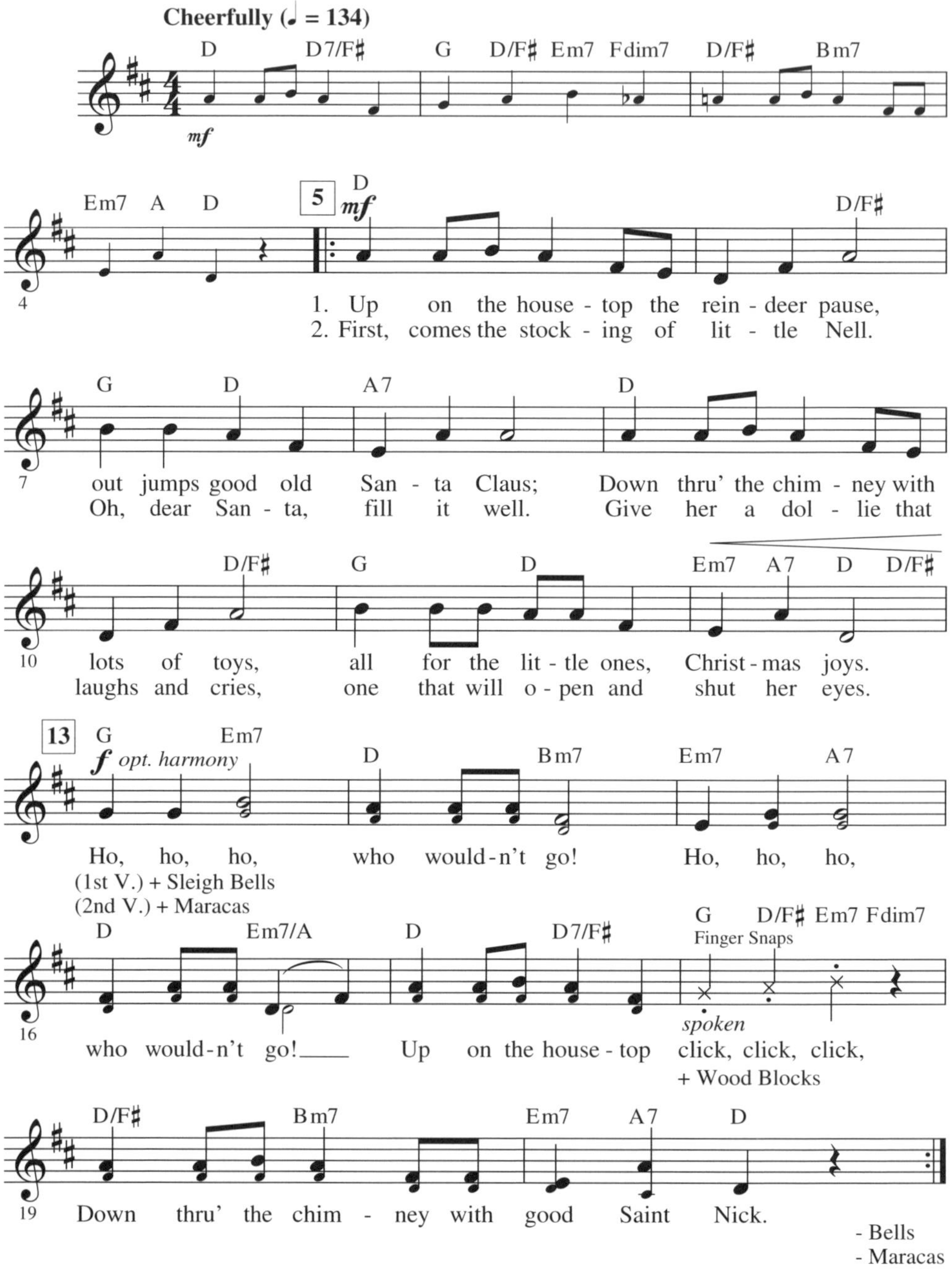

21 mf D
3. Next, comes the stock - ing of lit - tle Will;
G D A7
Oh, just see what a glo - rious fill!
D D/F#
Here is a ham - mer and lots of tacks,
G D Em7 A7 D Whip Crack D/F#
al - so a ball and a whip that cracks.
29 f G Em7 D Bm7
Ho, ho, ho, who would - n't go!
+ S. B. and Mar.
Em7 A7 D Em7/A
Ho, ho, ho, who would - n't go!
Finger Snaps
D D7/F# G D/F# Em7 Fdim7
Up on the house - top spoken click, click, click,
+ W. B.
D/F# Bm7 Em7 A7 D Whip Crack N.C.
Down thru' the chim - ney with good Saint Nick.

We Wish You a Merry Christmas

Traditional English Carol
Arranged by TOM ANDERSON

22
G   G/B   C   C/B   A7sus   A7
wish you a mer - ry Christ - mas, We wish you a mer - ry
+ Tri./F. C., H. D., Tamb.

D   D/C   B7sus   B7   Em   G/B
25
Christ - mas, We wish you a mer - ry Christ - mas, and a
- Tri./F. C.
- H. D.
- Tamb.

C6   Am7 cresc.   Am7/D   D9
28
hap - py New

ff G   G2/B   C   Am7   D9   G6/9
32
Year!
+ Tri./F. C., H. D., Tamb.

We Wish You a Merry Christmas

TRIANGLE/FINGER CYMBALS

Traditional English Carol
Arranged by TOM ANDERSON

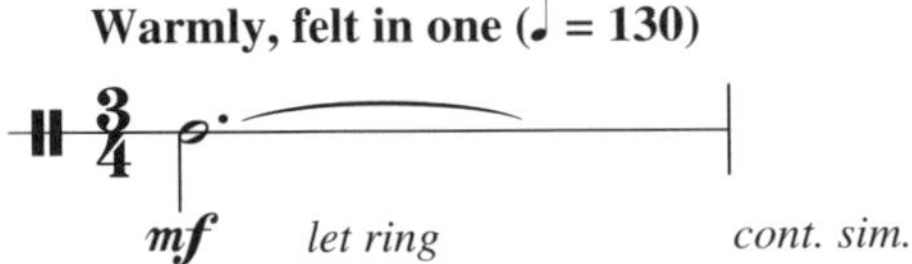

We Wish You a Merry Christmas

HAND DRUM

Traditional English Carol
Arranged by TOM ANDERSON

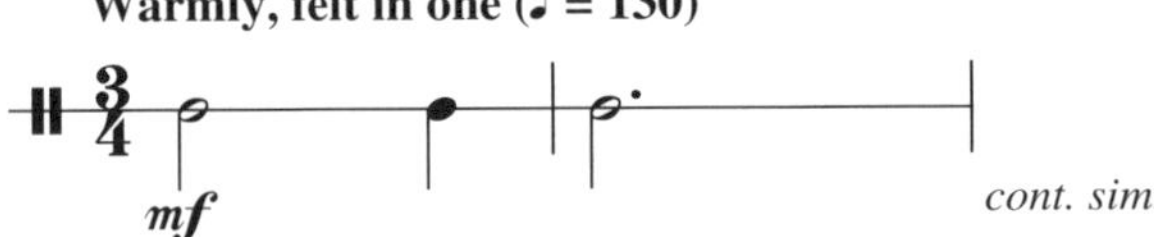

We Wish You a Merry Christmas

TAMBOURINE

Traditional English Carol
Arranged by TOM ANDERSON

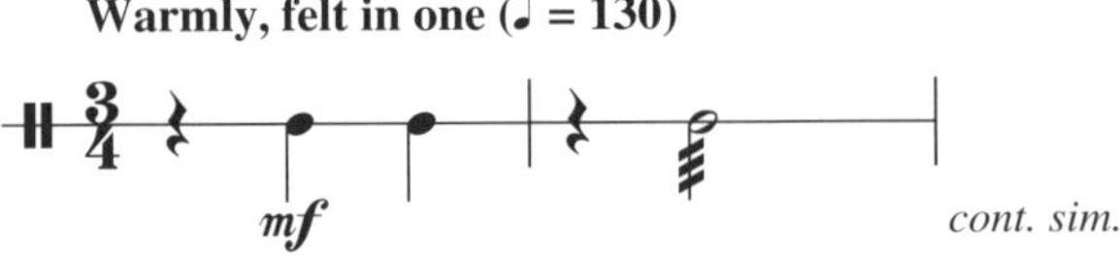

Disney
Mickey's Caroling Book
HOLIDAY FUN WITH MICKEY AND HIS FRIENDS

Table of Contents

HAL•LEONARD® CORPORATION
7777 W. BLUEMOUND RD. P.O. BOX 13819 MILWAUKEE, WI 53213

Visit Hal Leonard Online at
www.halleonard.com

Angels We Have Heard on High

Traditional French Carol
Arranged by TOM ANDERSON

Copyright © 2012 by HAL LEONARD CORPORATION
International Copyright Secured   All Rights Reserved

19 D/F# B7/D# B7 Em7 A/C# A7 D G/B G
Glo -
Asus A D A/D D/G G D/A A7
mel.
22
- ri - a in ex - cel - sis De -
D5 2 1, 2 3
25
o.

Angels We Have Heard on High

HAND DRUM

Traditional French Carol
Arranged by TOM ANDERSON

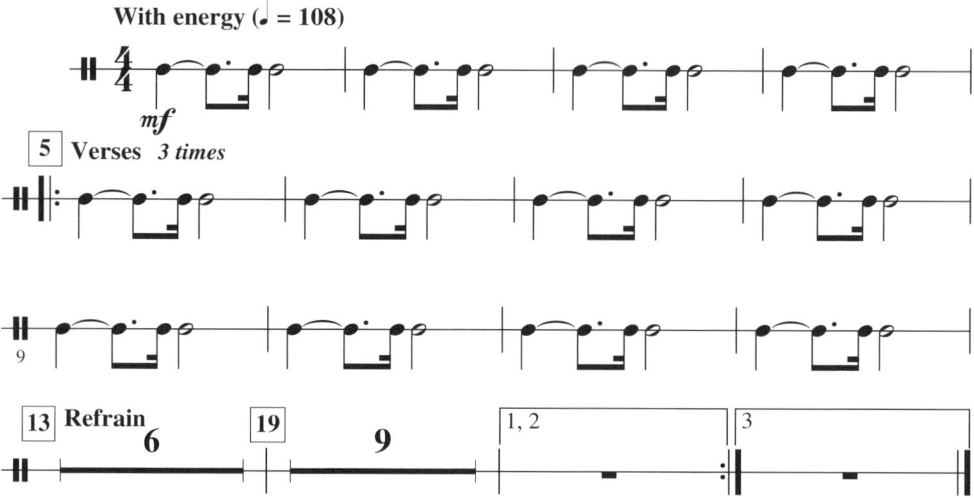

Angels We Have Heard on High

FINGER CYMBALS

Traditional French Carol
Arranged by TOM ANDERSON

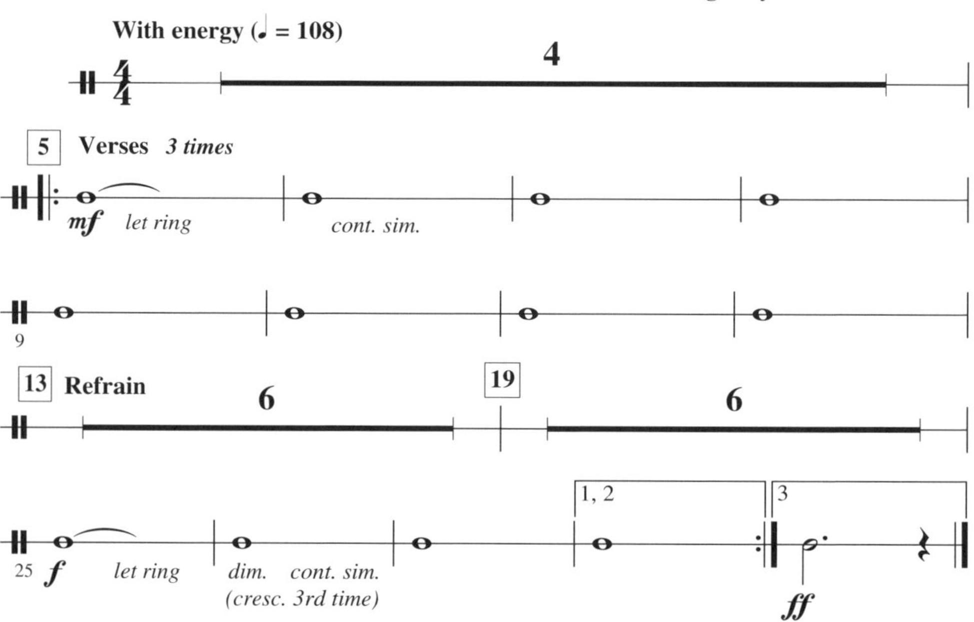

Angels We Have Heard on High

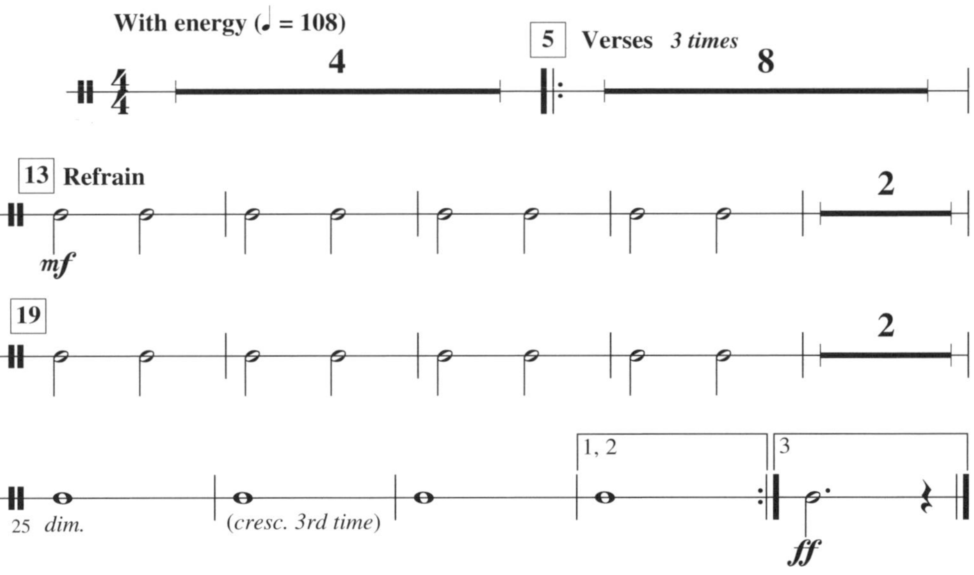

Angels We Have Heard on High

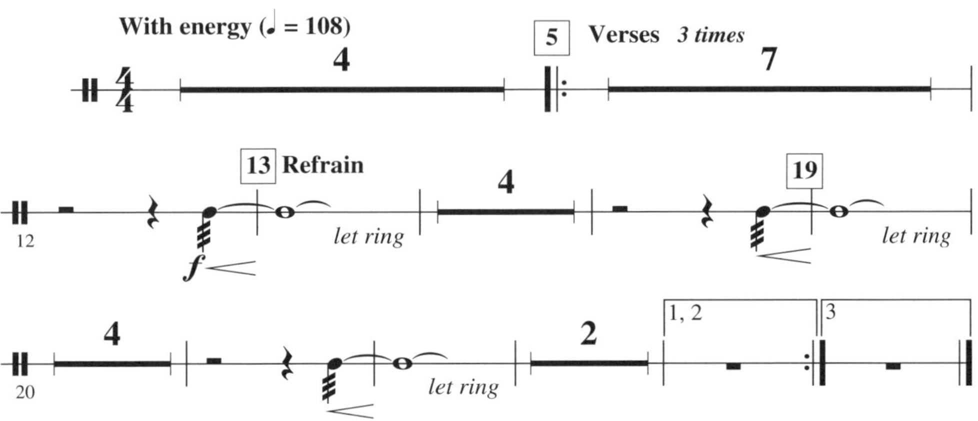

Angels We Have Heard on High

Away in a Manger

Music by JAMES R. MURRAY
Words, Stanza 1, 2, Anonymous
Stanza 3, JOHN THOMAS McFARLAND
Arranged by TOM ANDERSON

(5 clicks on recording)
With Motion ($\quarternote$ = 86)

mf

(opt. harmony, 2nd time)

1. A -

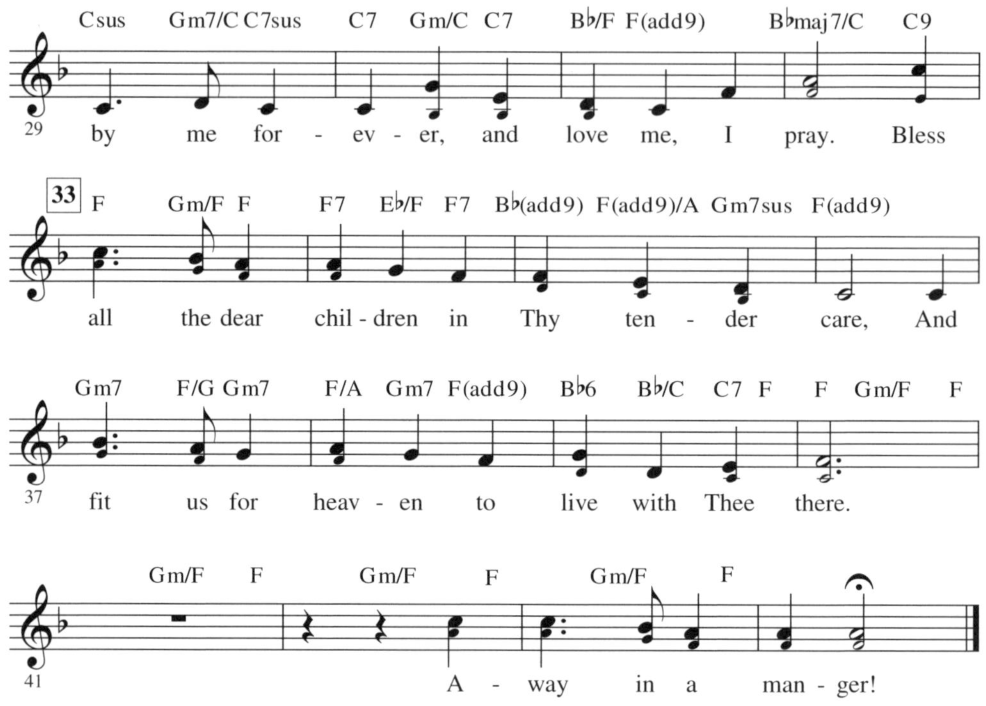

by me for - ev - er, and love me, I pray. Bless
all the dear chil - dren in Thy ten - der care, And
fit us for heav - en to live with Thee there.
A - way in a man - ger!

Away in a Manger

25
let ring
cont. sim.
let ring
cont. sim.
let ring
cont. sim.
33
30
35
40
let ring
let ring
let ring

Away in a Manger

SUSPENDED CRASH CYMBAL

Music by JAMES R. MURRAY
Words, Stanza 1, 2, Anonymous
Stanza 3, JOHN THOMAS McFARLAND
Arranged by TOM ANDERSON

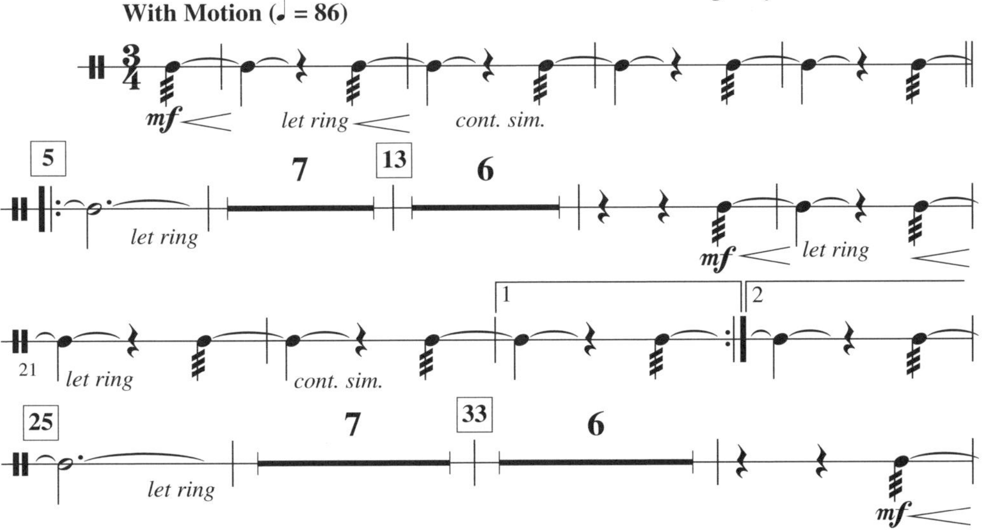

Away in a Manger

TIMPANI or TOM TOMS

Music by JAMES R. MURRAY
Words, Stanza 1, 2, Anonymous
Stanza 3, JOHN THOMAS McFARLAND
Arranged by TOM ANDERSON

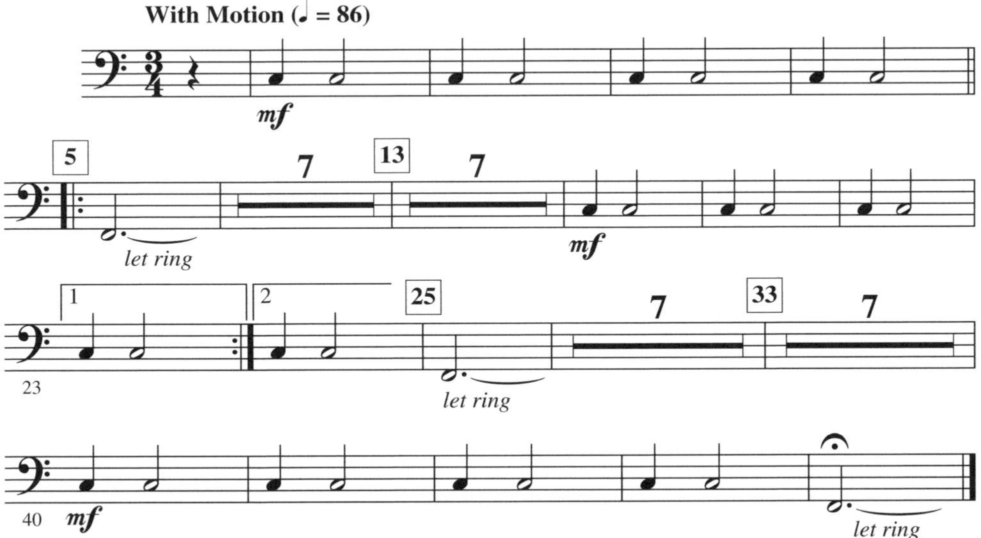

Deck the Halls

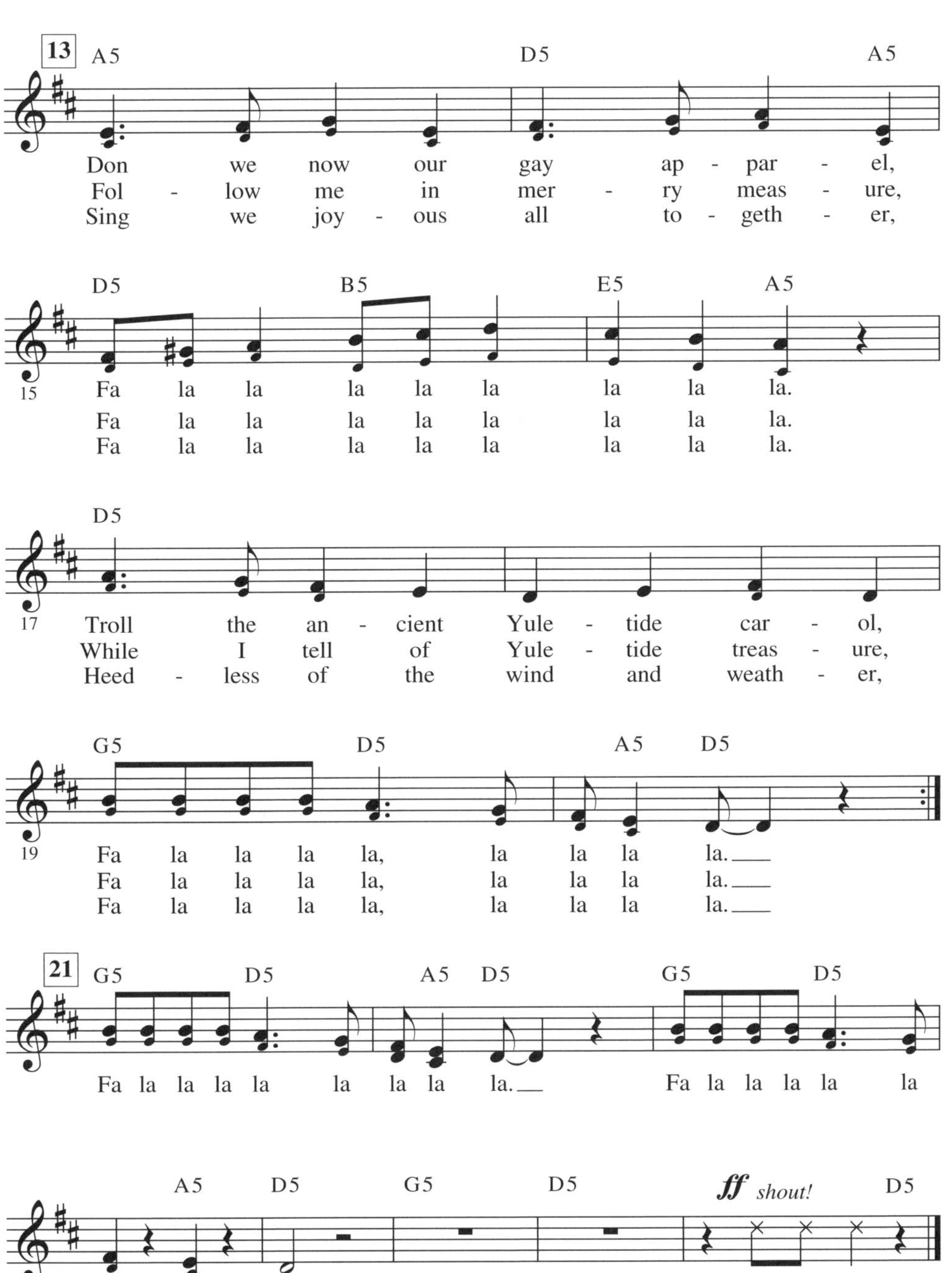

13 A5 D5 A5
Don we now our gay ap - par - el,
Fol - low me in mer - ry meas - ure,
Sing we joy - ous all to - geth - er,
D5 B5 E5 A5
15 Fa la la la la la la la la.
Fa la la la la la la la la.
Fa la la la la la la la la.
D5
17 Troll the an - cient Yule - tide car - ol,
While I tell of Yule - tide treas - ure,
Heed - less of the wind and weath - er,
G5 D5 A5 D5
19 Fa la la la la, la la la la.___
Fa la la la la, la la la la.___
Fa la la la la, la la la la.___
21 G5 D5 A5 D5 G5 D5
Fa la la la la la la la la.___ Fa la la la la la
A5 D5 G5 D5 ff shout! D5
24 la la la. Deck the halls!

Deck the Halls

BONGO/CONGA DRUMS

Traditional Welsh Carol
Arranged by TOM ANDERSON

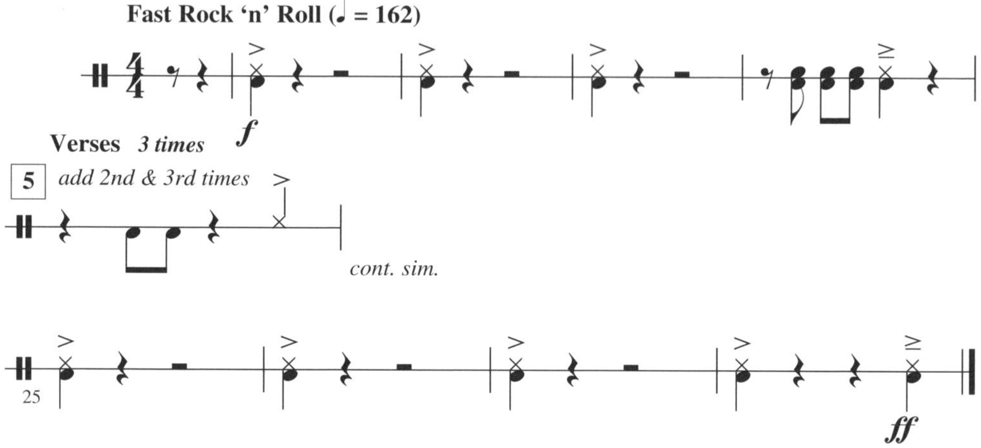

Deck the Halls

TAMBOURINE

Traditional Welsh Carol
Arranged by TOM ANDERSON

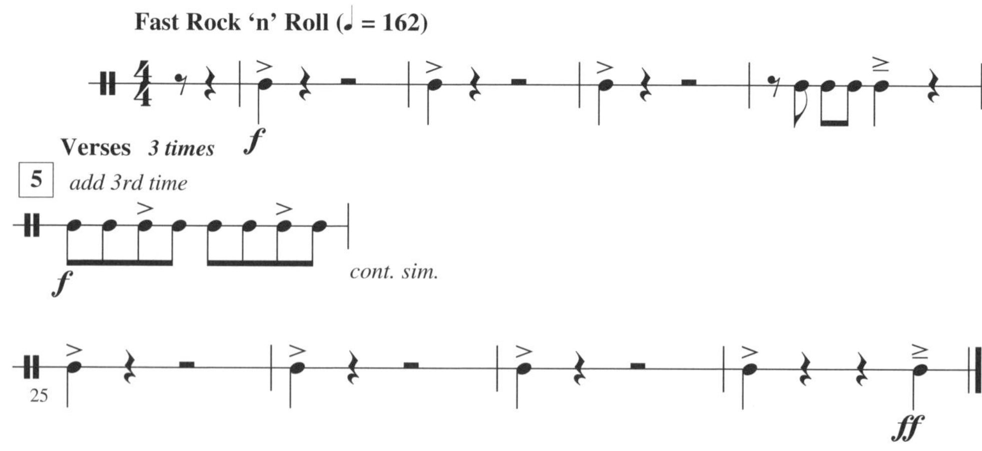

Here We Come A-Caroling

English Wassail Song
Arranged by TOM ANDERSON

Here We Come A-Caroling

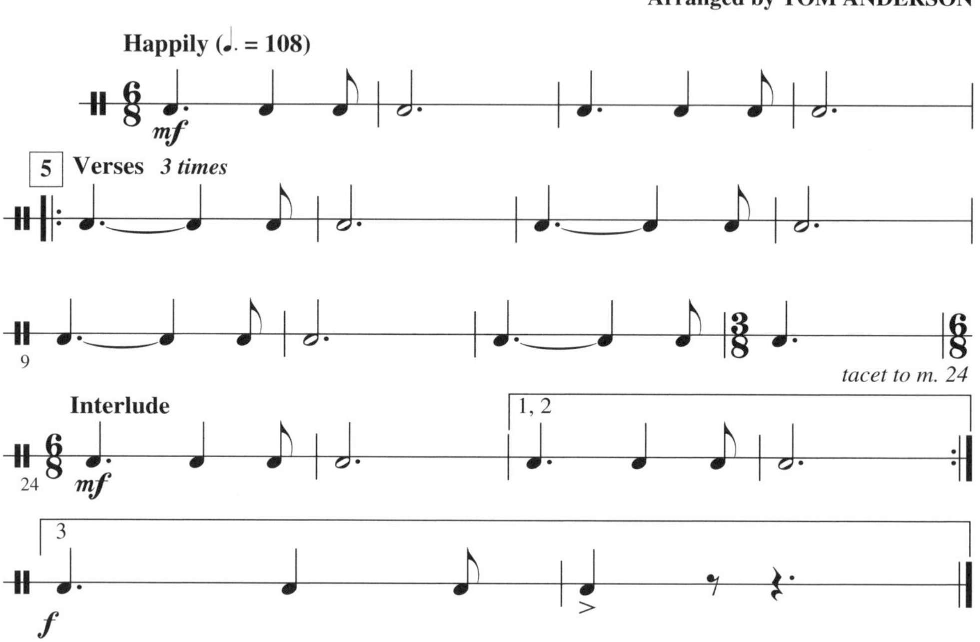

Here We Come A-Caroling

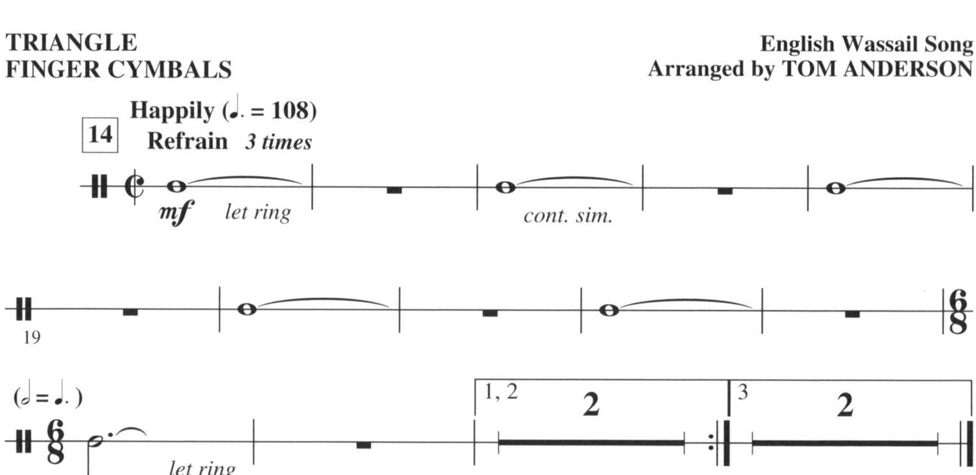

16   Mickey's Caroling Book – Singer

Jingle Bells

Words and Music by JAMES PIERPONT
Arranged by TOM ANDERSON

1. Dash-ing through the snow   in a one horse o - pen sleigh,
2. Now the ground is white,   Go it while you're young;
+ Wood or Temple Blocks

O'er the fields we go   laugh-ing all the way.
Take the girls to-night,   And sing this sleigh-ing song;   Just

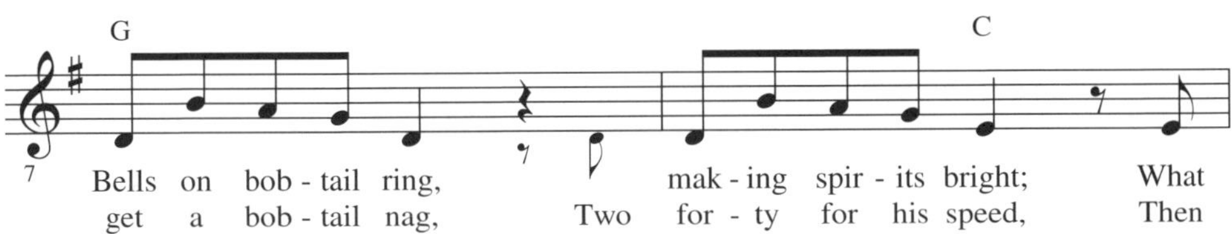

Bells on bob - tail ring,   mak-ing spir - its bright;   What
get a bob - tail nag,   Two for - ty for his speed,   Then

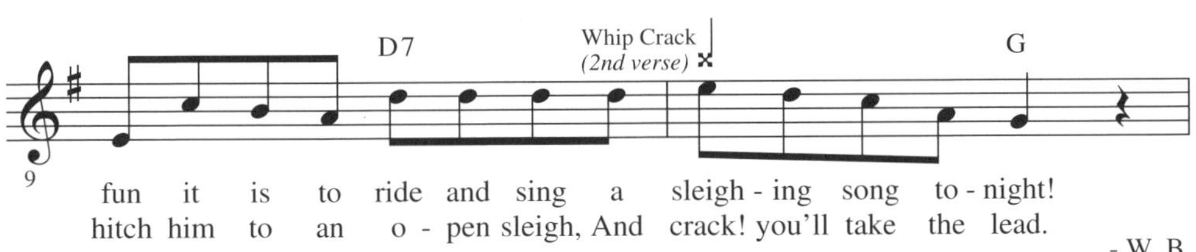

fun it is to ride and sing a sleigh - ing song to - night!
hitch him to an o - pen sleigh, And crack! you'll take the lead.

— W. B.

11 G
opt. harmony
Jin - gle bells! Jin - gle bells! Jin - gle all the way!
+ Jingle Bells
C G A7 Am7 D7
13 Oh, what fun it is to ride in a one - horse o - pen sleigh!___
G
15 Jin - gle bells! Jin - gle bells! Jin - gle all the way!
C G 1 D7 G
17 Oh, what fun it is to ride in a one - horse o - pen sleigh!
- J. B.
2 D7 G Whip N. C.
shout!
19 one - horse o - pen sleigh! Hey!

Jolly Old St. Nicholas

Traditional American Carol
Arranged by TOM ANDERSON

Straight Ahead Swing (♩ = 130) (♫ = ♩ ♪ triplet)

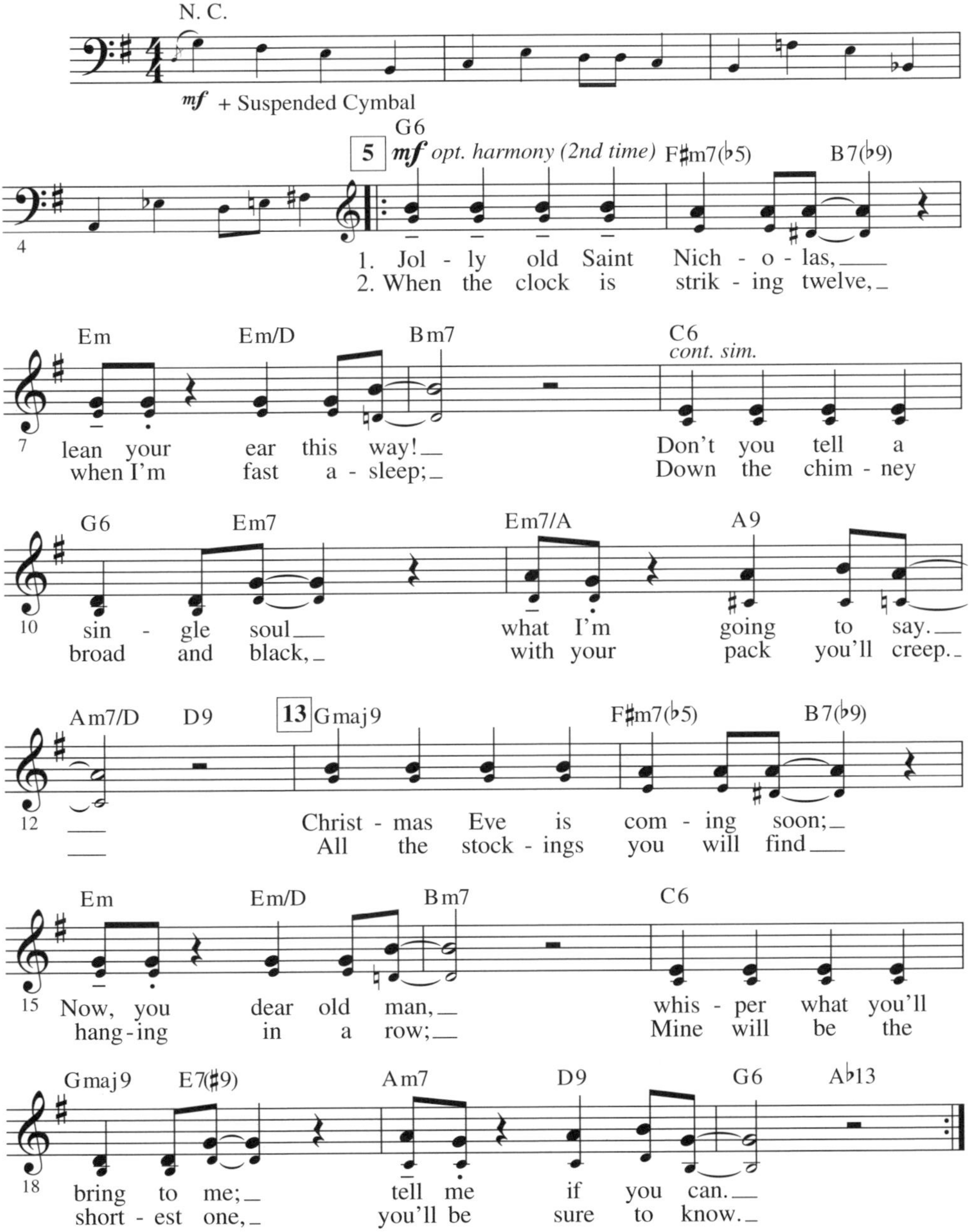

21 Recorder or Other Pitched Inst.
mf
29
27
- Recorder
32
37 f
3. John - ny wants a pair of skates, __ Su - sy wants a sled; __
+ Jingle Bells
41 Nel - lie wants a pic - ture book; __ yel-low, blue and red. __
45
44 __ Now I think I'll leave to you __
47 what to give the rest; __ Choose for me, dear San - ta Claus, __
53 cresc.
51 you will know the best. __ You will know the best. __
2
55 You will know the best! __

Jolly Old St. Nicholas

Jolly Old St. Nicholas

Jolly Old St. Nicholas

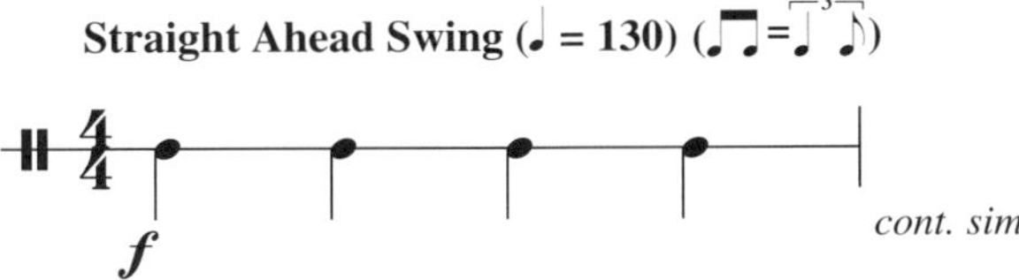

Joy to the World

Words by ISAAC WATTS
Music by GEORGE F. HANDEL
Arranged by TOM ANDERSON

(4-measure rhythm intro. on recording)

Mod. Gospel Shuffle (𝅗𝅥 = 86)

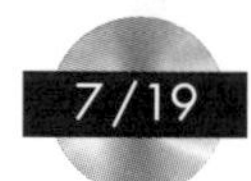

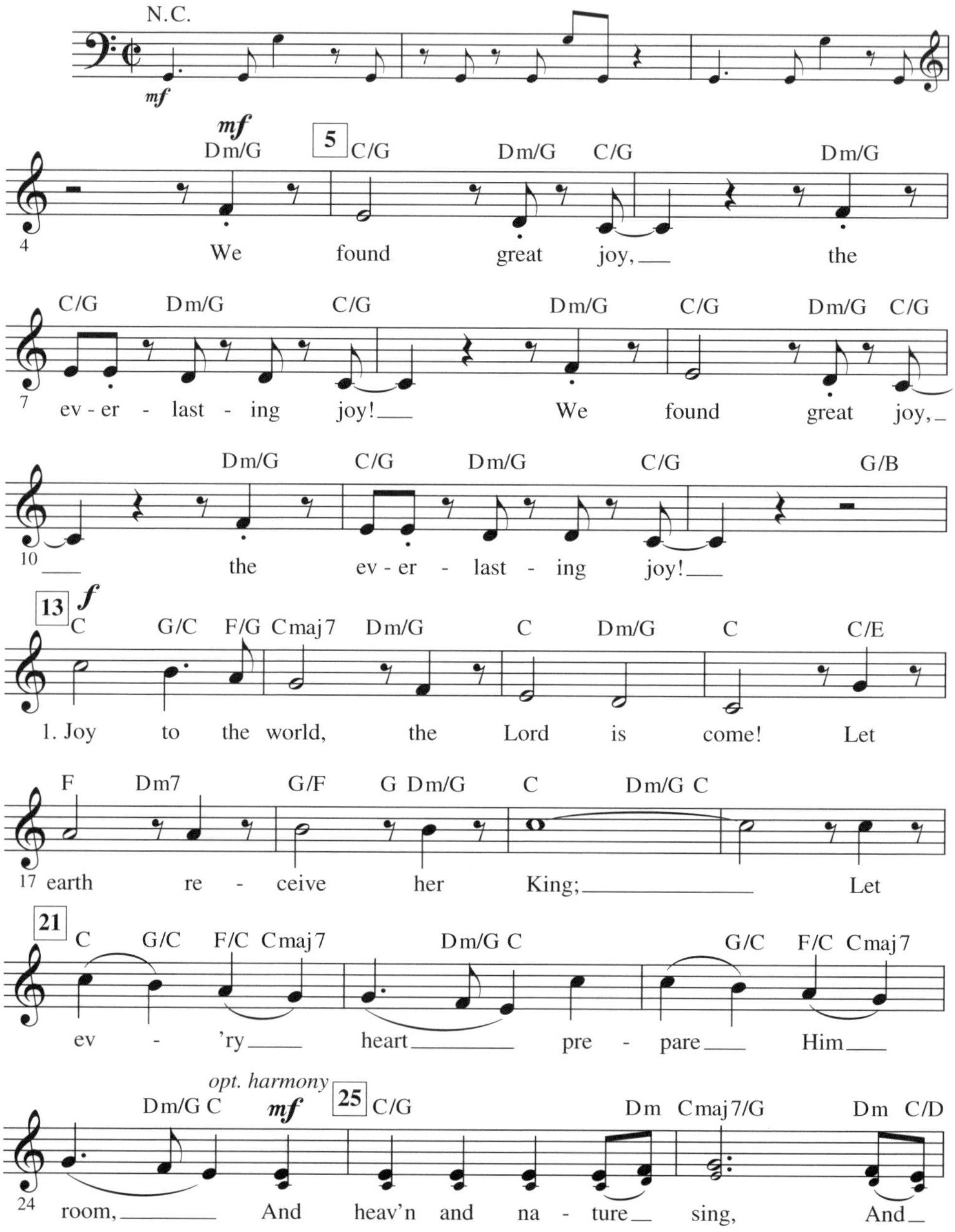

Dm7/G   C/D Dm7(b5)/G Dm7(b5)/Ab   Am7   Am7/G
heav'n and na - ture sing, And heav'n and

F(add9)   C/E F2/A C/G Dm/G   32 C   Dm/C C   Dm/C
opt. small group We found great joy, ___
mel.
heav'n and na - ture sing. the
+ Hand Claps on beat 2

C   Dm7(b5)/C   C   Dm/C   C   Dm/C C
ev - er - last - ing joy! ___ We found great joy, ___

Dm/C   C   Dm7(b5)/C   C   G/B
___ the ev - er - last - ing joy! ___   - Claps

40 f opt. harmony
C   G/C F/G Cmaj7 Dm/G   C   Dm/G   C   C/E
mel.
2. He rules the world with truth and grace, And

F   Dm7   G/F G Dm/G   C   Dm/G C
na - tions prove ___
makes the We found great joy! ___ The

48 C   G/C F/C Cmaj7   Dm/G C   G/C F/C Cmaj7
glo - ries ___ of ___ His right - eous -

Dm/G C   mf   52 C/G   Dm Cmaj7/G   Dm C/D
ness, ___ And won - ders of His ___ love, And ___

Dm7/G
C/D Dm7(b5)/G Dm7(b5)/Ab
Am7
Am7/G
54
won - ders of His__ love, And__ won - ders,
F(add9) C/E F2/A
C/G
Dm/G
59 C
Dm/C C
We found great joy,__
57
mel.
won - ders of His love.
+ Claps
Dm/C C Dm7(b5)/C C
Dm/C
60
the ev - er - last - ing joy!__ We
C Dm/C C
Dm/C C Dm7(b5)/C C
63 found great joy,__ the ev - er - last - ing joy!__
build intensity
f Dm/C
67 C
Dm/C C
Dm/C
66 __ We found great joy,__ the
+ Tambourine on beat 2
C Dm7(b5)/C C
Dm/C C Dm/C C
69 ev - er - last - ing joy!__ We found great joy,_
Dm/C C Dm7(b5)/C C
72 __ the ev - er - last - ing joy!__
ff

O Christmas Tree
(O Tannenbaum)

Traditional German Carol
Arranged by TOM ANDERSON

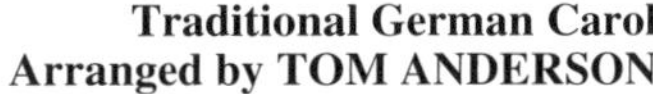

24
F2/A   D7(#9/#5)   Gm7sus Gm7   B♭/C   C7(#5)
more motion opt. harmony
sight of you   at Christ-mas-time, spreads hope and glad - ness
- W. C.
Gm7/F F   B♭(add9)/C F6   C7(♭9) Am7/D   D7(♭9)
dim.
27   far and wide.   O   Christ-mas tree,   O   Christ - mas tree,   how
Gm7   B♭/C   C7(♭9)   C7(♭9)/F   F6   E♭13(#11)
mp
30   love - ly   are   your   branch - es!   + F. C.
relaxed
F6/9   E♭13(#11)   F6/9
33
O   Christ - mas tree!________
+ W. C.

Pat-a-Pan
(Willie, Take Your Little Drum)

Words and Music by
BERNARD de la MONNOYE
Arranged by TOM ANDERSON

mf
28 E5
27 3. God and man to - day be - come close-ly joined as
B5
30 flute and drum. Let the joy - ous tune play
E5
B5
33 on! Tu - re - lu - re - lu, pat - a - pat - a - pan. As the
E5
B5
36 in - stru - ments you play, we will sing, this Christ - mas
39 Ending
E5
6
Day.

Pat-a-Pan
(Willie, Take Your Little Drum)

Pat-a-Pan
(Willie, Take Your Little Drum)

ALTO METALLOPHONE

Words and Music by
BERNARD de la MONNOYE
Arranged by TOM ANDERSON

Pat-a-Pan
(Willie, Take Your Little Drum)

Pat-a-Pan
(Willie, Take Your Little Drum)

Copyright © 2012 by HAL LEONARD CORPORATION
International Copyright Secured   All Rights Reserved

32   Mickey's Caroling Book – Singer

Silent Night

Words by JOSEPH MOHR
Music by FRANZ GRUBER
Arranged by TOM ANDERSON

more motion
29 C Cmaj7 C6 C Dm7/G
mf
3. Si - lent night, ho - ly night, Son of
+ Descant/Recorder
G9 C(add9) Gm7/C C9 37 F(add9) C/E Dm7 G9
34 God, love's pure light; ra - diant beams from
+ Sus. Cym.
C Dm/G C C7 F(add9) F6/9 C(add9)
39 Thy ho - ly face, with the dawn of re - deem - ing
45 Dm7 Dm7/G G/F C2/E Am7
44 grace, Je - sus, Lord, at Thy birth,
+ Sus. Cym.
C/G Dm7 G9 C(add9)
dim. slight rit. mp
49 Je - sus, Lord at Thy birth.
+ W. C.

Silent Night

Words by JOSEPH MOHR
Music by FRANZ GRUBER
Arranged by TOM ANDERSON

Up on the Housetop

Words and Music by B. R. HANDY
Arranged by TOM ANDERSON

21
mf
D
D/F♯
3. Next, comes the stock - ing of lit - tle Will;
G
D
A7
23 Oh, just see what a glo - rious fill!
D
D/F♯
25 Here is a ham - mer and lots of tacks,
G
D
Em7
A7
D
Whip Crack
D/F♯
27 al - so a ball and a whip that cracks.
29
f
G
Em7
D
Bm7
Ho, ho, ho, who would - n't go!
+ S. B. and Mar.
Em7
A7
D
Em7/A
31 Ho, ho, ho, who would - n't go!
Finger Snaps
D
D7/F♯
G
D/F♯
Em7
Fdim7
spoken
33 Up on the house - top click, click, click,
+ W. B.
D/F♯
Bm7
Em7
A7
D
Whip Crack
N.C.
35 Down thru' the chim - ney with good Saint Nick.

We Wish You a Merry Christmas

Traditional English Carol
Arranged by TOM ANDERSON

22
G   G/B   C   C/B   A7sus   A7
wish   you   a   mer - ry   Christ - mas,   We   wish   you   a   mer - ry
+ Tri./F. C., H. D., Tamb.
D   D/C   B7sus   B7   Em   G/B
25   Christ - mas,   We   wish   you   a   mer - ry   Christ - mas,   and   a
- Tri./F. C.
- H. D.
- Tamb.
C6   Am7   cresc.   Am7/D   D9
28   hap   -   py   New
ff   G   G2/B   C   Am7   D9   G6/9
32   Year!
+ Tri./F. C., H. D., Tamb.

We Wish You a Merry Christmas

TRIANGLE/FINGER CYMBALS

Traditional English Carol
Arranged by TOM ANDERSON

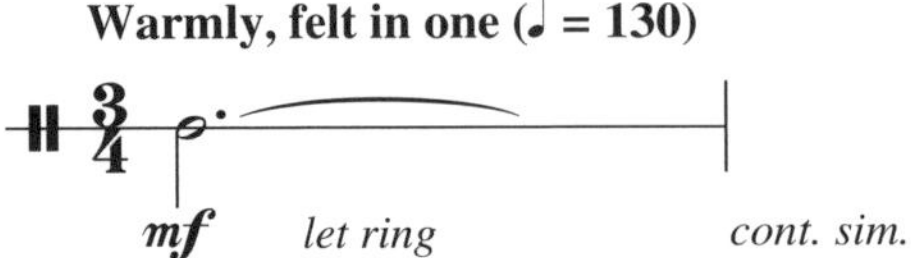

We Wish You a Merry Christmas

HAND DRUM

Traditional English Carol
Arranged by TOM ANDERSON

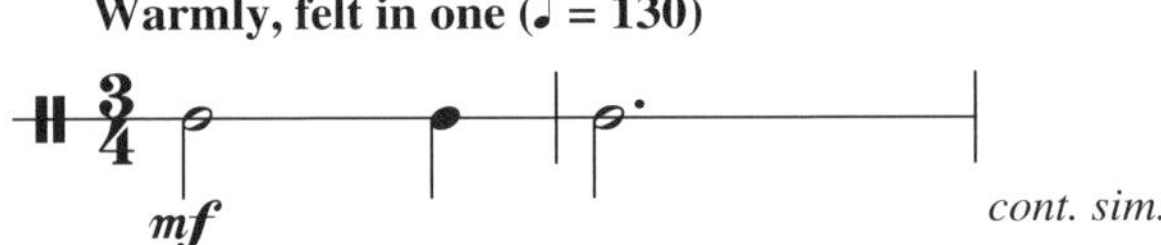

We Wish You a Merry Christmas

TAMBOURINE

Traditional English Carol
Arranged by TOM ANDERSON

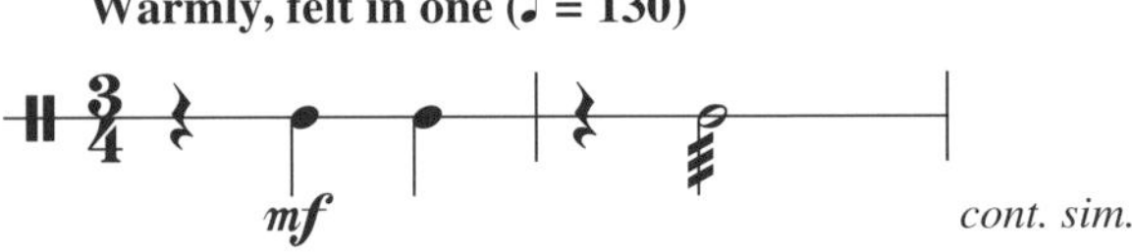

Disney Mickey's Caroling Book

HOLIDAY FUN WITH MICKEY AND HIS FRIENDS

Table of Contents

No part of this publication may be reproduced in any form or by any means without the prior written permission of the Publisher.

7777 W. BLUEMOUND RD. P.O. BOX 13819 MILWAUKEE, WI 53213

Visit Hal Leonard Online at
www.halleonard.com

Angels We Have Heard on High

Traditional French Carol
Arranged by TOM ANDERSON

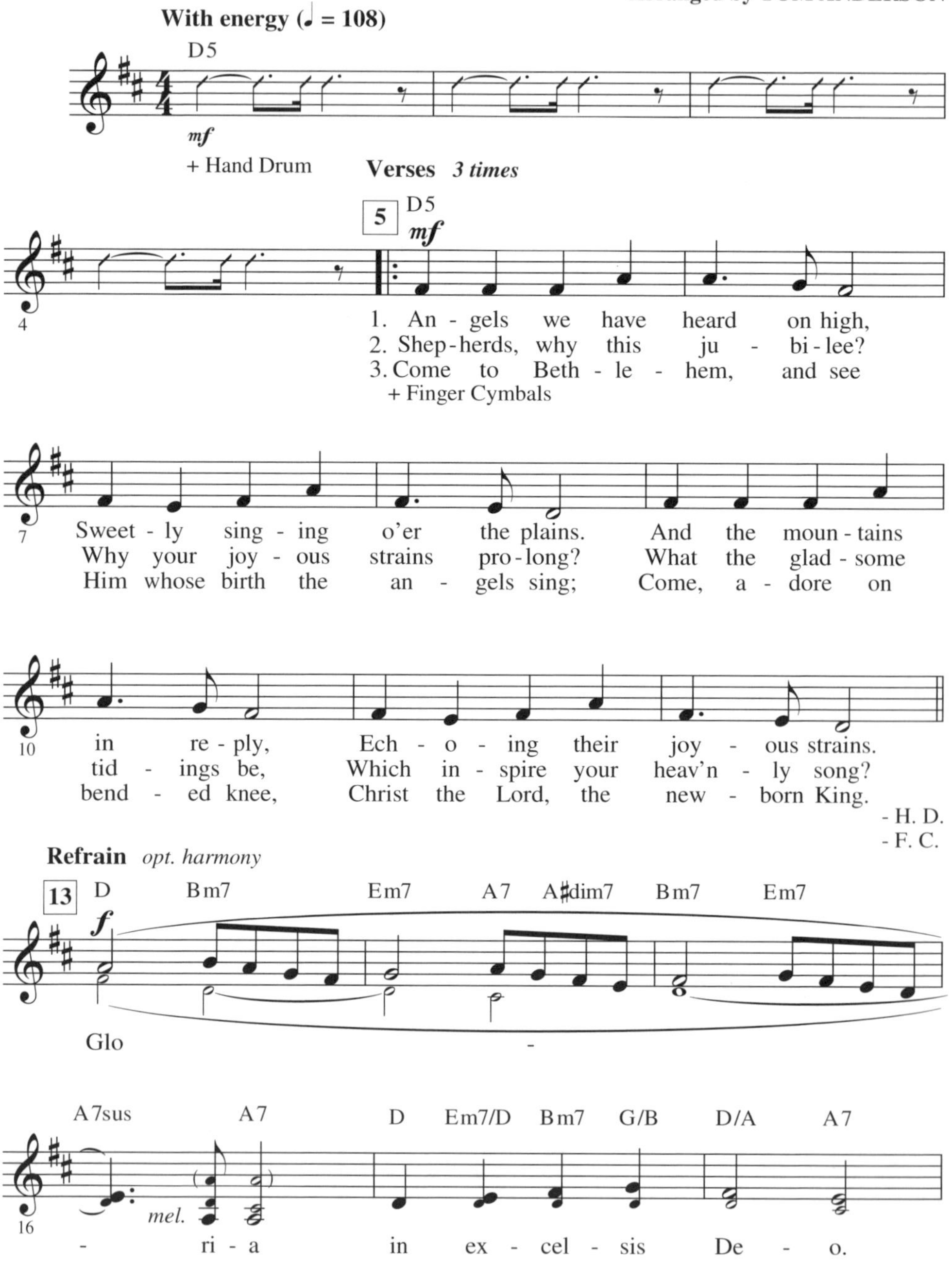

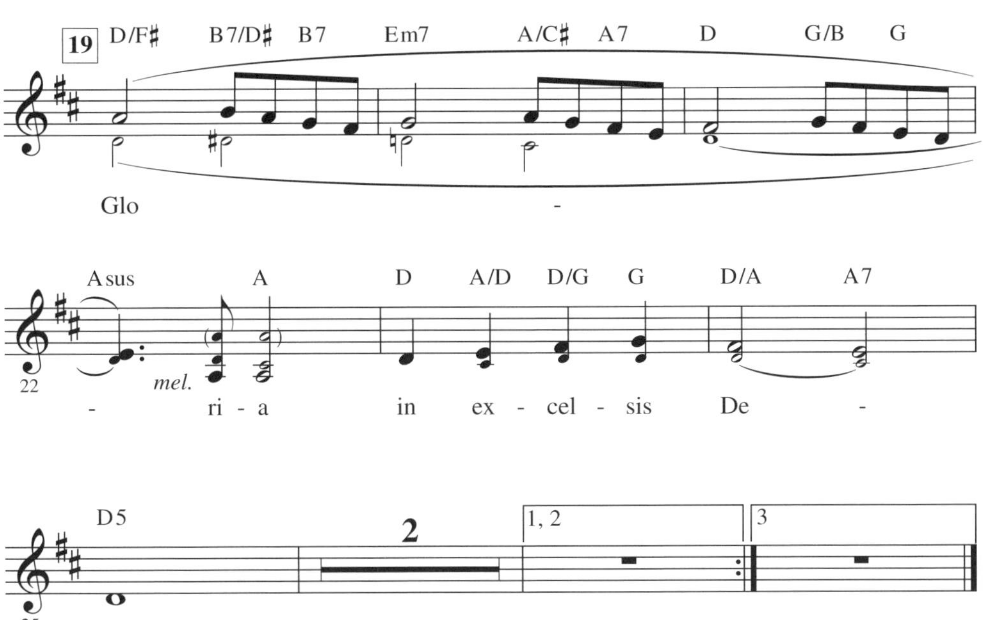

19 D/F# B7/D# B7 Em7 A/C# A7 D G/B G
Glo -
A sus A D A/D D/G G D/A A7
mel.
- ri - a in ex - cel - sis De -
D5 2 1, 2 3
o.
22
25

Angels We Have Heard on High

HAND DRUM

Traditional French Carol
Arranged by TOM ANDERSON

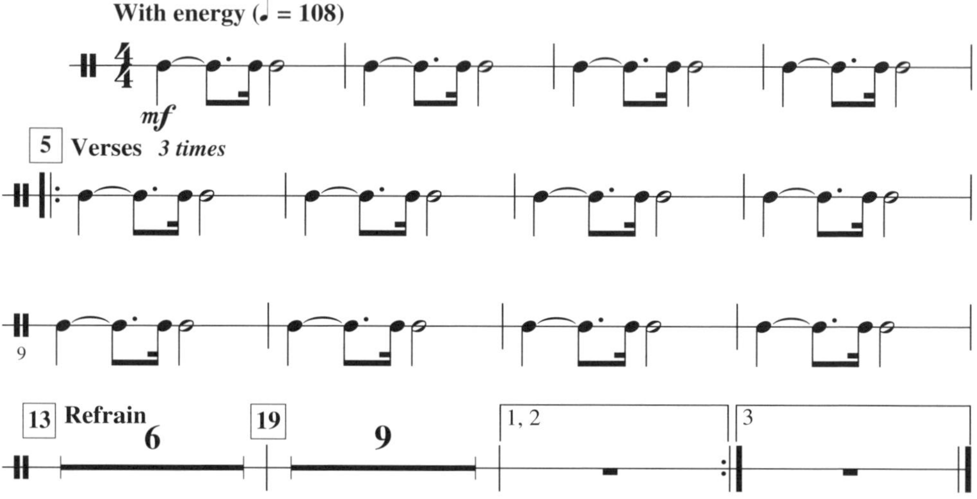

Angels We Have Heard on High

FINGER CYMBALS

Traditional French Carol
Arranged by TOM ANDERSON

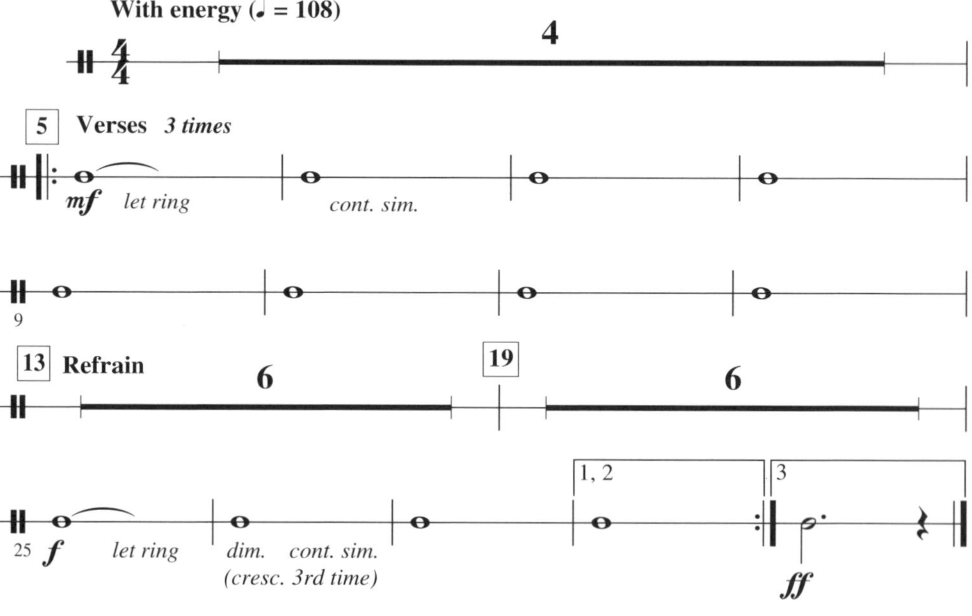

Angels We Have Heard on High

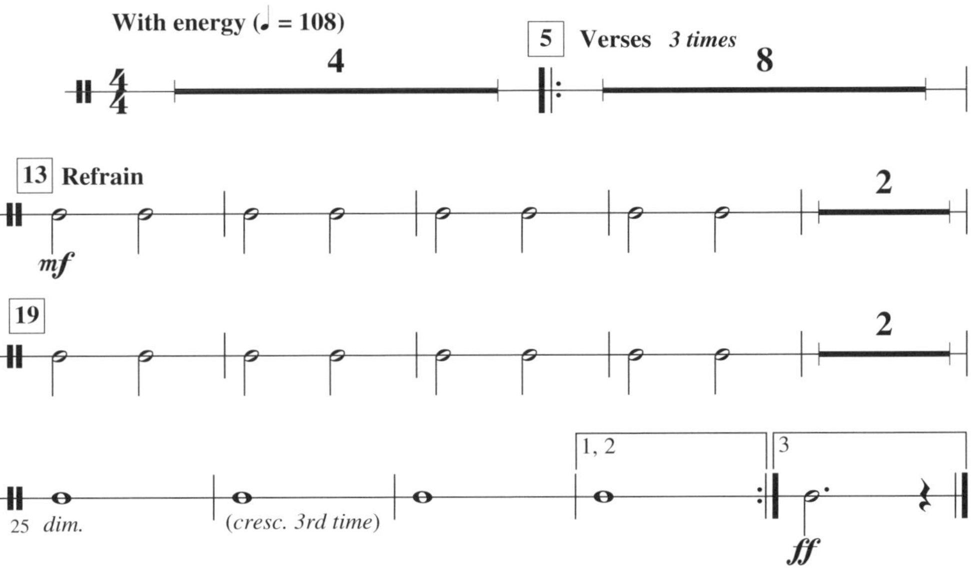

Angels We Have Heard on High

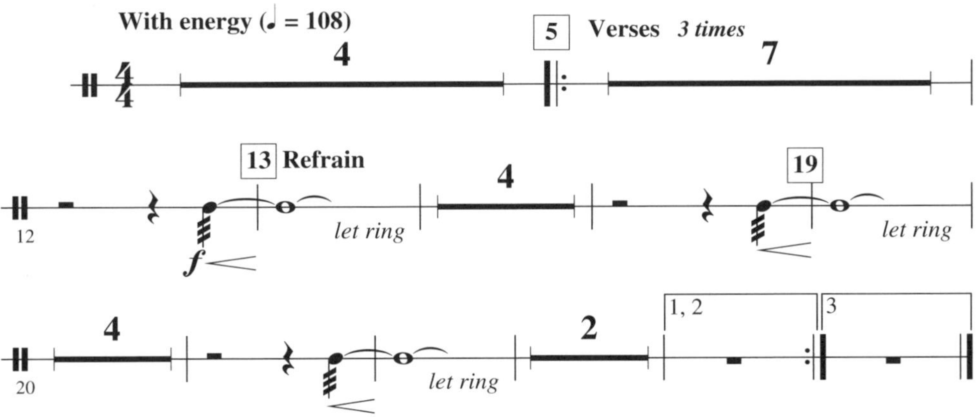

Angels We Have Heard on High

Away in a Manger

Music by JAMES R. MURRAY
Words, Stanza 1, 2, Anonymous
Stanza 3, JOHN THOMAS McFARLAND
Arranged by TOM ANDERSON

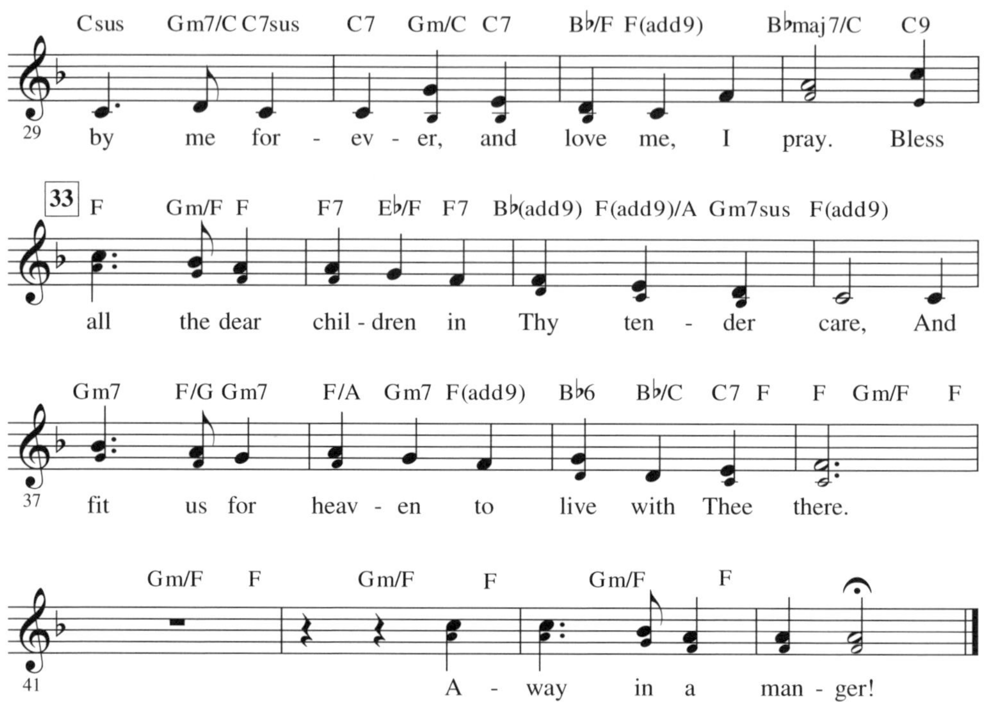

Csus Gm7/C C7sus C7 Gm/C C7 Bb/F F(add9) Bbmaj7/C C9
29
by me for - ev - er, and love me, I pray. Bless
33 F Gm/F F F7 Eb/F F7 Bb(add9) F(add9)/A Gm7sus F(add9)
all the dear chil - dren in Thy ten - der care, And
Gm7 F/G Gm7 F/A Gm7 F(add9) Bb6 Bb/C C7 F F Gm/F F
37 fit us for heav - en to live with Thee there.
Gm/F F Gm/F F Gm/F F
41 A - way in a man - ger!

Away in a Manger

25
let ring
cont. sim.
let ring
cont. sim.
let ring
cont. sim.
33
30
35
40
let ring
let ring
let ring
let ring

Away in a Manger

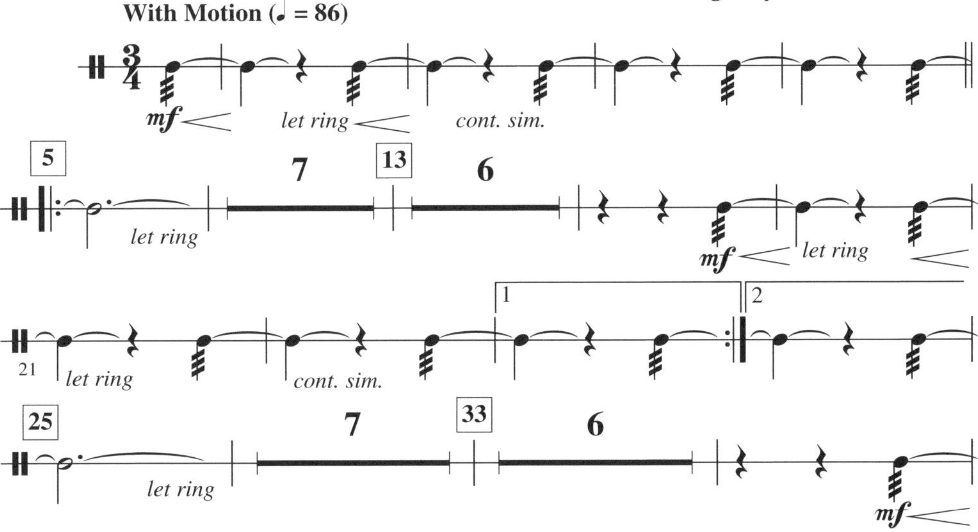

Away in a Manger

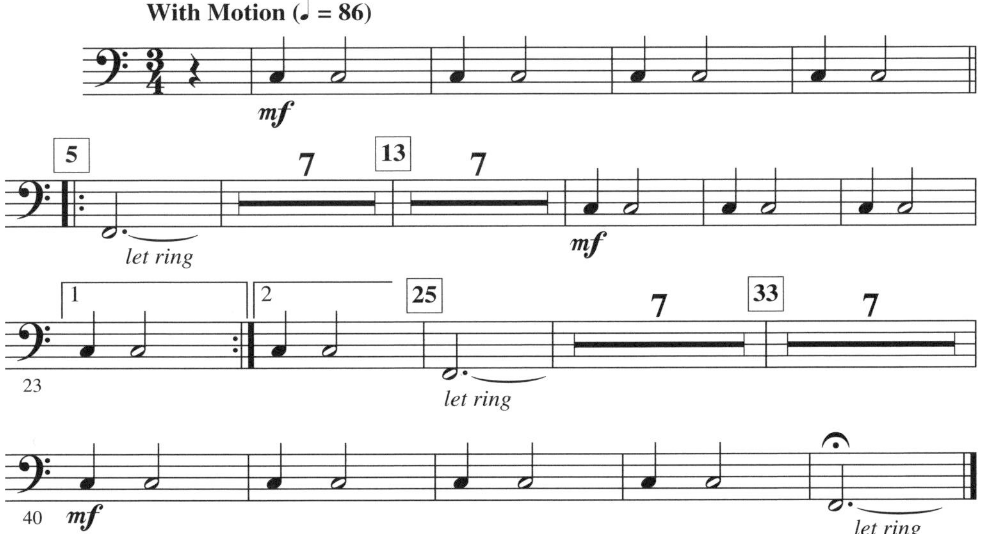

3/15

Deck the Halls

Traditional Welsh Carol
Arranged by TOM ANDERSON

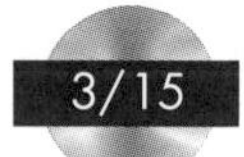

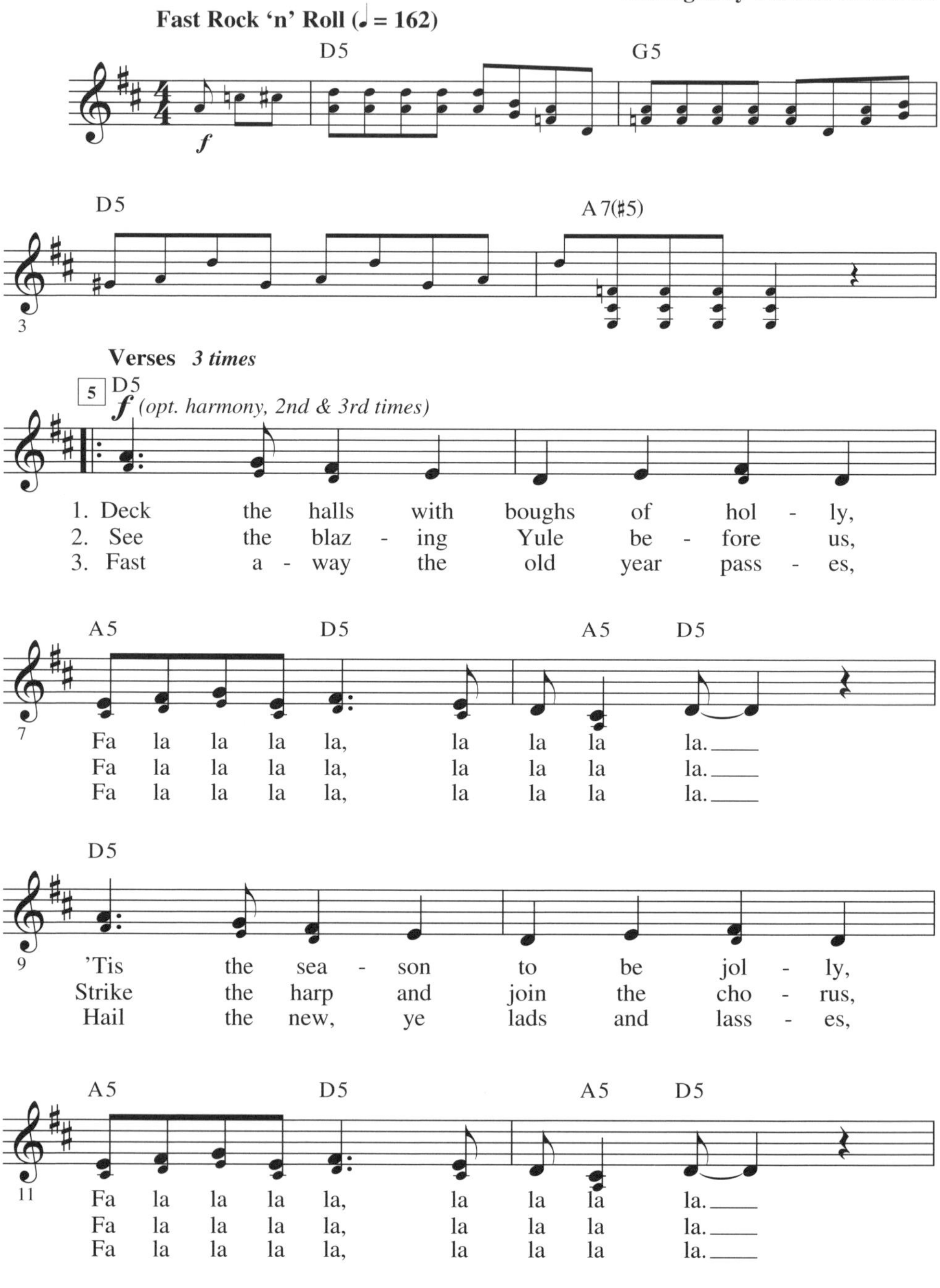

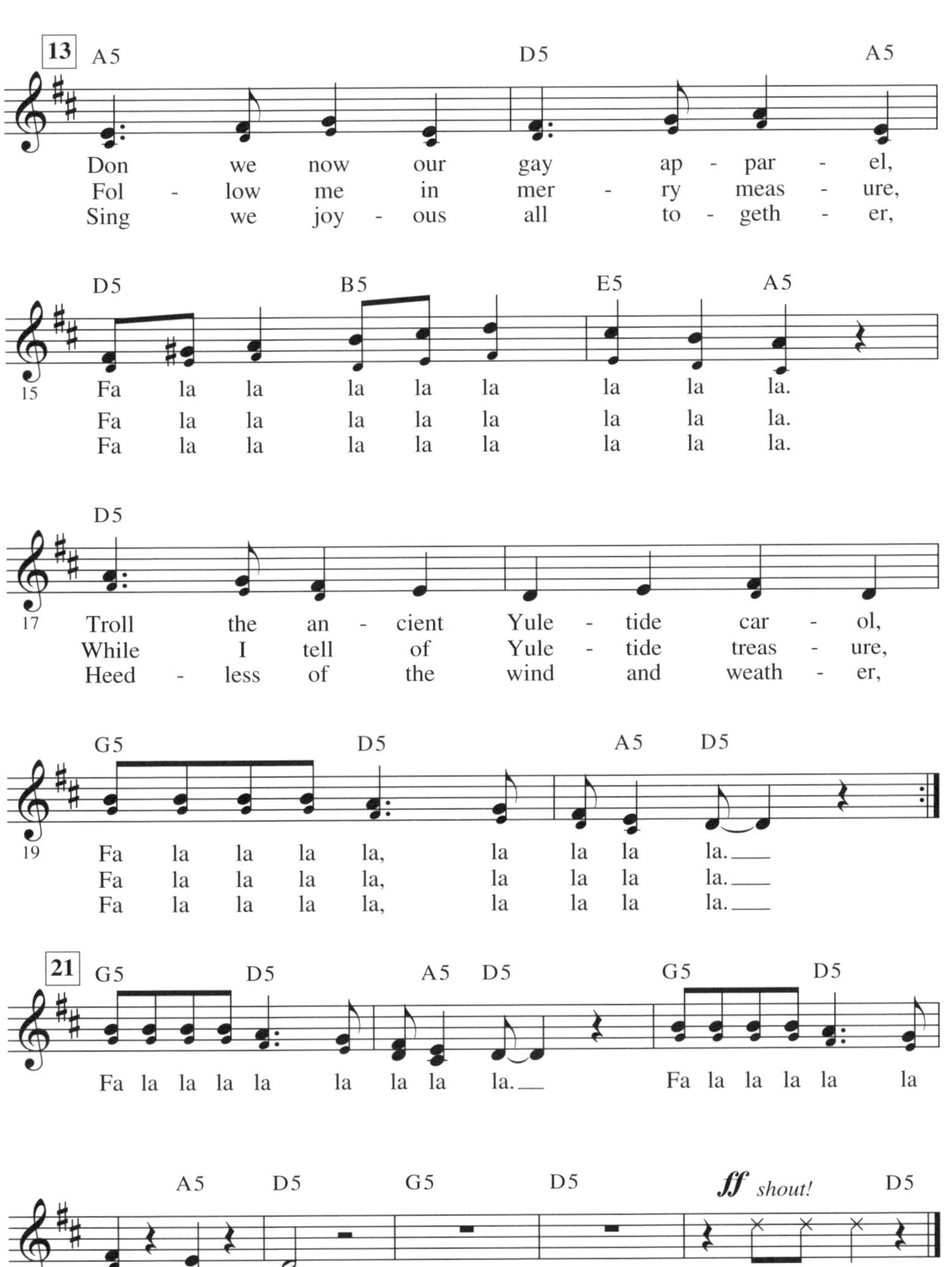

13
A5
D5
A5
Don we now our gay ap - par - el,
Fol - low me in mer - ry meas - ure,
Sing we joy - ous all to - geth - er,
D5
B5
E5
A5
15
Fa la la la la la la la la.
Fa la la la la la la la la.
Fa la la la la la la la la.
D5
17
Troll the an - cient Yule - tide car - ol,
While I tell of Yule - tide treas - ure,
Heed - less of the wind and weath - er,
G5
D5
A5
D5
19
Fa la la la la, la la la la.___
Fa la la la la, la la la la.___
Fa la la la la, la la la la.___
21
G5
D5
A5
D5
G5
D5
Fa la la la la la la la la.__ Fa la la la la la
A5
D5
G5
D5
ff shout!
D5
24
la la la. Deck the halls!

Deck the Halls

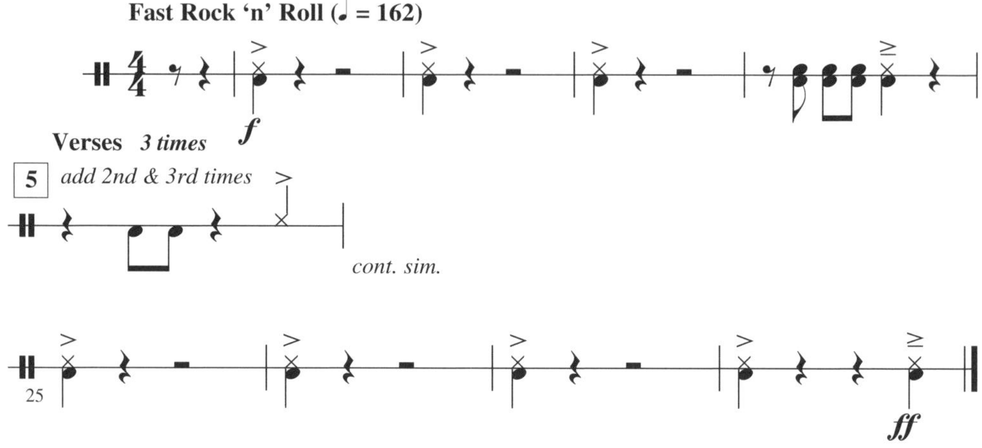

Deck the Halls

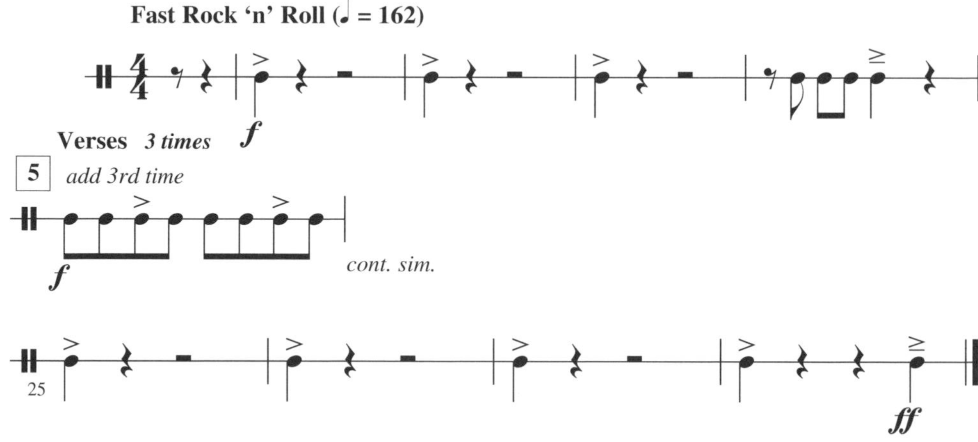

Here We Come A-Caroling

English Wassail Song
Arranged by TOM ANDERSON

Here We Come A-Caroling

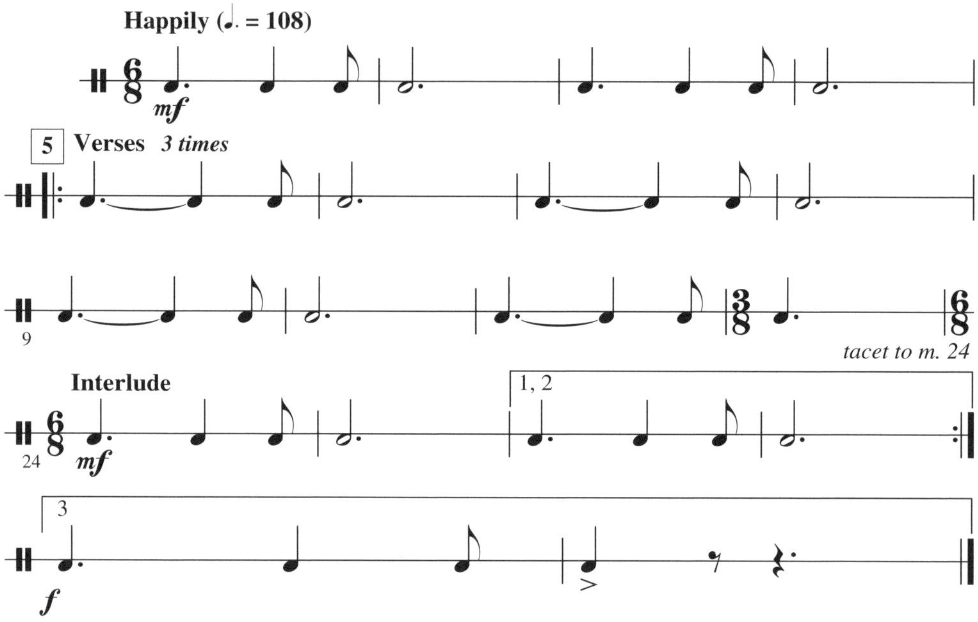

Here We Come A-Caroling

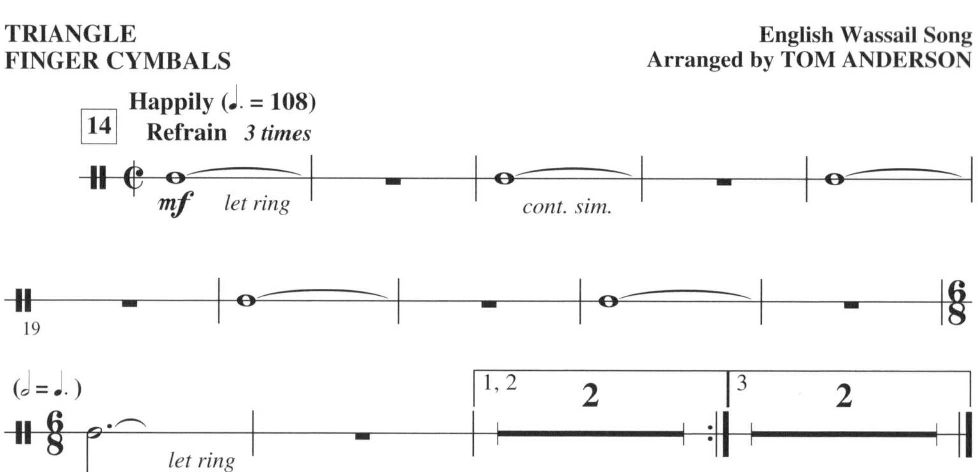

Jingle Bells

Words and Music by JAMES PIERPONT
Arranged by TOM ANDERSON

With Joy! (♩ = 106)

Verses

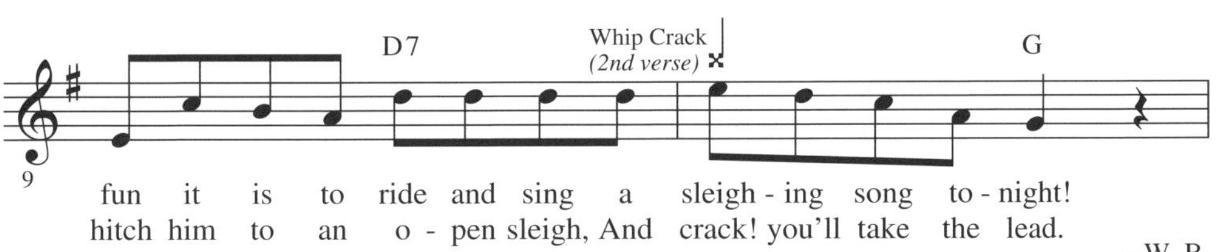

Copyright © 2012 by HAL LEONARD CORPORATION
International Copyright Secured   All Rights Reserved

Refrain
11
G
opt. harmony
f
Jin - gle bells! Jin - gle bells! Jin - gle all the way!
+ Jingle Bells
C
G
A 7
Am7
D 7
13
Oh, what fun it is to ride in a one - horse o - pen sleigh!___
G
15
Jin - gle bells! Jin - gle bells! Jin - gle all the way!
C
G
1
D 7
G
17
Oh, what fun it is to ride in a one - horse o - pen sleigh!
- J. B.
2
D 7
G
Whip
N. C.
shout!
19
one - horse o - pen sleigh! Hey!

Jolly Old St. Nicholas

Traditional American Carol
Arranged by TOM ANDERSON

21 Recorder or Other Pitched Inst.
G6 F#m7(b5) B7(b9) Em Em/D Bm7 C6 G6 Em7
mf
29
Em7/A A9 Am7/D D9 Gmaj9 F#m7(b5) B7(b9) Em Em/D
27
- Recorder
Bm7 C6 Gmaj9 E7(#9) Am7 D9 G6 Ab13
32
37 G6 F#m7(b5) B7(b9) Em Em/D Bm7
f
3. John - ny wants a pair of skates,__ Su - sy wants a sled;__
+ Jingle Bells
C6 G6 Em7 Em7/A A9
41
Nel - lie wants a pic - ture book;__ yel-low, blue and red.__
Am7/D D9 45 Gmaj9 F#m7(b5) B7(b9)
44
Now I think I'll leave to you__
Em Em/D Bm7 C6 Gmaj9 E7(#9)
47
what to give the rest;__ Choose for me, dear San - ta Claus,__
Am7 D9 G6 Bb13 53 Am7 D7(#9 #5) G6 E7(#9)
cresc.
51
you will know the best.__ You will know the best.__
Am7 Am7/D D7(#9) G6 2 N.C.
55
You will know the best!________

Jolly Old St. Nicholas

Jolly Old St. Nicholas

Jolly Old St. Nicholas

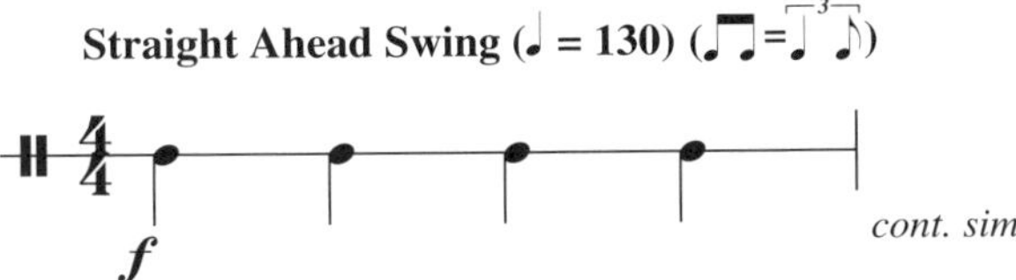

Joy to the World

Copyright © 2012 by HAL LEONARD CORPORATION
International Copyright Secured   All Rights Reserved

Dm7/G   C/D Dm7(b5)/G Dm7(b5)/Ab   Am7   Am7/G
27
heav'n and na - ture sing,   And heav'n and

F(add9) C/E F2/A C/G Dm/G   32 C   Dm/C C   Dm/C
opt. small group We   found   great   joy,___
30
heav'n and na - ture sing.   the
mel.
+ Hand Claps on beat 2

C   Dm7(b5)/C   C   Dm/C   C   Dm/C C
34 ev - er - last - ing joy!___   We   found   great   joy,_

Dm/C   C   Dm7(b5)/C   C   G/B
37 ___   the   ev - er - last - ing   joy!___   - Claps

40 f opt. harmony
C   G/C   F/G Cmaj7 Dm/G   C   Dm/G   C   C/E
2. He   rules   the world   with   truth   and   grace,   And
mel.

F   Dm7   G/F   G Dm/G   C   Dm/G C
na - tions   prove______
44 makes   the   We   found   great   joy!___   The

48 C   G/C   F/C Cmaj7   Dm/G C   G/C   F/C Cmaj7
glo - ries___   of_____   His   right - eous -

Dm/G C   mf   52 C/G   Dm Cmaj7/G   Dm C/D
51 ness,_______   And   won - ders   of   His_ love,   And_

Dm7/G
C/D Dm7(b5)/G Dm7(b5)/Ab
Am7
Am7/G
54
won - ders   of   His___ love,   And___ won - ders,

F(add9) C/E F2/A
C/G
Dm/G
59 C
Dm/C C
We   found   great   joy,___
57
won - ders   of   His   love.
mel.
+ Claps

Dm/C C Dm7(b5)/C C
Dm/C
60
the   ev - er - last - ing   joy!___   We

C Dm/C C
Dm/C C Dm7(b5)/C C
63 found   great   joy,___   the   ev - er - last - ing   joy!__

build intensity
67 C Dm/C C
Dm/C
f Dm/C
66 ___   We   found   great   joy,___   the
+ Tambourine on beat 2

C Dm7(b5)/C C
Dm/C C Dm/C C
69 ev - er - last - ing   joy!___   We   found   great   joy,_

Dm/C C Dm7(b5)/C C
72 ___   the   ev - er - last - ing   joy!___
ff

O Christmas Tree
(O Tannenbaum)

Traditional German Carol
Arranged by TOM ANDERSON

Gentle Waltz ($\quarternote = 72$)

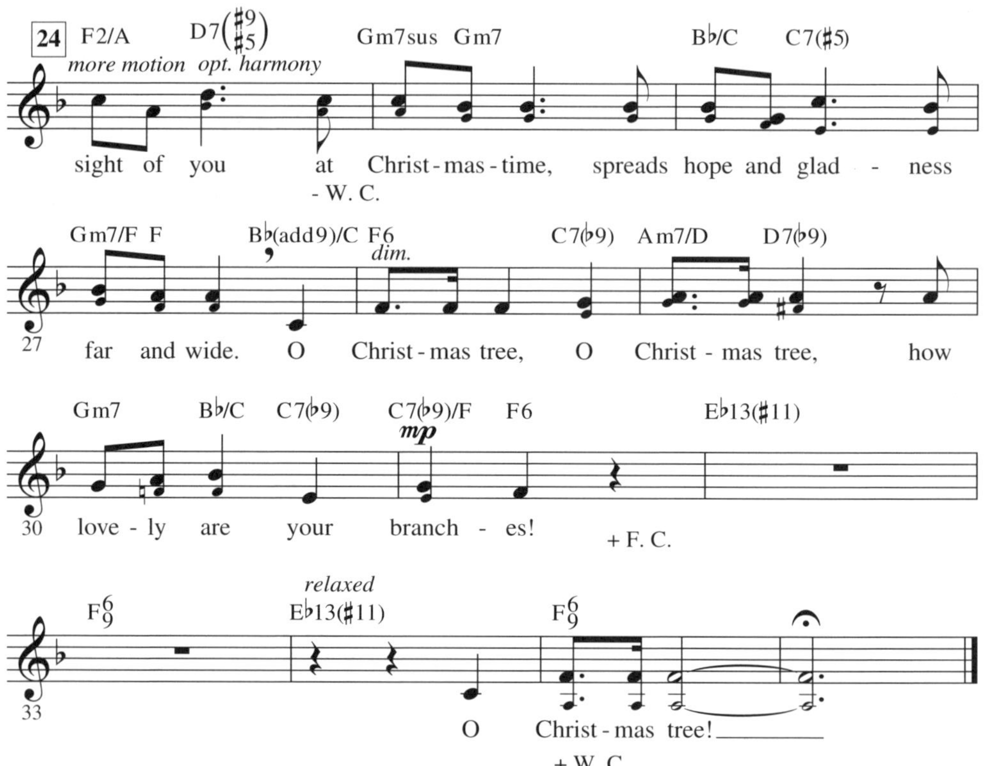
24
more motion opt. harmony
F2/A   D7(#9/#5)   Gm7sus Gm7   Bb/C   C7(#5)
sight of you   at Christ-mas-time,   spreads hope and glad - ness
- W. C.
Gm7/F F   Bb(add9)/C F6   C7(b9) Am7/D   D7(b9)
dim.
27 far and wide.   O   Christ-mas tree,   O   Christ-mas tree,   how
Gm7   Bb/C   C7(b9)   C7(b9)/F F6   Eb13(#11)
mp
30 love-ly are your branch-es!   + F. C.
relaxed
F6/9   Eb13(#11)   F6/9
33   O   Christ-mas tree!
+ W. C.

9/21

Pat-a-Pan

(Willie, Take Your Little Drum)

Words and Music by
BERNARD de la MONNOYE
Arranged by TOM ANDERSON

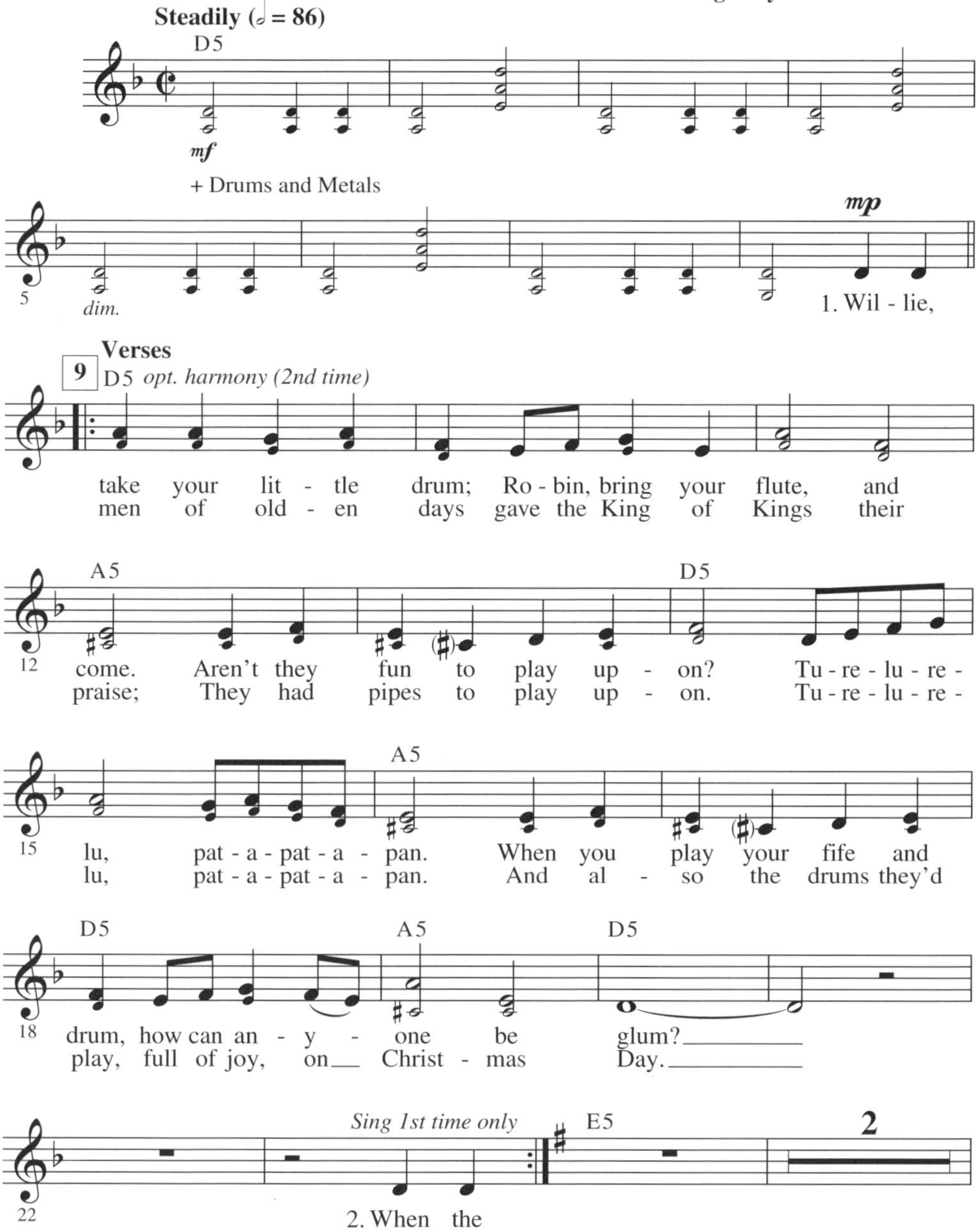

mf
28 E5
3. God and man to - day be - come close-ly joined as
B5
flute and drum. Let the joy - ous tune play
E5
on! Tu - re - lu - re - lu, pat - a - pat - a - pan. As the
E5
B5
in - stru - ments you play, we will sing, this Christ - mas
39 Ending
E5
6
Day.

Pat-a-Pan
(Willie, Take Your Little Drum)

Pat-a-Pan
(Willie, Take Your Little Drum)

Pat-a-Pan
(Willie, Take Your Little Drum)

Pat-a-Pan
(Willie, Take Your Little Drum)

32   Mickey's Caroling Book – Singer

10/22

Silent Night

Words by JOSEPH MOHR
Music by FRANZ GRUBER
Arranged by TOM ANDERSON

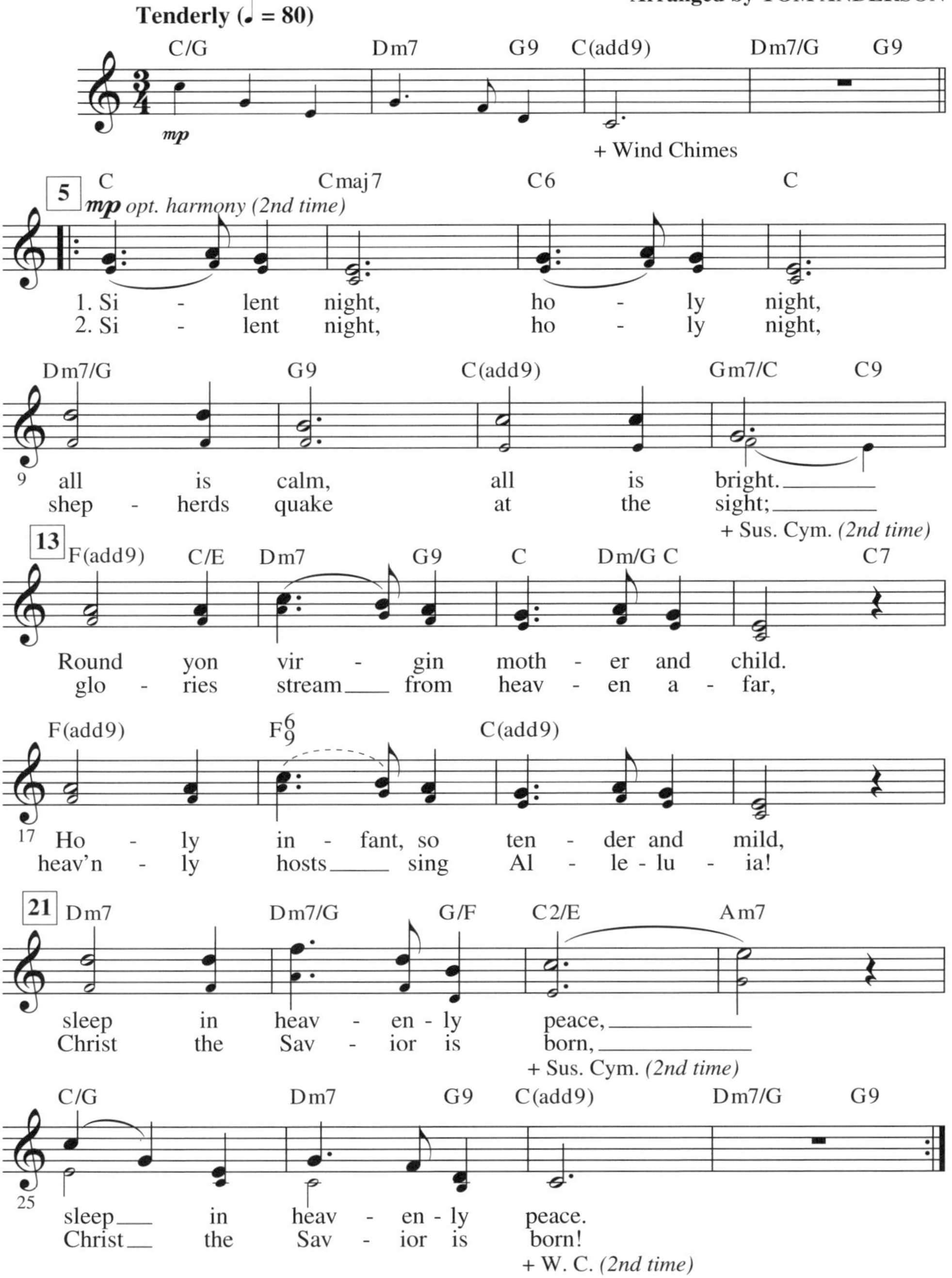

more motion
29 C   Cmaj7   C6   C   Dm7/G
mf
3. Si - lent night, ho - ly night, Son of
+ Descant/Recorder

G9   C(add9)   Gm7/C   C9   37 F(add9)   C/E Dm7   G9
34 God, love's pure light;________ ra - diant beams__ from
+ Sus. Cym.

C Dm/G C   C7   F(add9)   F6/9   C(add9)
39 Thy ho - ly face, with the dawn of re - deem - ing

45 Dm7   Dm7/G   G/F   C2/E   Am7
44 grace, Je - sus, Lord, at Thy birth,________
+ Sus. Cym.

C/G   Dm7   G9   C(add9)
dim.   slight rit.   mp
49 Je - sus, Lord at Thy birth.
+ W. C.

Silent Night

Words by JOSEPH MOHR
Music by FRANZ GRUBER
Arranged by TOM ANDERSON

RECORDER
(or Sing on "loo")

Up on the Housetop

Words and Music by B. R. HANDY
Arranged by TOM ANDERSON

21
mf
D
D/F#
3. Next, comes the stock - ing of lit - tle Will;

G
D
A7
23
Oh, just see what a glo - rious fill!

D
D/F#
25
Here is a ham - mer and lots of tacks,

G
D
Em7
A7
D
Whip
Crack
D/F#
27
al - so a ball and a whip that cracks.

29
f
G
Em7
D
Bm7
Ho, ho, ho, who would - n't go!
+ S. B. and Mar.

Em7
A7
D
Em7/A
31
Ho, ho, ho, who would - n't go!

Finger Snaps
D
D7/F#
G
D/F#
Em7
Fdim7
33
spoken
Up on the house - top click, click, click,
+ W. B.

N.C.
D/F#
Bm7
Em7
A7
D
Whip
Crack
35
Down thru' the chim - ney with good Saint Nick.

We Wish You a Merry Christmas

Traditional English Carol
Arranged by TOM ANDERSON

22
G   G/B   C   C/B   A7sus   A7
wish you a mer-ry Christ-mas, We wish you a mer-ry
+ Tri./F. C., H. D., Tamb.
D   D/C   B7sus   B7   Em   G/B
25
Christ-mas, We wish you a mer-ry Christ-mas, and a
- Tri./F. C.
- H. D.
- Tamb.
C6   Am7 cresc.   Am7/D   D9
28
hap - py New
ff G   G2/B   C   Am7   D9   G6/9
32
Year!
+ Tri./F. C., H. D., Tamb.

We Wish You a Merry Christmas

TRIANGLE/FINGER CYMBALS

Traditional English Carol
Arranged by TOM ANDERSON

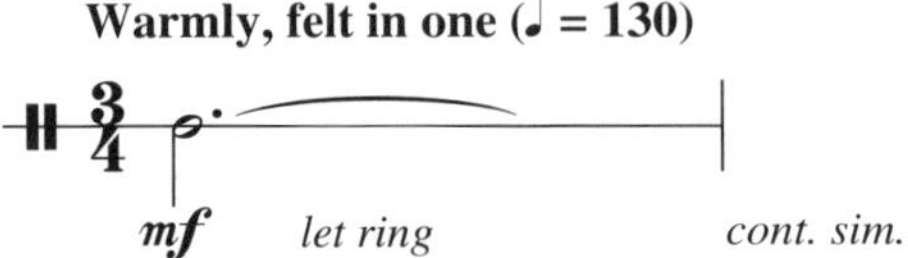

We Wish You a Merry Christmas

HAND DRUM

Traditional English Carol
Arranged by TOM ANDERSON

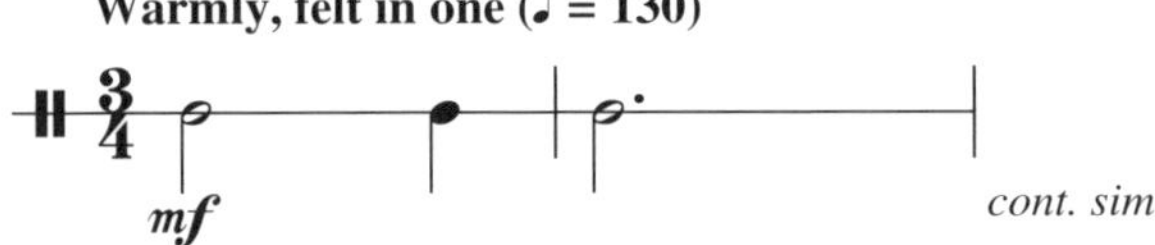

We Wish You a Merry Christmas

TAMBOURINE

Traditional English Carol
Arranged by TOM ANDERSON

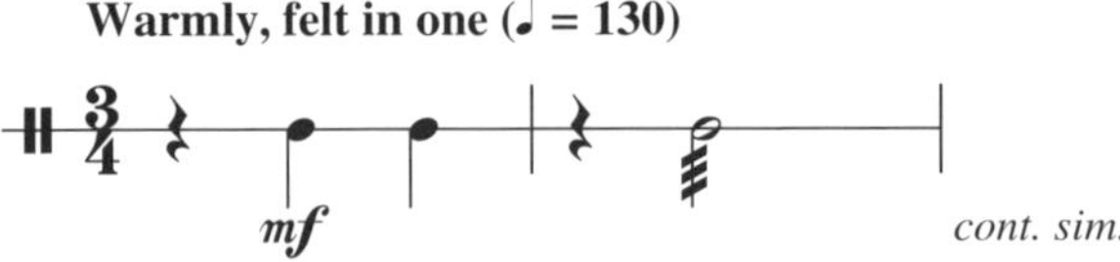

Disney
Mickey's Caroling Book
HOLIDAY FUN WITH MICKEY AND HIS FRIENDS

Table of Contents

7777 W. BLUEMOUND RD. P.O. BOX 13819 MILWAUKEE, WI 53213

Visit Hal Leonard Online at
www.halleonard.com

Angels We Have Heard on High

Traditional French Carol
Arranged by TOM ANDERSON

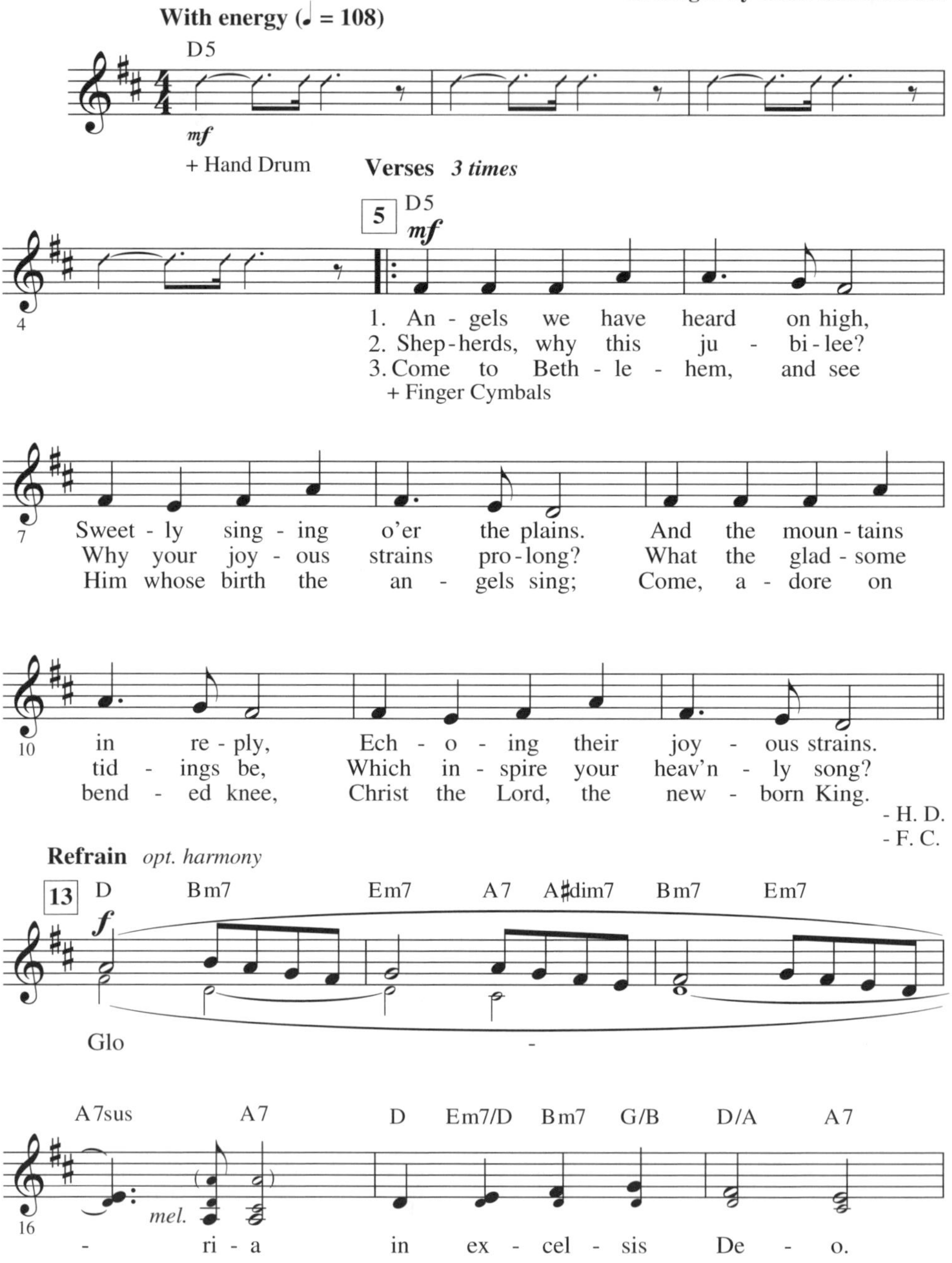

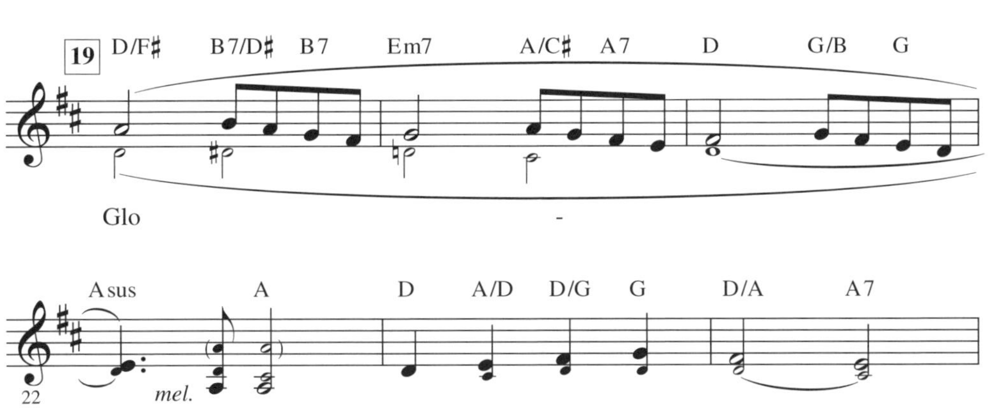

19
D/F# B7/D# B7 Em7 A/C# A7 D G/B G
Glo -
Asus A D A/D D/G G D/A A7
22
mel.
- ri - a in ex - cel - sis De -

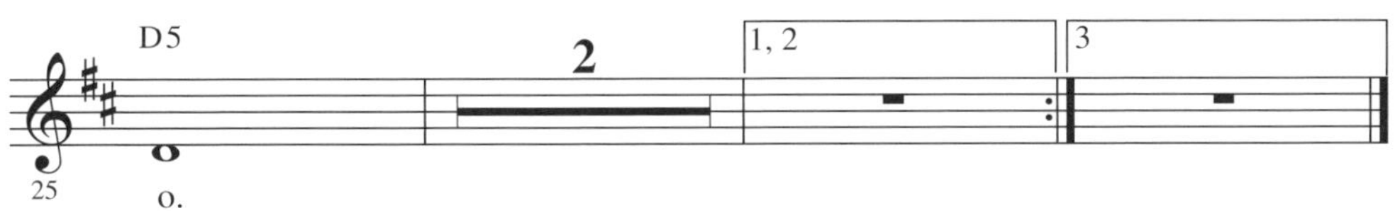

D5
2
1, 2
3
25
o.

Angels We Have Heard on High

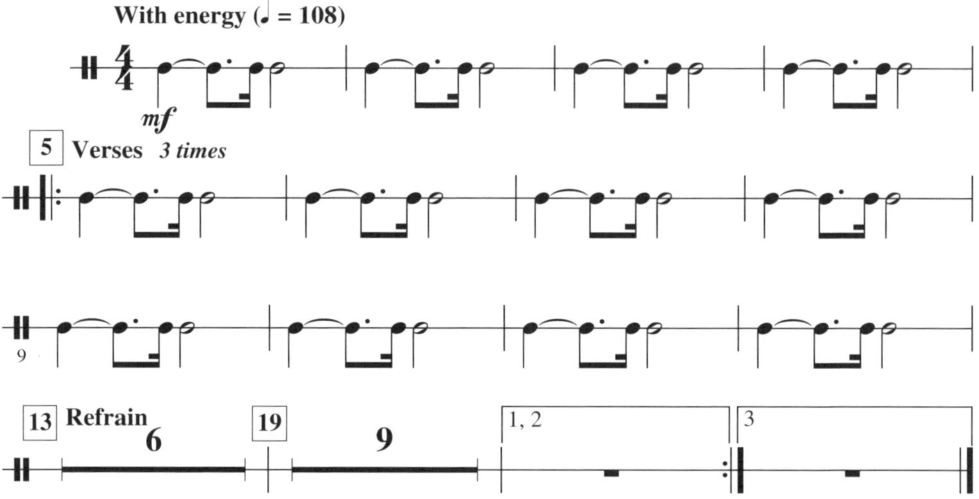

Angels We Have Heard on High

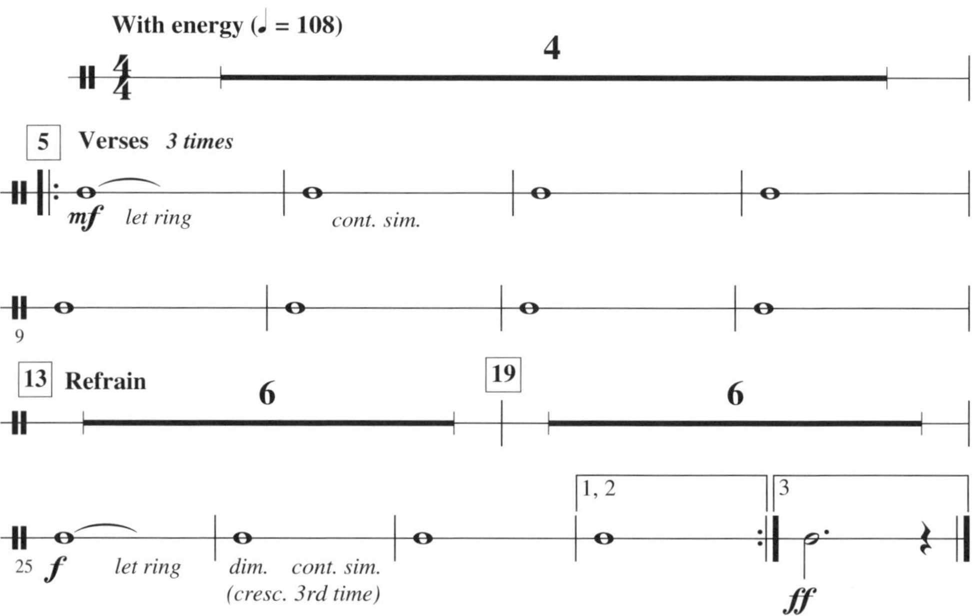

Angels We Have Heard on High

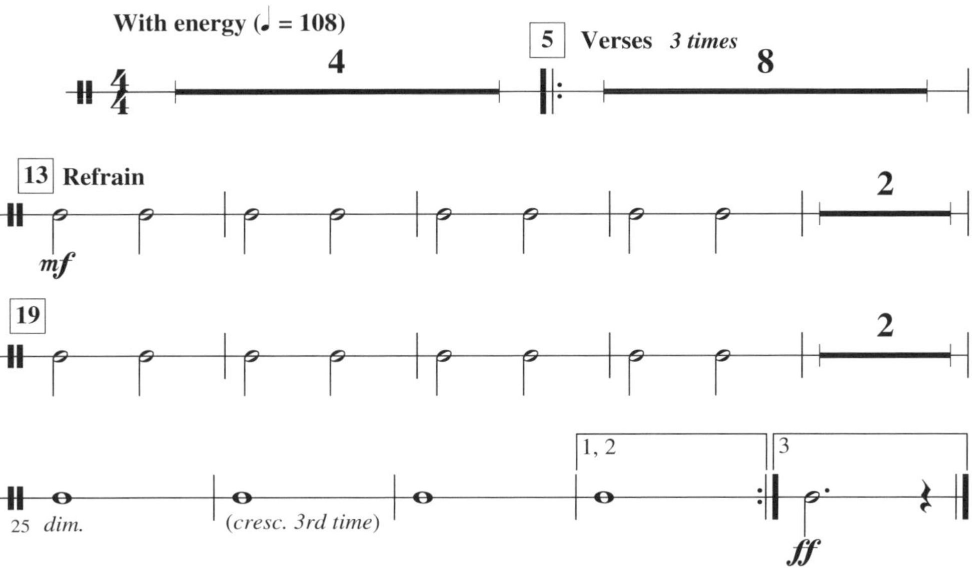

Angels We Have Heard on High

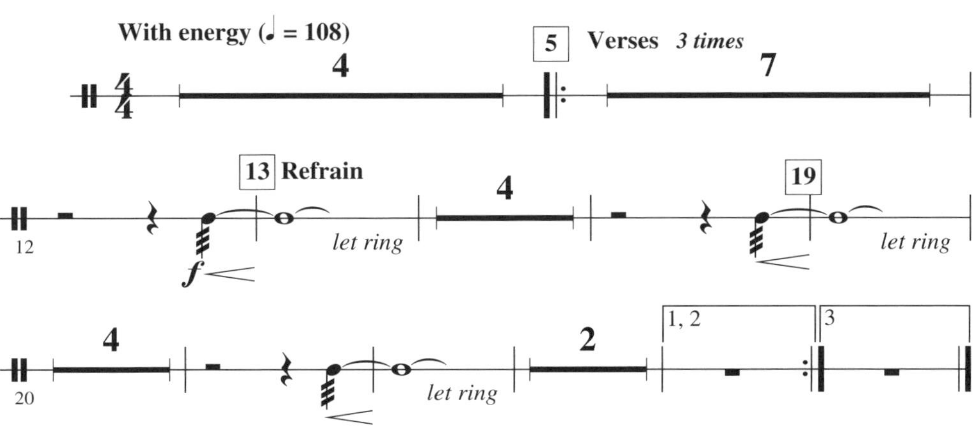

Angels We Have Heard on High

Away in a Manger

Music by JAMES R. MURRAY
Words, Stanza 1, 2, Anonymous
Stanza 3, JOHN THOMAS McFARLAND
Arranged by TOM ANDERSON

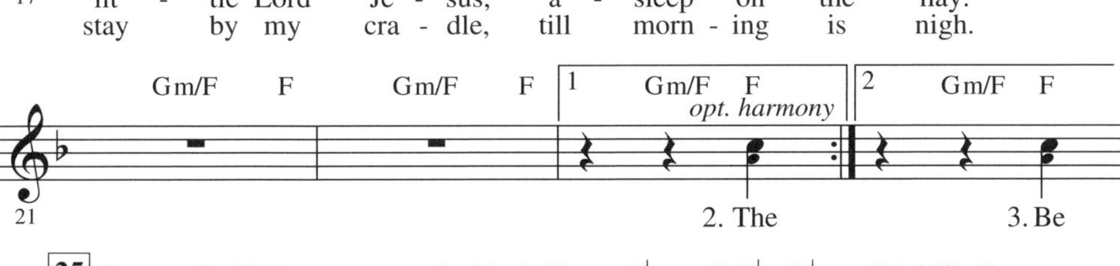

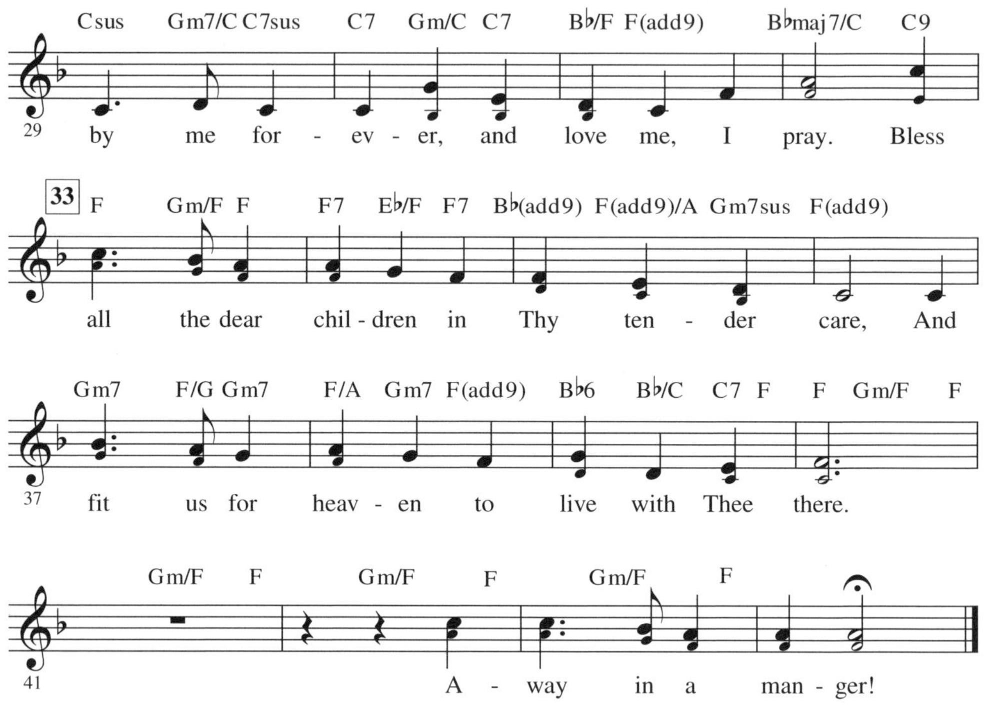

Csus   Gm7/C C7sus   C7   Gm/C C7   Bb/F F(add9)   Bbmaj7/C   C9
29 by   me   for - ev - er,   and   love   me,   I   pray.   Bless
33 F   Gm/F F   F7   Eb/F F7   Bb(add9) F(add9)/A Gm7sus   F(add9)
all   the dear   chil - dren   in   Thy   ten - der   care,   And
Gm7   F/G Gm7   F/A Gm7 F(add9)   Bb6   Bb/C   C7 F   F Gm/F   F
37 fit   us   for   heav - en   to   live   with   Thee   there.
Gm/F   F   Gm/F   F   Gm/F   F
41 A - way   in   a   man - ger!

Away in a Manger

25
let ring
cont. sim.
let ring
cont. sim.
let ring
cont. sim.
33
30
35
40
let ring
let ring
let ring

Away in a Manger

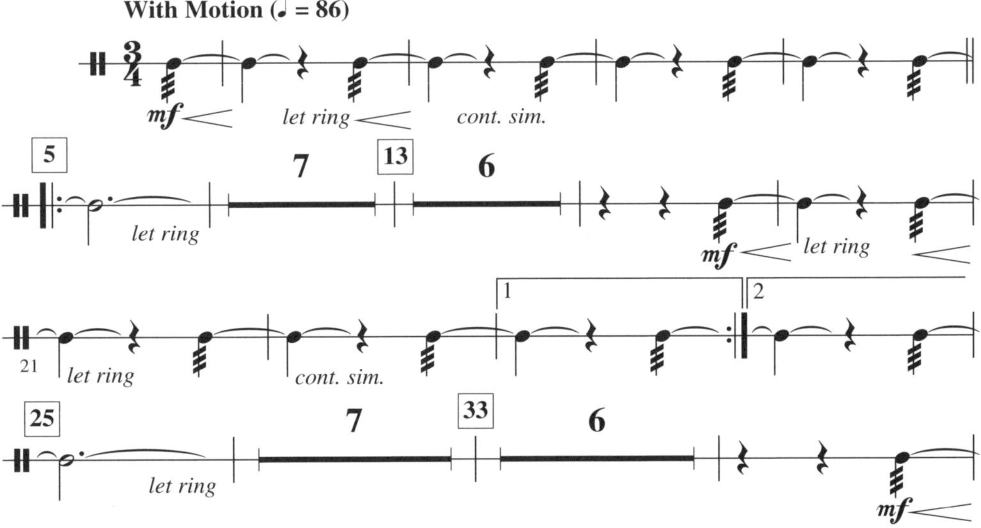

Away in a Manger

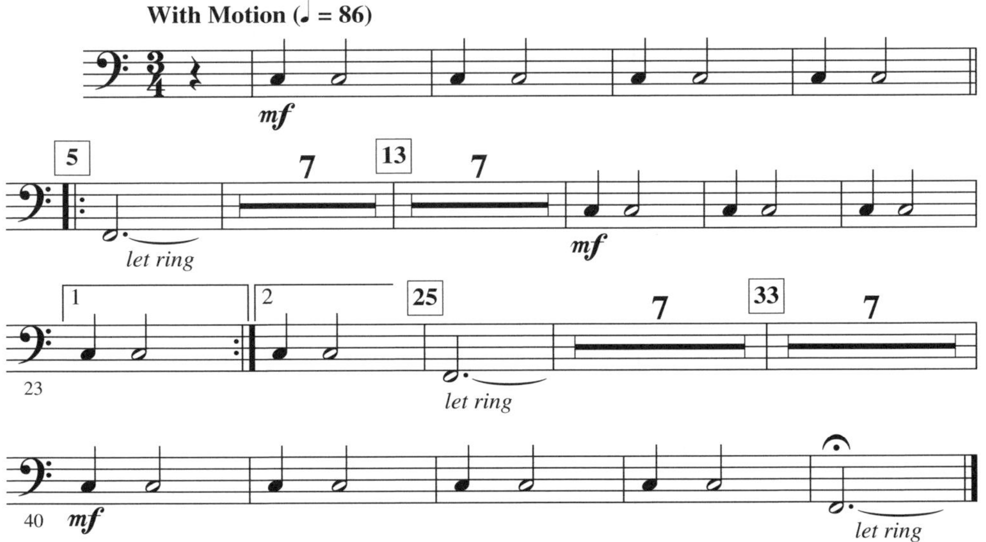

Deck the Halls

Traditional Welsh Carol
Arranged by TOM ANDERSON

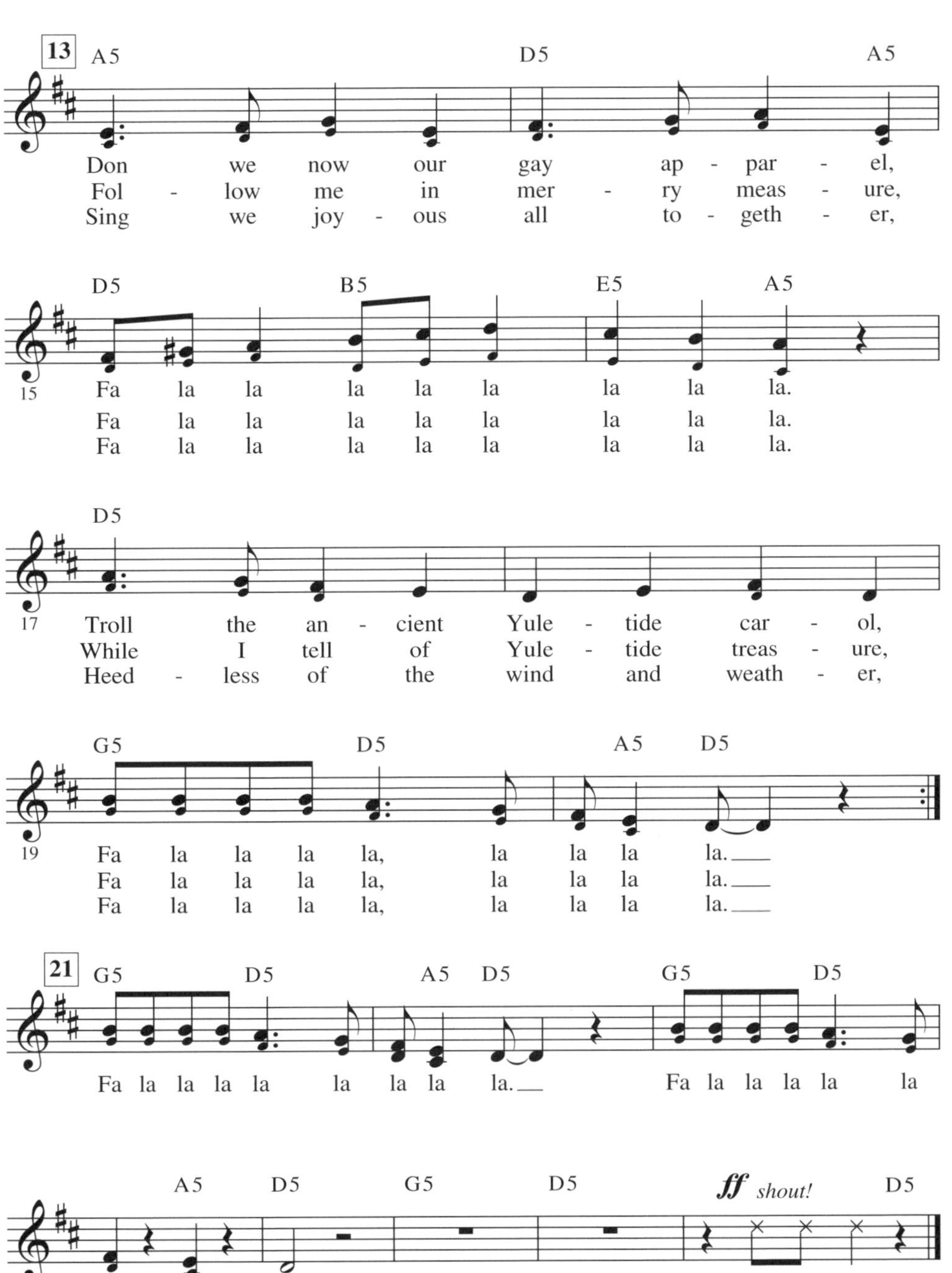

13
A5   D5   A5
Don we now our gay ap - par - el,
Fol - low me in mer - ry meas - ure,
Sing we joy - ous all to - geth - er,

D5   B5   E5   A5
15
Fa la la la la la la la la.
Fa la la la la la la la la.
Fa la la la la la la la la.

D5
17
Troll the an - cient Yule - tide car - ol,
While I tell of Yule - tide treas - ure,
Heed - less of the wind and weath - er,

G5   D5   A5   D5
19
Fa la la la la, la la la la.____
Fa la la la la, la la la la.____
Fa la la la la, la la la la.____

21
G5   D5   A5   D5   G5   D5
Fa la la la la la la la la.____ Fa la la la la la

A5   D5   G5   D5   ff shout!   D5
24
la la la. Deck the halls!

Deck the Halls

BONGO/CONGA DRUMS

Traditional Welsh Carol
Arranged by TOM ANDERSON

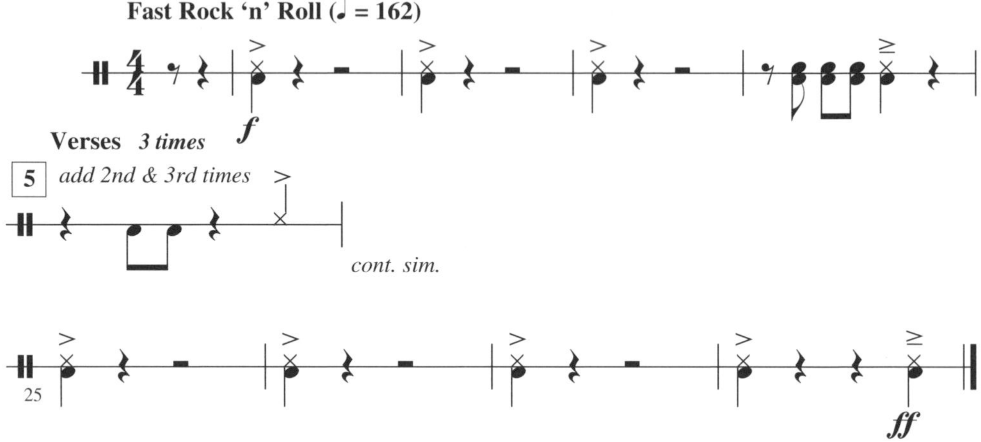

Deck the Halls

TAMBOURINE

Traditional Welsh Carol
Arranged by TOM ANDERSON

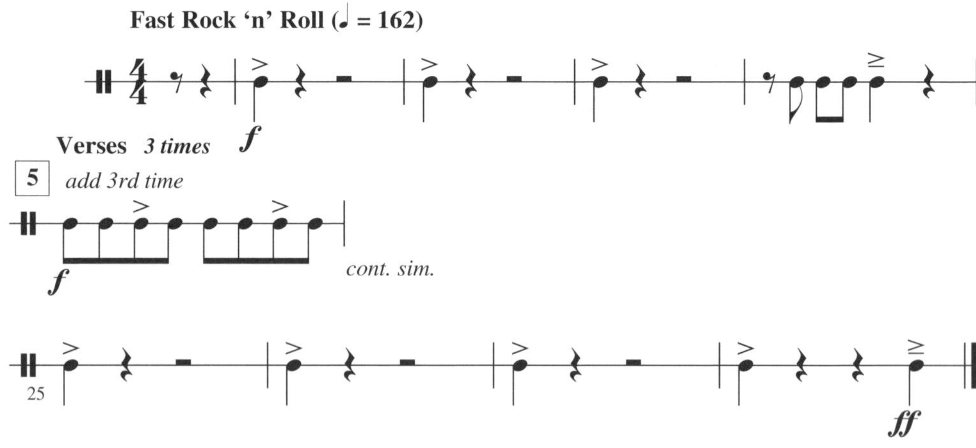

Here We Come A-Caroling

English Wassail Song
Arranged by TOM ANDERSON

Here We Come A-Caroling

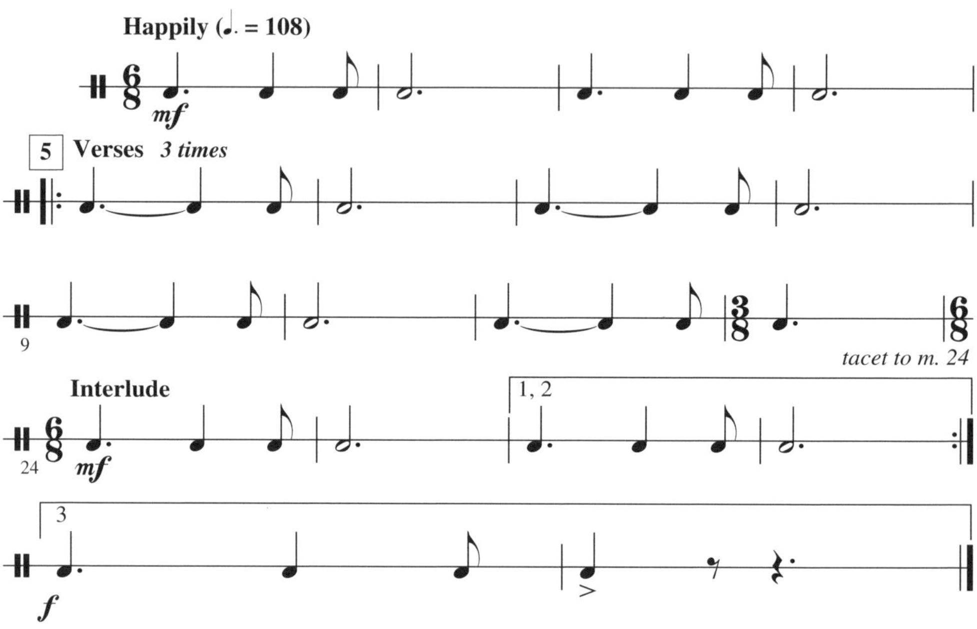

Here We Come A-Caroling

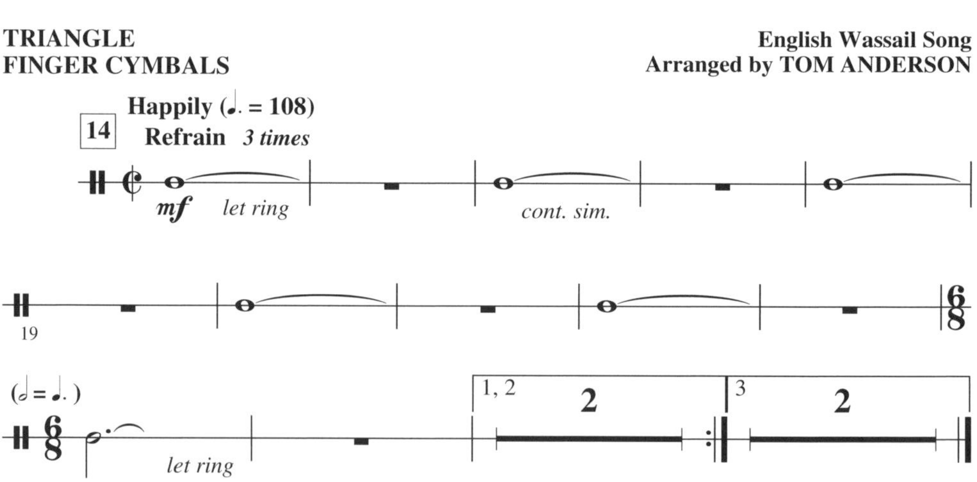

Copyright © 2012 by HAL LEONARD CORPORATION
International Copyright Secured   All Rights Reserved

Jingle Bells

Words and Music by JAMES PIERPONT
Arranged by TOM ANDERSON

Verses

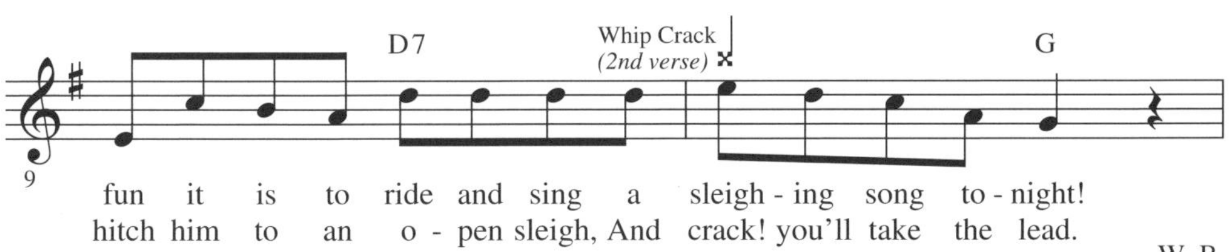

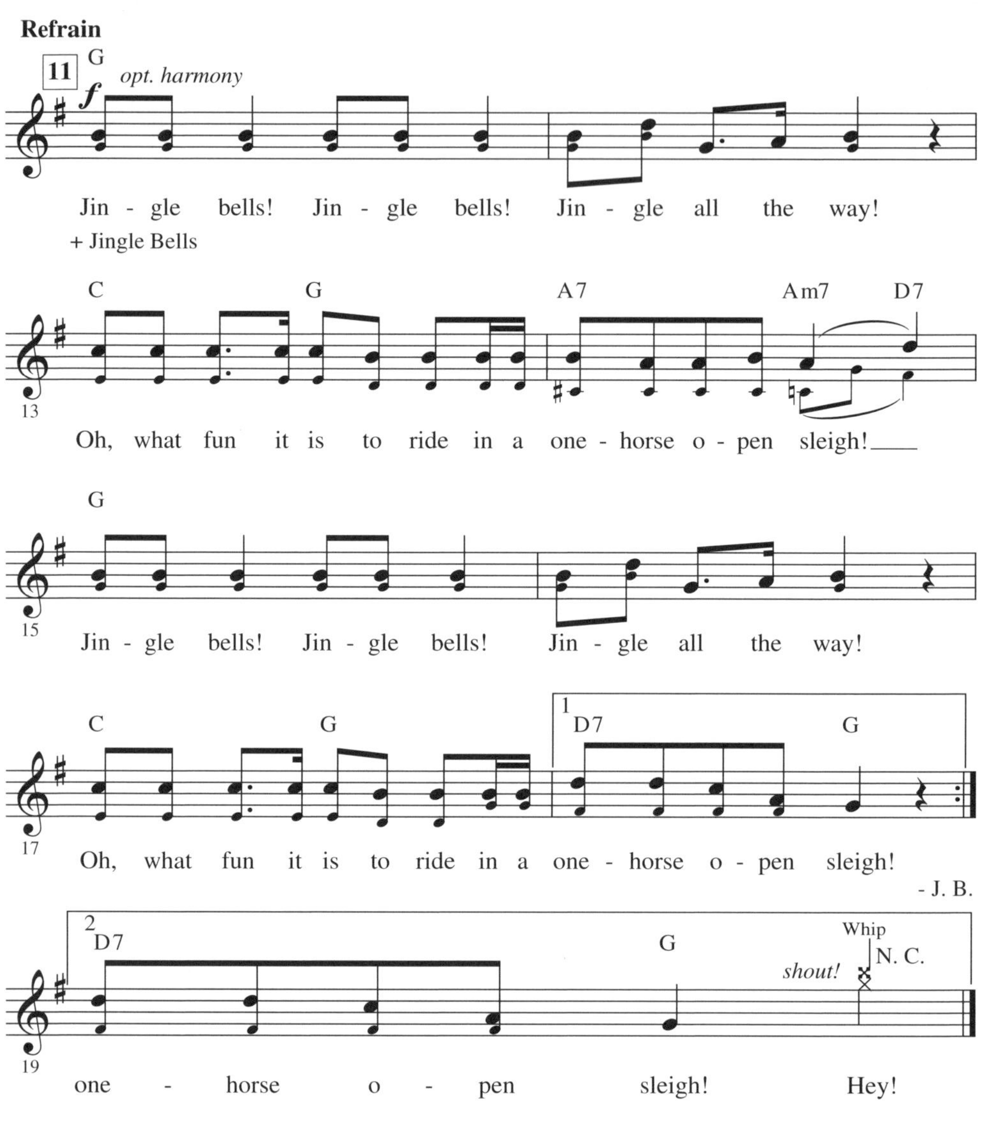

Refrain
11
G
opt. harmony
f
Jin - gle bells! Jin - gle bells! Jin - gle all the way!
+ Jingle Bells
C
G
A7
Am7
D7
13
Oh, what fun it is to ride in a one - horse o - pen sleigh!___
G
15
Jin - gle bells! Jin - gle bells! Jin - gle all the way!
C
G
1
D7
G
17
Oh, what fun it is to ride in a one - horse o - pen sleigh!
- J. B.
2
D7
G
Whip
N. C.
shout!
19
one - horse o - pen sleigh! Hey!

6/18

Jolly Old St. Nicholas

Traditional American Carol
Arranged by TOM ANDERSON

Straight Ahead Swing (♩ = 130) (♫ = ♩ ♪ triplet)

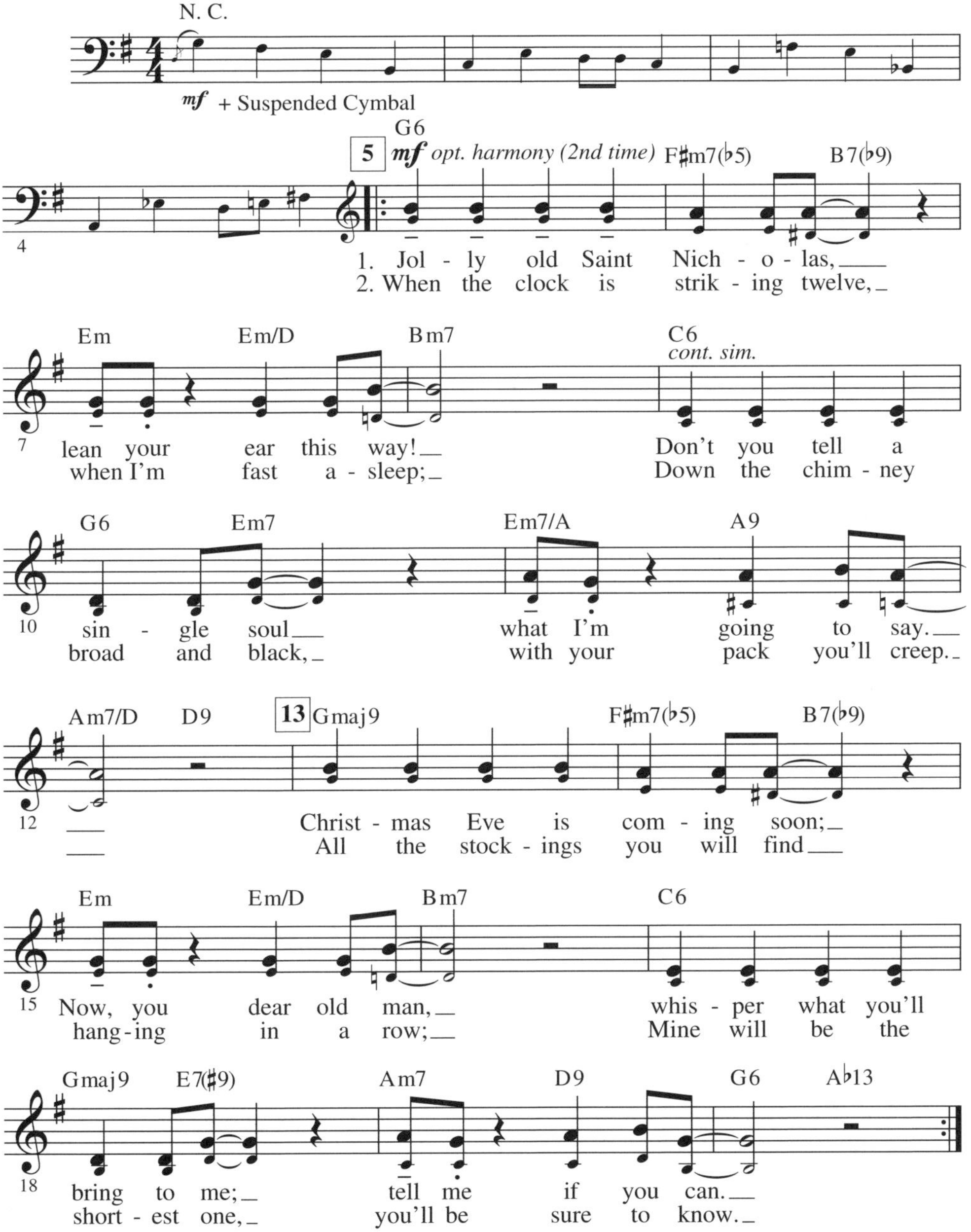

Recorder or Other Pitched Inst.
3. John-ny wants a pair of skates,__ Su-sy wants a sled;__
+ Jingle Bells
Nel - lie wants a pic - ture book;__ yel-low, blue and red..
Now I think I'll leave to you__
what to give the rest;__ Choose for me, dear San - ta Claus,__
you will know the best.__ You will know the best.__
You will know the best!________
- Recorder

Jolly Old St. Nicholas

Jolly Old St. Nicholas

Jolly Old St. Nicholas

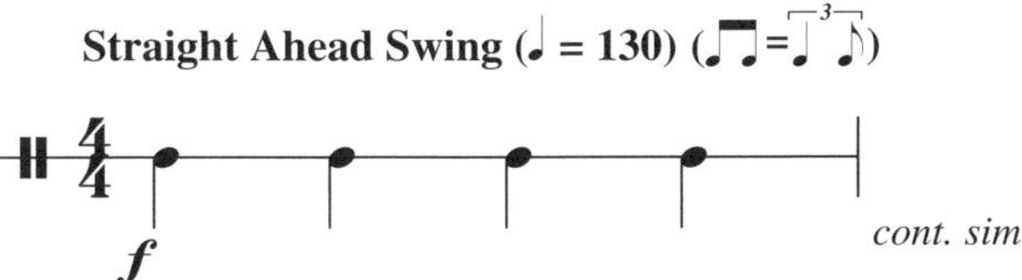

Joy to the World

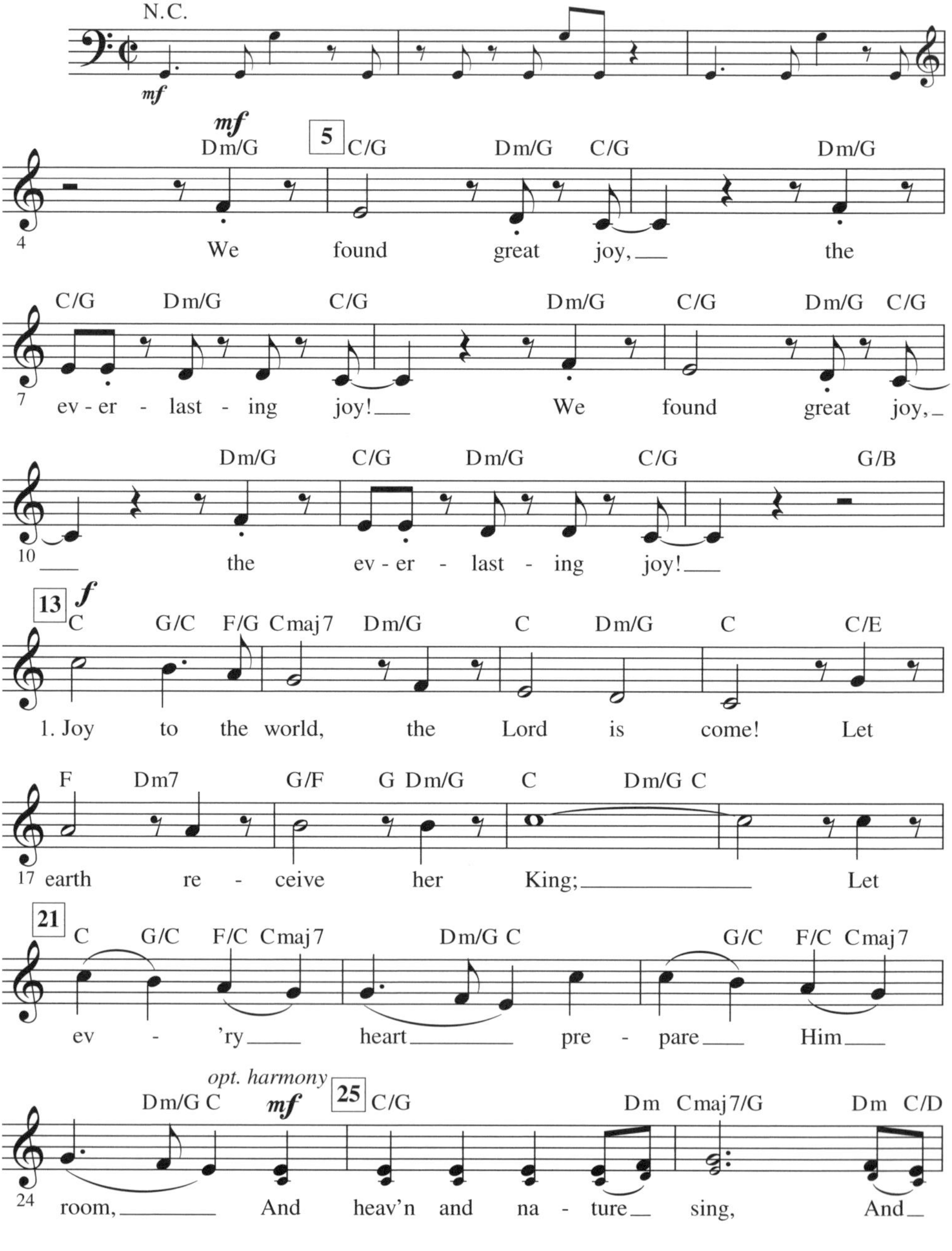

Dm7/G   C/D Dm7(b5)/G Dm7(b5)/Ab   Am7   Am7/G
27
heav'n and na - ture sing,   And heav'n and

F(add9) C/E F2/A C/G Dm/G   32 C   Dm/C C   Dm/C
opt. small group We found great joy, ___
30
heav'n and na - ture sing.   the
mel.
+ Hand Claps on beat 2

C   Dm7(b5)/C   C   Dm/C   C   Dm/C C
34
ev - er - last - ing joy! ___   We found great joy, ___

Dm/C   C   Dm7(b5)/C   C   G/B
37
the ev - er - last - ing joy! ___   - Claps

40 f opt. harmony
C   G/C F/G Cmaj7 Dm/G   C   Dm/G   C   C/E
2. He rules the world with truth and grace, And
mel.

F   Dm7   G/F G Dm/G C   Dm/G C
na - tions prove ___
44 makes the   We found great joy! ___   The

48 C   G/C F/C Cmaj7   Dm/G C   G/C F/C Cmaj7
glo - ries ___ of ___ His right - eous -

Dm/G C   mf   52 C/G   Dm Cmaj7/G   Dm C/D
51
ness, ___   And won - ders of His __ love, And __

Dm7/G
C/D Dm7(♭5)/G Dm7(♭5)/A♭
Am7
Am7/G
54
won - ders   of   His___ love,   And__ won - ders,
F(add9) C/E F2/A
C/G
Dm/G
59 C
Dm/C   C
We   found   great   joy,___
57
won - ders   of   His   love.
mel.
+ Claps
Dm/C   C   Dm7(♭5)/C   C
Dm/C
60
the   ev - er - last - ing   joy!___   We
C   Dm/C C   Dm/C   C   Dm7(♭5)/C   C
63 found   great   joy,___   the   ev - er - last - ing   joy!__
build intensity
f Dm/C
67 C   Dm/C   C   Dm/C
66 ___   We   found   great   joy,___   the
+ Tambourine on beat 2
C   Dm7(♭5)/C   C   Dm/C   C   Dm/C C
69 ev - er - last - ing   joy!___   We   found   great   joy,_
Dm/C   C   Dm7(♭5)/C   C
72 ___   the   ev - er - last - ing   joy!___
ff

O Christmas Tree
(O Tannenbaum)

Traditional German Carol
Arranged by TOM ANDERSON

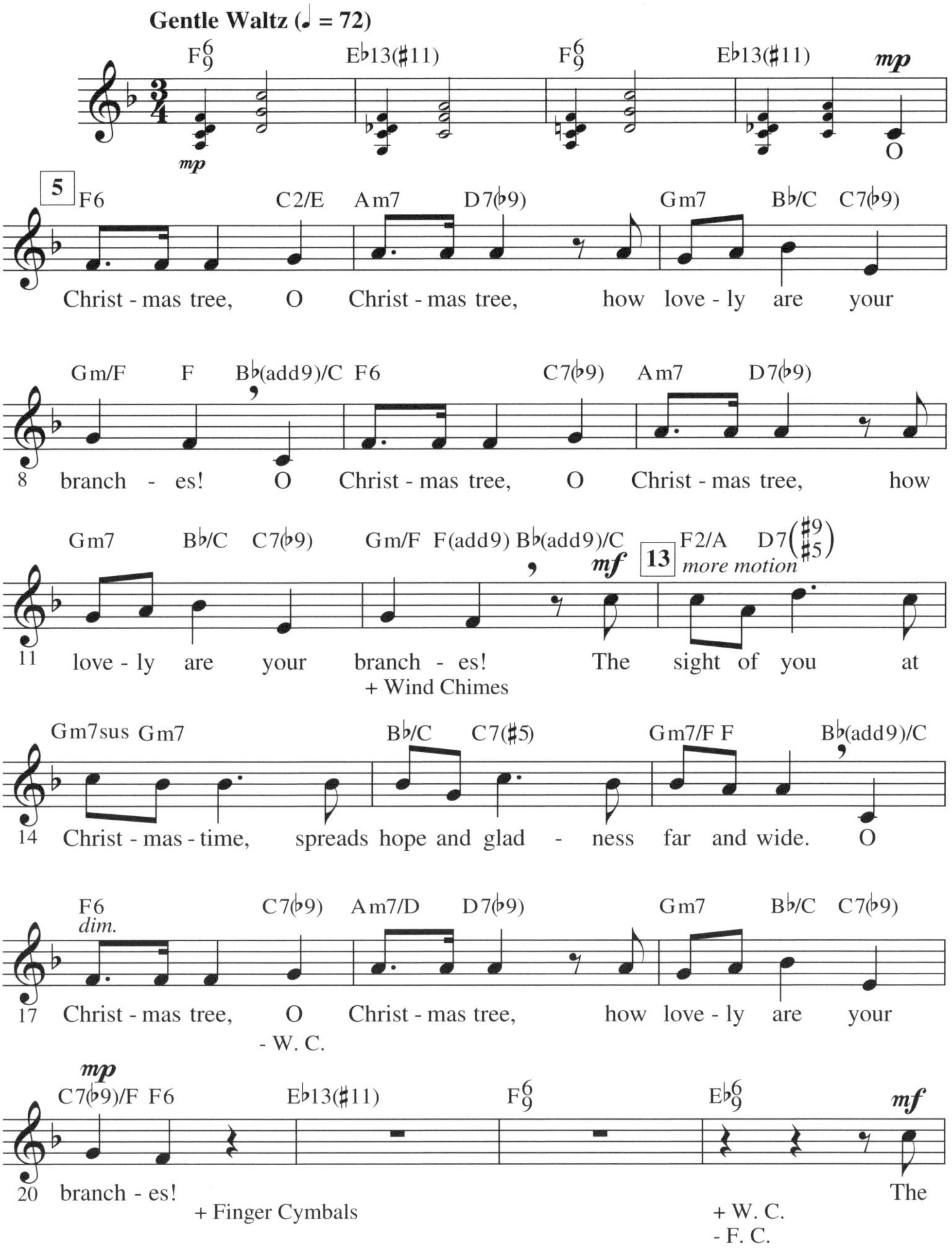

24 F2/A   D7(#9/#5)   Gm7sus Gm7   Bb/C   C7(#5)
more motion   opt. harmony
sight of you   at Christ-mas-time,   spreads hope and glad - ness
- W. C.
Gm7/F F   Bb(add9)/C F6   C7(b9) Am7/D   D7(b9)
dim.
27   far and wide.   O   Christ-mas tree,   O   Christ - mas tree,   how
Gm7   Bb/C   C7(b9)   C7(b9)/F   F6   Eb13(#11)
mp
30   love - ly   are   your   branch - es!   + F. C.
relaxed
F6/9   Eb13(#11)   F6/9
33   O   Christ - mas tree!
+ W. C.

Pat-a-Pan
(Willie, Take Your Little Drum)

Words and Music by
BERNARD de la MONNOYE
Arranged by TOM ANDERSON

28 E5
3. God and man to - day be - come close - ly joined as
B5
flute and drum. Let the joy - ous tune play
E5 B5
on! Tu - re - lu - re - lu, pat - a - pat - a - pan. As the
E5 B5
in - stru - ments you play, we will sing, this Christ - mas
39 Ending
E5
6
Day.

Pat-a-Pan
(Willie, Take Your Little Drum)

Pat-a-Pan
(Willie, Take Your Little Drum)

Copyright © 2012 by HAL LEONARD CORPORATION
International Copyright Secured   All Rights Reserved

30   Mickey's Caroling Book – Singer

Pat-a-Pan
(Willie, Take Your Little Drum)

Pat-a-Pan
(Willie, Take Your Little Drum)

Silent Night

Words by JOSEPH MOHR
Music by FRANZ GRUBER
Arranged by TOM ANDERSON

29 C more motion Cmaj7 C6 C Dm7/G
mf
3. Si - lent night, ho - ly night, Son of
+ Descant/Recorder
G9 C(add9) Gm7/C C9 37 F(add9) C/E Dm7 G9
34 God, love's pure light;____ ra - diant beams__ from
+ Sus. Cym.
C Dm/G C C7 F(add9) F6/9 C(add9)
39 Thy ho - ly face, with the dawn of re - deem - ing
45 Dm7 Dm7/G G/F C2/E Am7
44 grace, Je - sus, Lord, at Thy birth,____
+ Sus. Cym.
C/G Dm7 G9 C(add9)
dim. slight rit. mp
49 Je - sus, Lord at Thy birth.
+ W. C.

Silent Night

Up on the Housetop

Words and Music by B. R. HANDY
Arranged by TOM ANDERSON

Cheerfully ($\quad$ = 134)

21
mf
D
D/F#
3. Next, comes the stock - ing of lit - tle Will;
G
D
A7
23
Oh, just see what a glo - rious fill!
D
D/F#
25
Here is a ham - mer and lots of tacks,
G
D
Em7
A7
D
Whip Crack
D/F#
27
al - so a ball and a whip that cracks.
29
f
G
Em7
D
Bm7
Ho, ho, ho, who would - n't go!
+ S. B. and Mar.
Em7
A7
D
Em7/A
31
Ho, ho, ho, who would - n't go!
Finger Snaps
D
D7/F#
G
D/F#
Em7
Fdim7
33
Up on the house - top
spoken
click, click, click,
+ W. B.
D/F#
Bm7
Em7
A7
D
Whip Crack
N.C.
35
Down thru' the chim - ney with good Saint Nick.

We Wish You a Merry Christmas

Traditional English Carol
Arranged by TOM ANDERSON

22
G   G/B   C   C/B   A7sus   A7
wish   you   a   mer - ry   Christ - mas,   We   wish   you   a   mer - ry
+ Tri./F. C., H. D., Tamb.
D   D/C   B7sus   B7   Em   G/B
25
Christ - mas,   We   wish   you   a   mer - ry   Christ - mas,   and a
- Tri./F. C.
- H. D.
- Tamb.
C6   Am7   cresc.   Am7/D   D9
28
hap   -   py   New
ff   G   G2/B   C   Am7   D9   G 6/9
32
Year!
+ Tri./F. C., H. D., Tamb.

We Wish You a Merry Christmas

TRIANGLE/FINGER CYMBALS

Traditional English Carol
Arranged by TOM ANDERSON

Warmly, felt in one (♩ = 130)

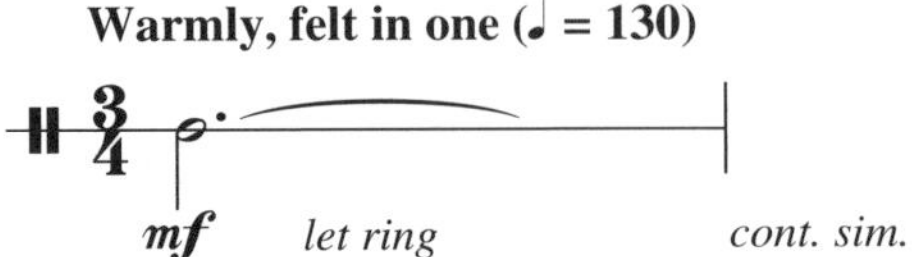

We Wish You a Merry Christmas

HAND DRUM

Traditional English Carol
Arranged by TOM ANDERSON

Warmly, felt in one (♩ = 130)

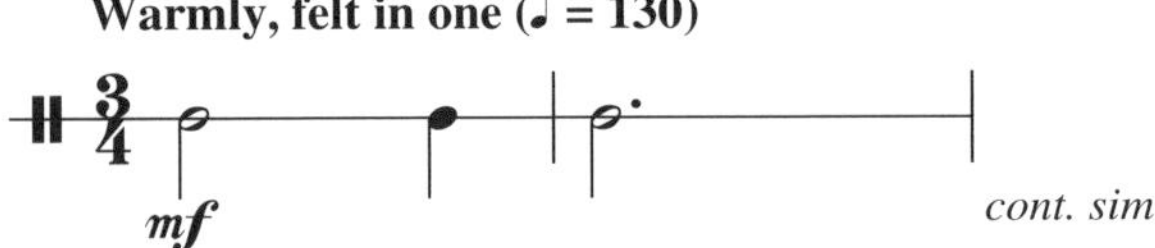

We Wish You a Merry Christmas

TAMBOURINE

Traditional English Carol
Arranged by TOM ANDERSON

Warmly, felt in one (♩ = 130)

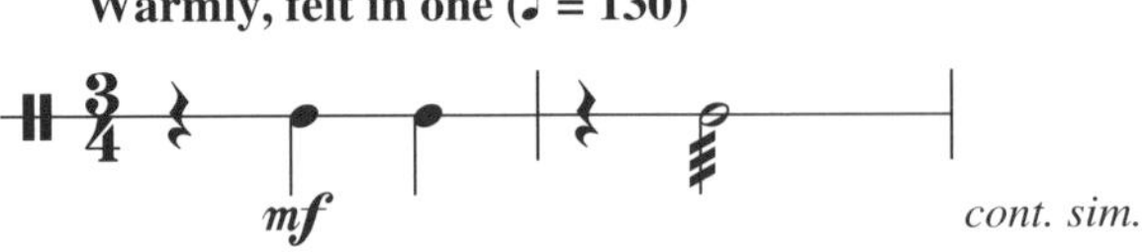

Disney
Mickey's Caroling Book
HOLIDAY FUN WITH MICKEY AND HIS FRIENDS

Table of Contents

HAL•LEONARD® CORPORATION

7777 W. BLUEMOUND RD. P.O. BOX 13819 MILWAUKEE, WI 53213

Visit Hal Leonard Online at
www.halleonard.com

Angels We Have Heard on High

Traditional French Carol
Arranged by TOM ANDERSON

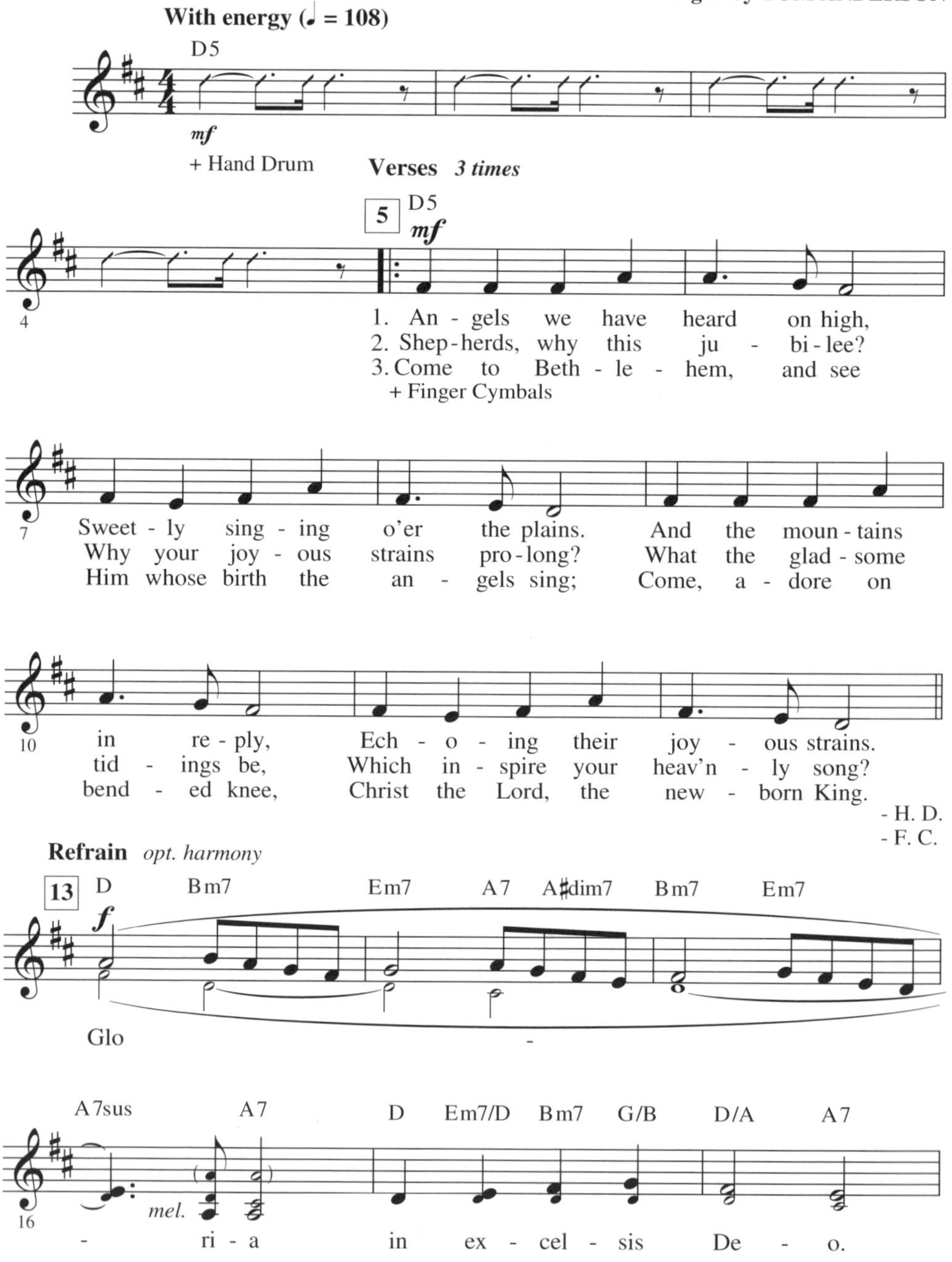

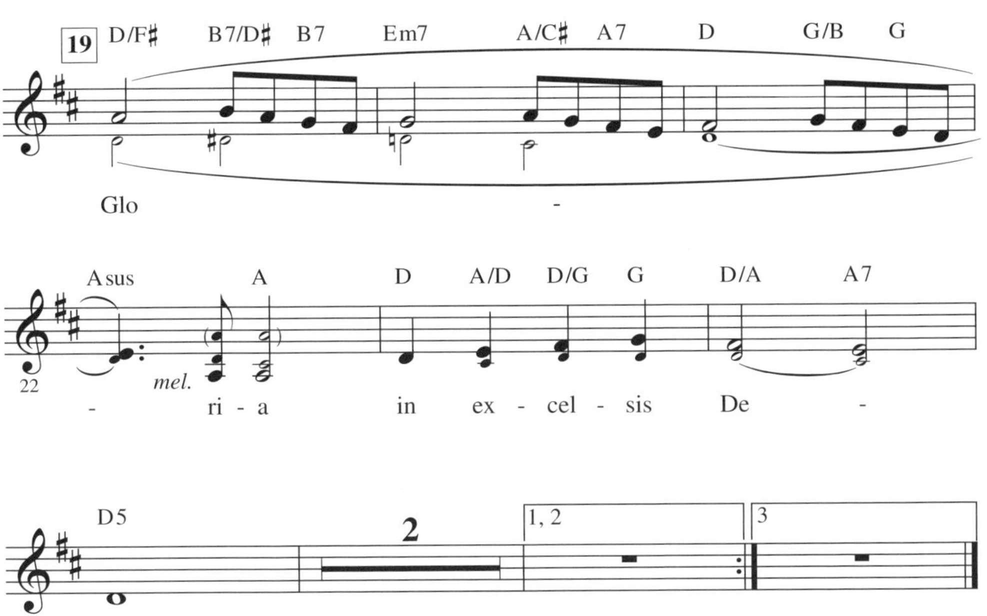

19
D/F♯ B7/D♯ B7 Em7 A/C♯ A7 D G/B G
Glo -
A sus A D A/D D/G G D/A A7
mel.
- ri - a in ex - cel - sis De -
D5
2
1, 2
3
o.

Angels We Have Heard on High

HAND DRUM

Traditional French Carol
Arranged by TOM ANDERSON

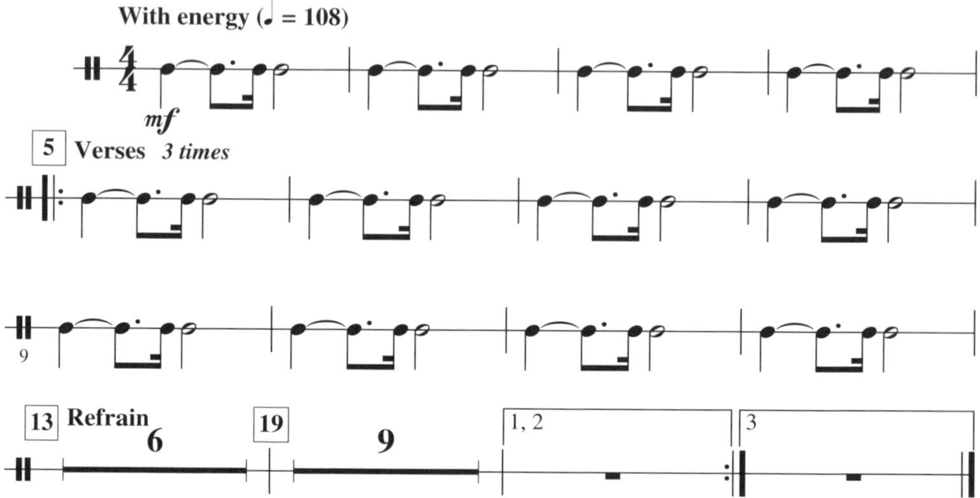

Angels We Have Heard on High

FINGER CYMBALS

Traditional French Carol
Arranged by TOM ANDERSON

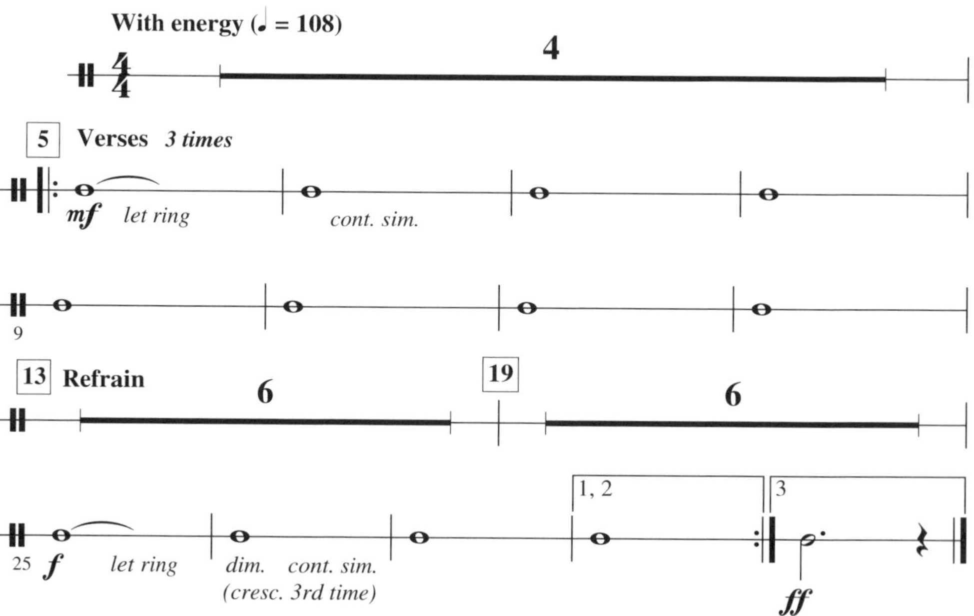

Angels We Have Heard on High

BASS DRUM

Traditional French Carol
Arranged by TOM ANDERSON

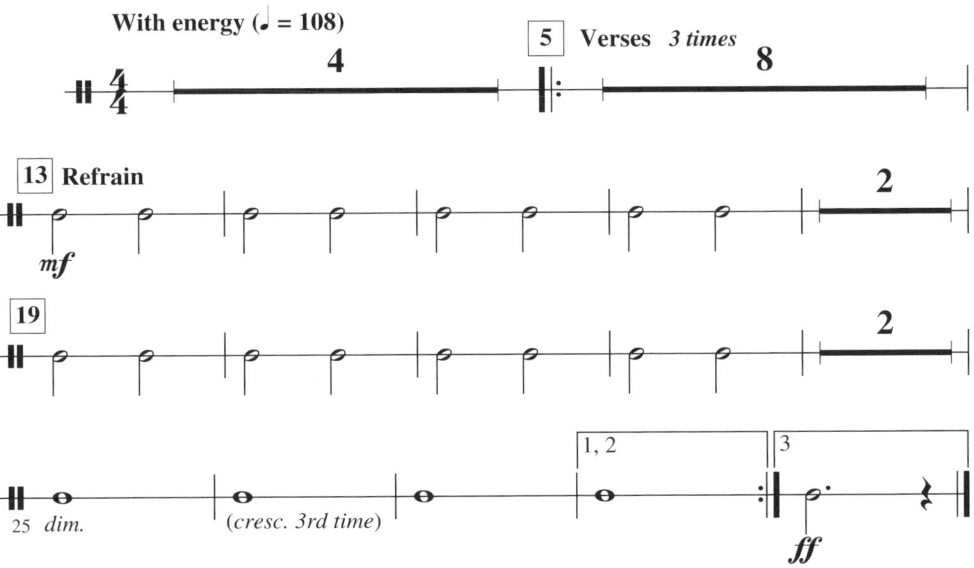

Angels We Have Heard on High

SUSPENDED CYMBAL

Traditional French Carol
Arranged by TOM ANDERSON

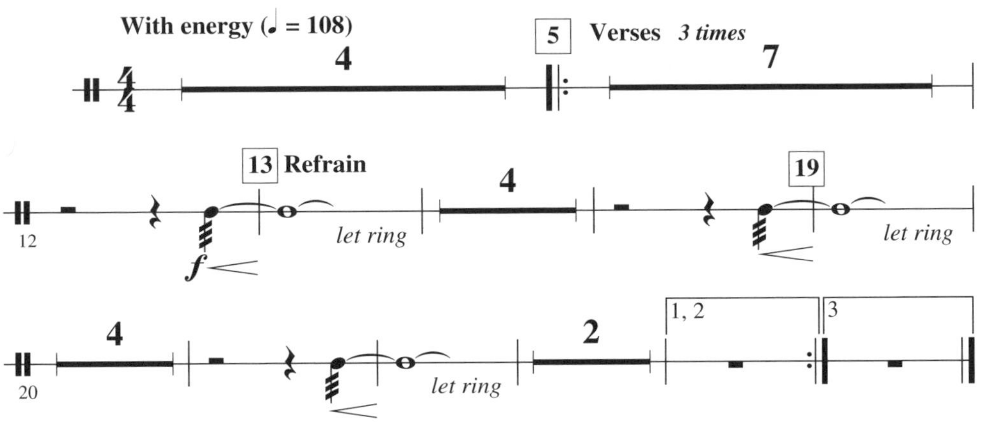

Angels We Have Heard on High

ORFF INSTRUMENTS

Traditional French Carol
Arranged by TOM ANDERSON

With energy (♩ = 108)

Away in a Manger

Music by JAMES R. MURRAY
Words, Stanza 1, 2, Anonymous
Stanza 3, JOHN THOMAS McFARLAND
Arranged by TOM ANDERSON

Copyright © 2012 by HAL LEONARD CORPORATION
International Copyright Secured   All Rights Reserved

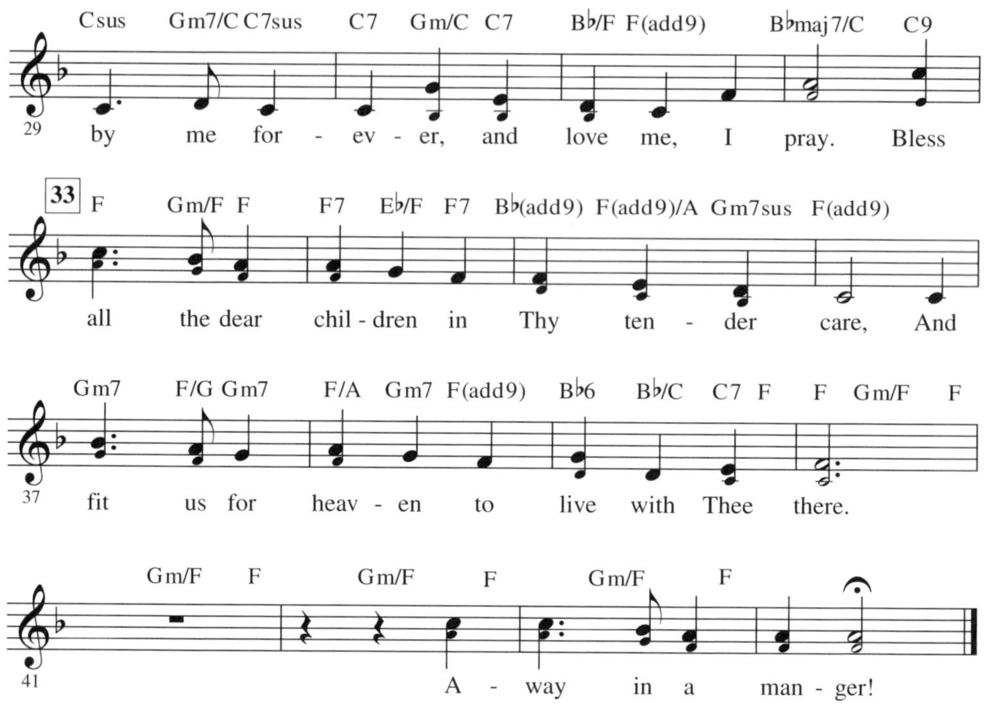

Csus Gm7/C C7sus C7 Gm/C C7 B♭/F F(add9) B♭maj7/C C9
by me for - ev - er, and love me, I pray. Bless
33 F Gm/F F F7 E♭/F F7 B♭(add9) F(add9)/A Gm7sus F(add9)
all the dear chil - dren in Thy ten - der care, And
Gm7 F/G Gm7 F/A Gm7 F(add9) B♭6 B♭/C C7 F F Gm/F F
fit us for heav - en to live with Thee there.
Gm/F F Gm/F F Gm/F F
A - way in a man - ger!

Away in a Manger

Music by JAMES R. MURRAY
Words, Stanza 1, 2, Anonymous
Stanza 3, JOHN THOMAS McFARLAND
Arranged by TOM ANDERSON

25
let ring
cont. sim.
let ring
cont. sim.
let ring
cont. sim.
33
30
35
40
let ring
let ring
let ring
let ring

Away in a Manger

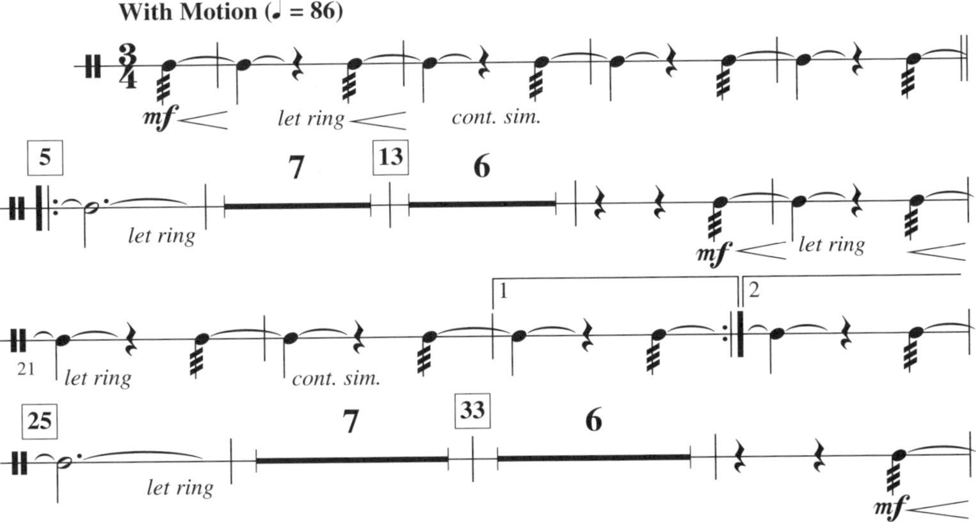

Away in a Manger

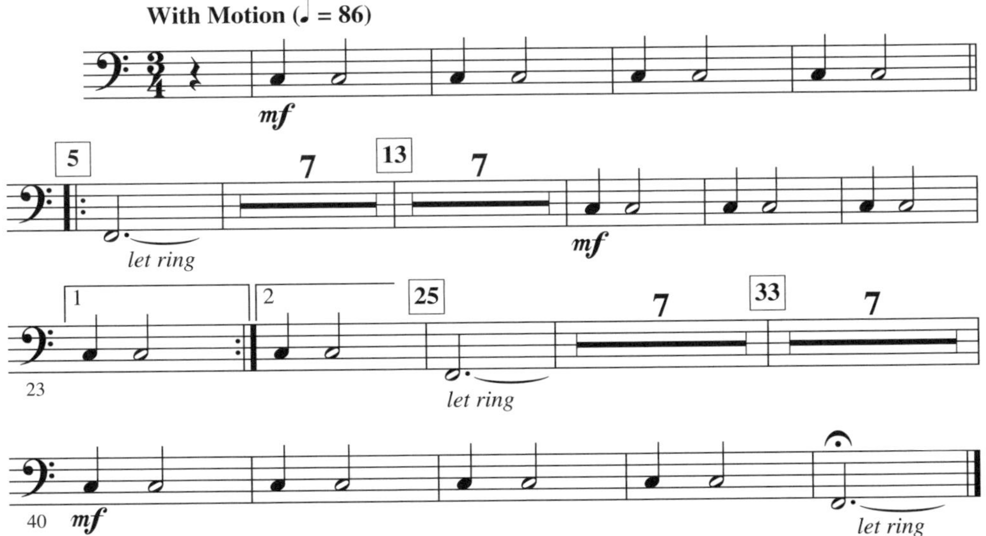

Deck the Halls

Traditional Welsh Carol
Arranged by TOM ANDERSON

Don we now our gay ap - par - el,
Fol - low me in mer - ry meas - ure,
Sing we joy - ous all to - geth - er,
Fa la la la la la la la la.
Fa la la la la la la la la.
Fa la la la la la la la la.
Troll the an - cient Yule - tide car - ol,
While I tell of Yule - tide treas - ure,
Heed - less of the wind and weath - er,
Fa la la la la, la la la la.
Fa la la la la, la la la la.
Fa la la la la, la la la la.
Fa la la la la la la la la.
Fa la la la la la
ff shout!
la la la.
Deck the halls!

Deck the Halls

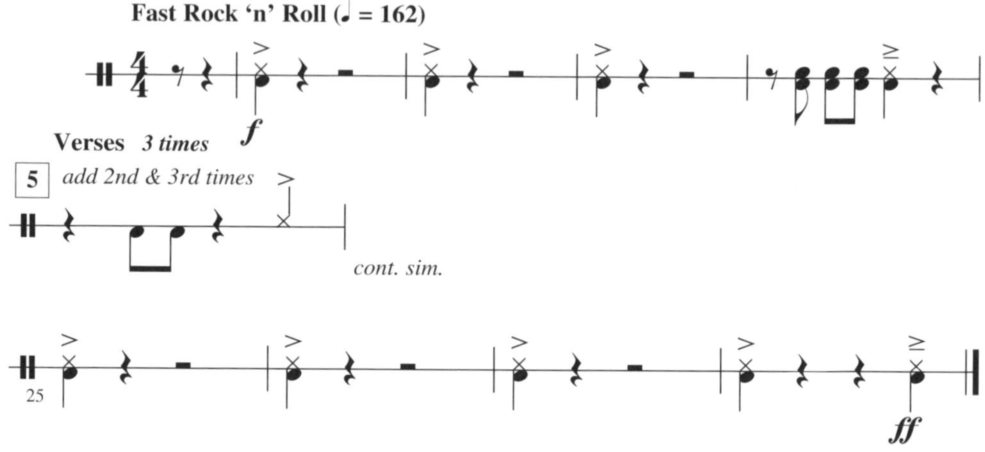

Deck the Halls

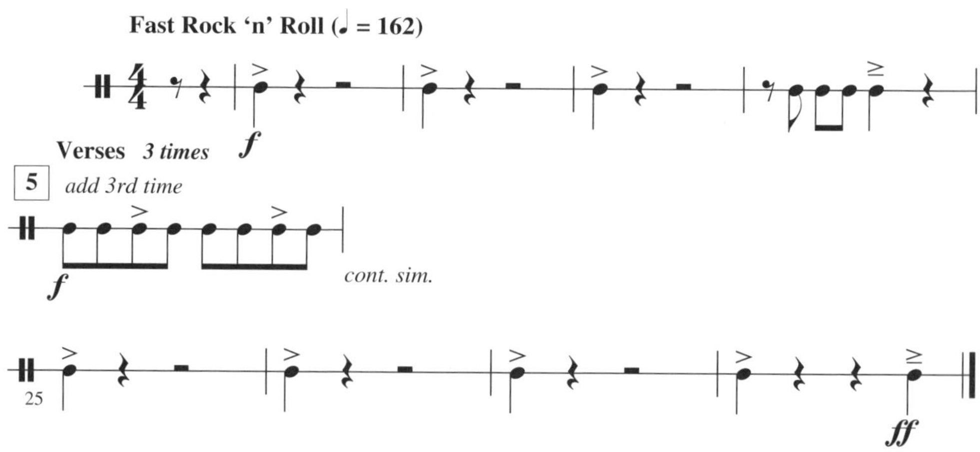

Here We Come A-Caroling

English Wassail Song
Arranged by TOM ANDERSON

Here We Come A-Caroling

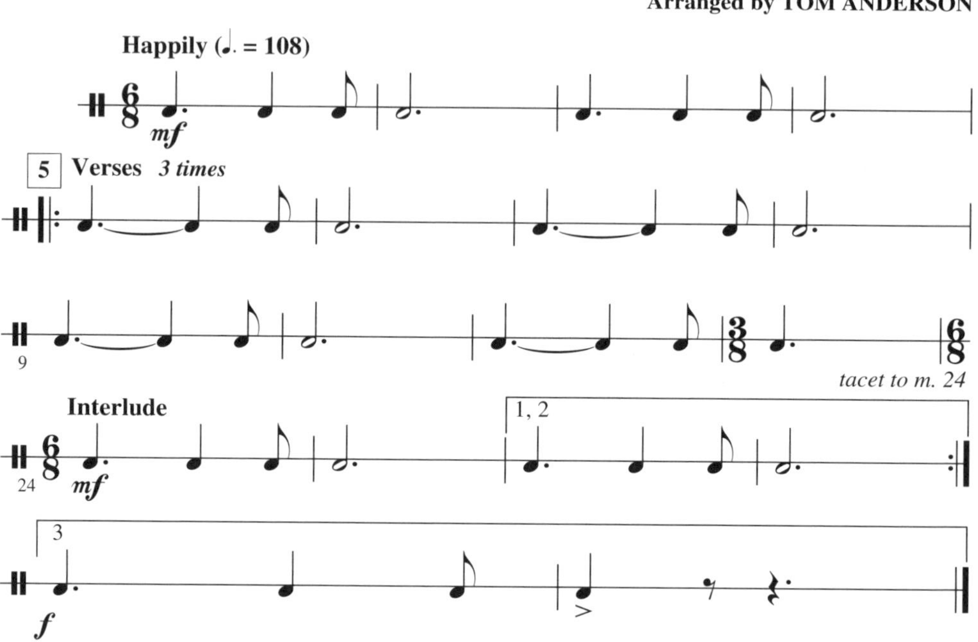

Here We Come A-Caroling

Here We Come A-Caroling

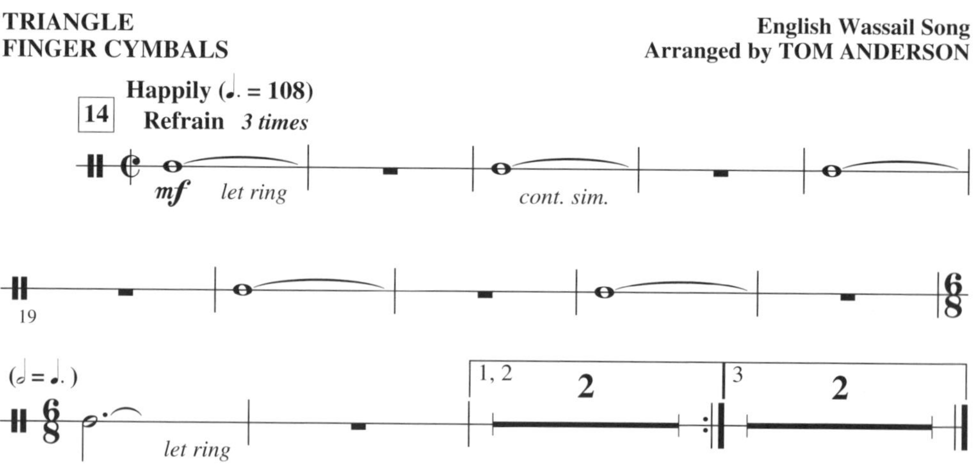

Jingle Bells

Words and Music by JAMES PIERPONT
Arranged by TOM ANDERSON

With Joy! (♩ = 106)

Verses

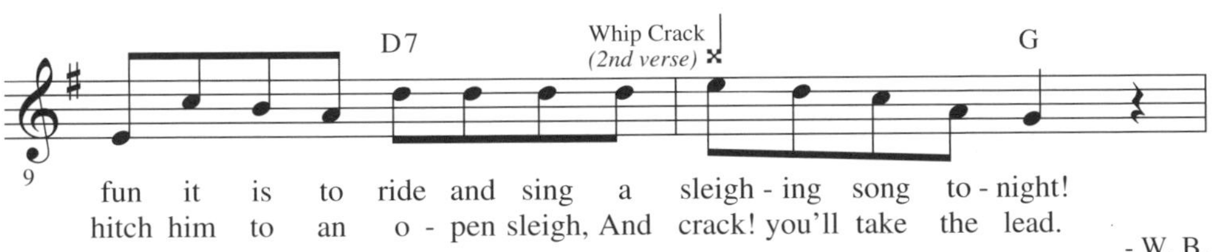

- W. B.

Refrain
11
G
opt. harmony
f
Jin - gle bells! Jin - gle bells! Jin - gle all the way!
+ Jingle Bells
C   G   A7   Am7   D7
13
Oh, what fun it is to ride in a one - horse o - pen sleigh!___
G
15
Jin - gle bells! Jin - gle bells! Jin - gle all the way!
C   G   1 D7   G
17
Oh, what fun it is to ride in a one - horse o - pen sleigh!
- J. B.
2 D7   G   Whip N. C.
shout!
19
one - horse o - pen sleigh! Hey!

6/18

Jolly Old St. Nicholas

Traditional American Carol
Arranged by TOM ANDERSON

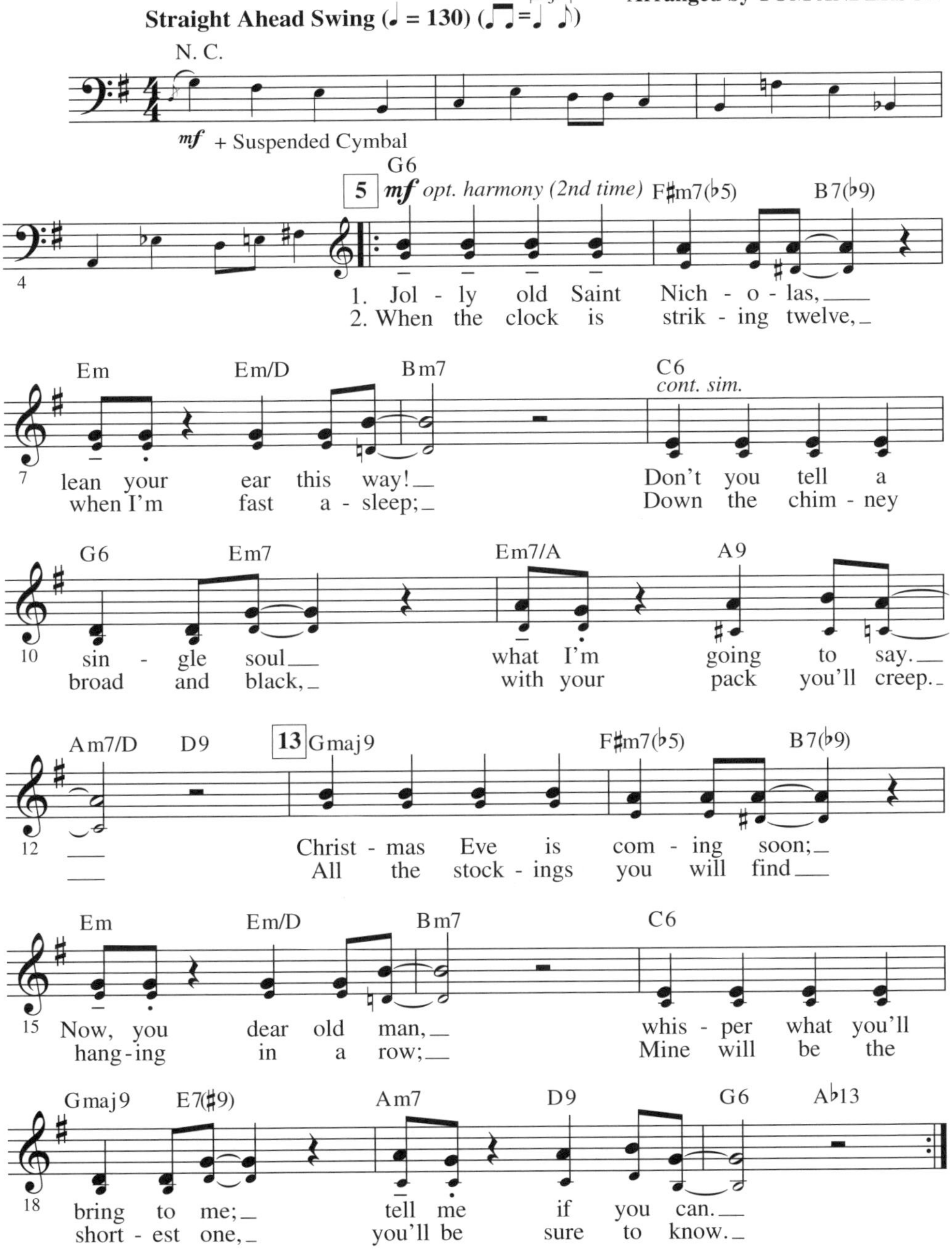

20   Mickey's Caroling Book – Singer

Jolly Old St. Nicholas

Jolly Old St. Nicholas

Jolly Old St. Nicholas

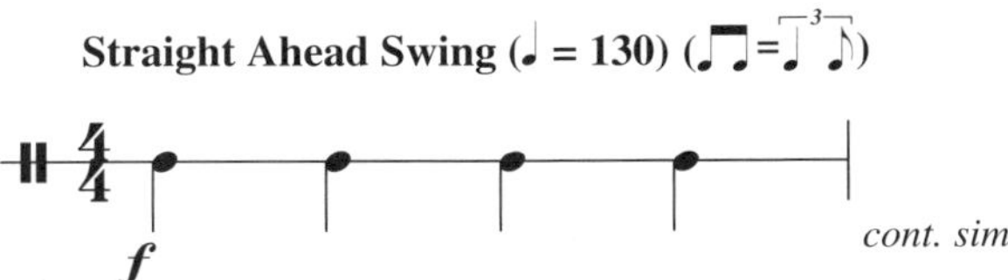

7/19

Joy to the World

Words by ISAAC WATTS
Music by GEORGE F. HANDEL
Arranged by TOM ANDERSON

(4-measure rhythm intro. on recording)

Mod. Gospel Shuffle (♩ = 86)

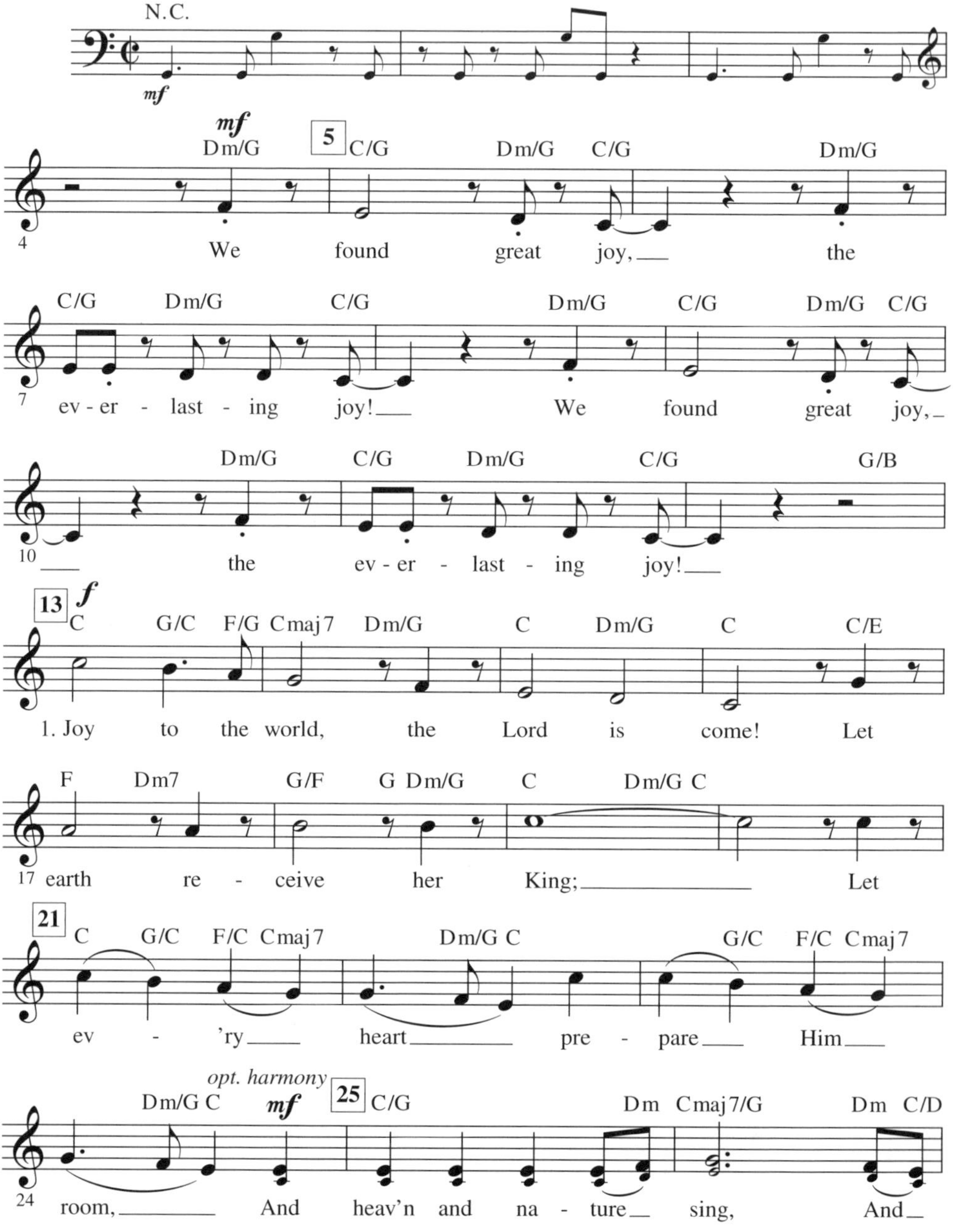

heav'n and na - ture sing, And heav'n and
heav'n and na - ture sing.
opt. small group We found great joy, the
ev - er - last - ing joy! We found great joy,
the ev - er - last - ing joy! - Claps
+ Hand Claps on beat 2
opt. harmony
2. He rules the world with truth and grace, And
na - tions prove We found great joy!
makes the The
glo - ries of His right - eous -
ness, And won - ders of His love, And

Dm7/G   C/D Dm7(b5)/G Dm7(b5)/Ab   Am7   Am7/G
54
won - ders   of   His__   love,   And__   won - ders,

F(add9)   C/E F2/A   C/G   Dm/G   59 C   Dm/C   C
We   found   great   joy,__
57
won - ders   of   His   love.
mel.   + Claps

Dm/C   C   Dm7(b5)/C   C   Dm/C
60
the   ev - er - last - ing   joy!__   We

C   Dm/C   C   Dm/C   C   Dm7(b5)/C   C
63 found   great   joy,__   the   ev - er - last - ing   joy!__

build intensity
f Dm/C   67 C   Dm/C   C   Dm/C
66
We   found   great   joy,__   the
+ Tambourine on beat 2

C   Dm7(b5)/C   C   Dm/C   C   Dm/C   C
69 ev - er - last - ing   joy!__   We   found   great   joy,_

Dm/C   C   Dm7(b5)/C   C
72
the   ev - er - last - ing   joy!__   ff

O Christmas Tree
(O Tannenbaum)

Traditional German Carol
Arranged by TOM ANDERSON

24 F2/A   D7(#9/#5)   Gm7sus Gm7   Bb/C   C7(#5)
more motion opt. harmony
sight of you   at Christ-mas-time,   spreads hope and glad - ness
- W. C.
Gm7/F F   Bb(add9)/C F6   C7(b9) Am7/D   D7(b9)
dim.
far and wide.   O   Christ-mas tree,   O   Christ-mas tree,   how
27
Gm7   Bb/C   C7(b9)   C7(b9)/F   F6   Eb13(#11)
mp
love-ly are your branch-es!   + F. C.
30
relaxed
F6/9   Eb13(#11)   F6/9
O   Christ-mas tree!
+ W. C.
33

Pat-a-Pan
(Willie, Take Your Little Drum)

Words and Music by
BERNARD de la MONNOYE
Arranged by TOM ANDERSON

mf
28 E5
27 3. God and man to - day be - come close-ly joined as
B5
30 flute and drum. Let the joy - ous tune play
E5 B5
33 on! Tu - re - lu - re - lu, pat - a - pat - a - pan. As the
E5 B5
36 in - stru - ments you play, we will sing, this Christ - mas
39 Ending
E5
6
Day.

Pat-a-Pan
(Willie, Take Your Little Drum)

Pat-a-Pan
(Willie, Take Your Little Drum)

Pat-a-Pan
(Willie, Take Your Little Drum)

Pat-a-Pan
(Willie, Take Your Little Drum)

10/22

Silent Night

Words by JOSEPH MOHR
Music by FRANZ GRUBER
Arranged by TOM ANDERSON

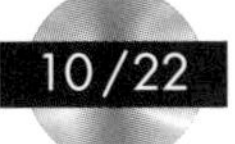

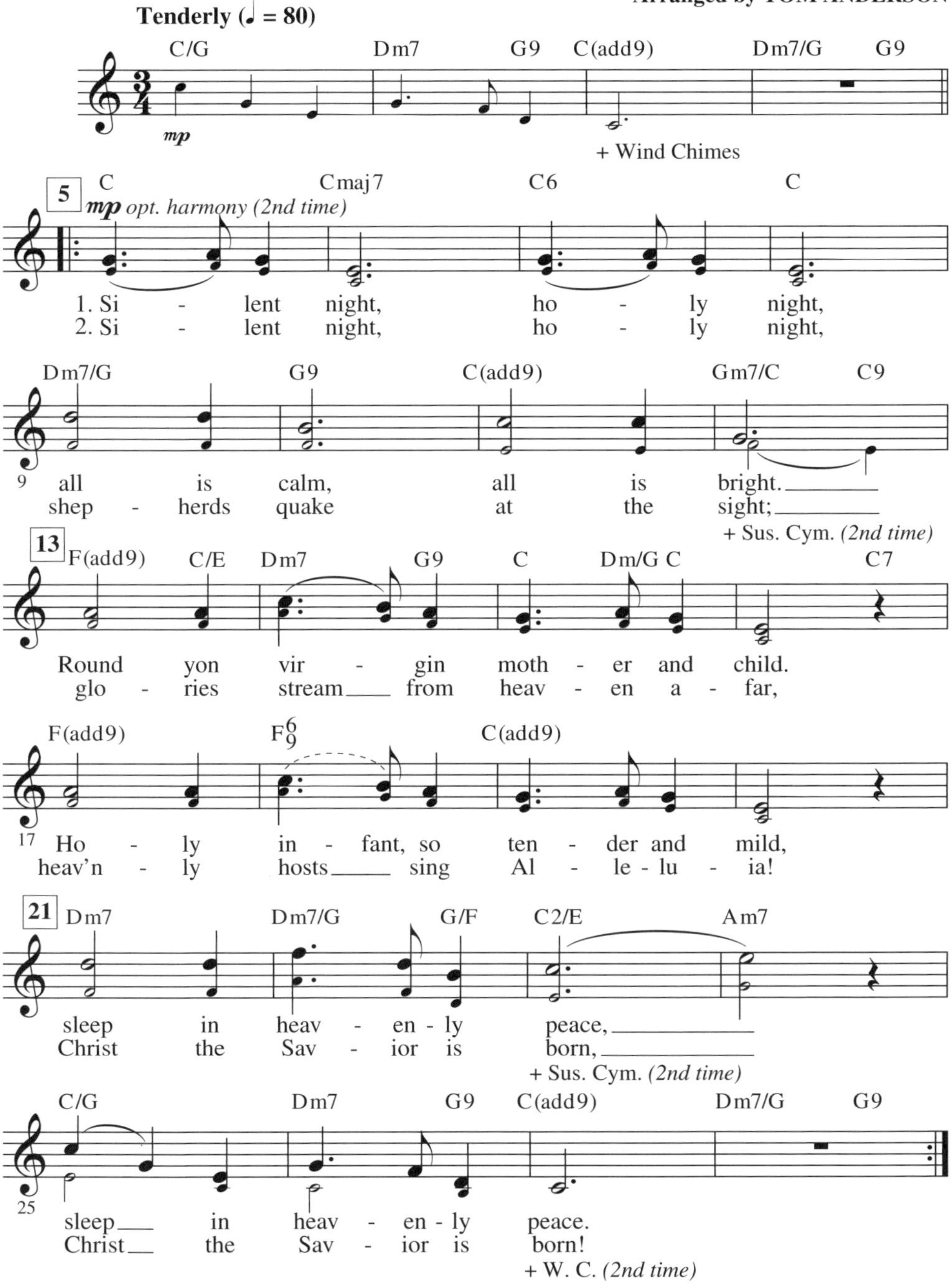

34   **Mickey's Caroling Book – Singer**

Silent Night

11/23

Up on the Housetop

Words and Music by B. R. HANDY
Arranged by TOM ANDERSON

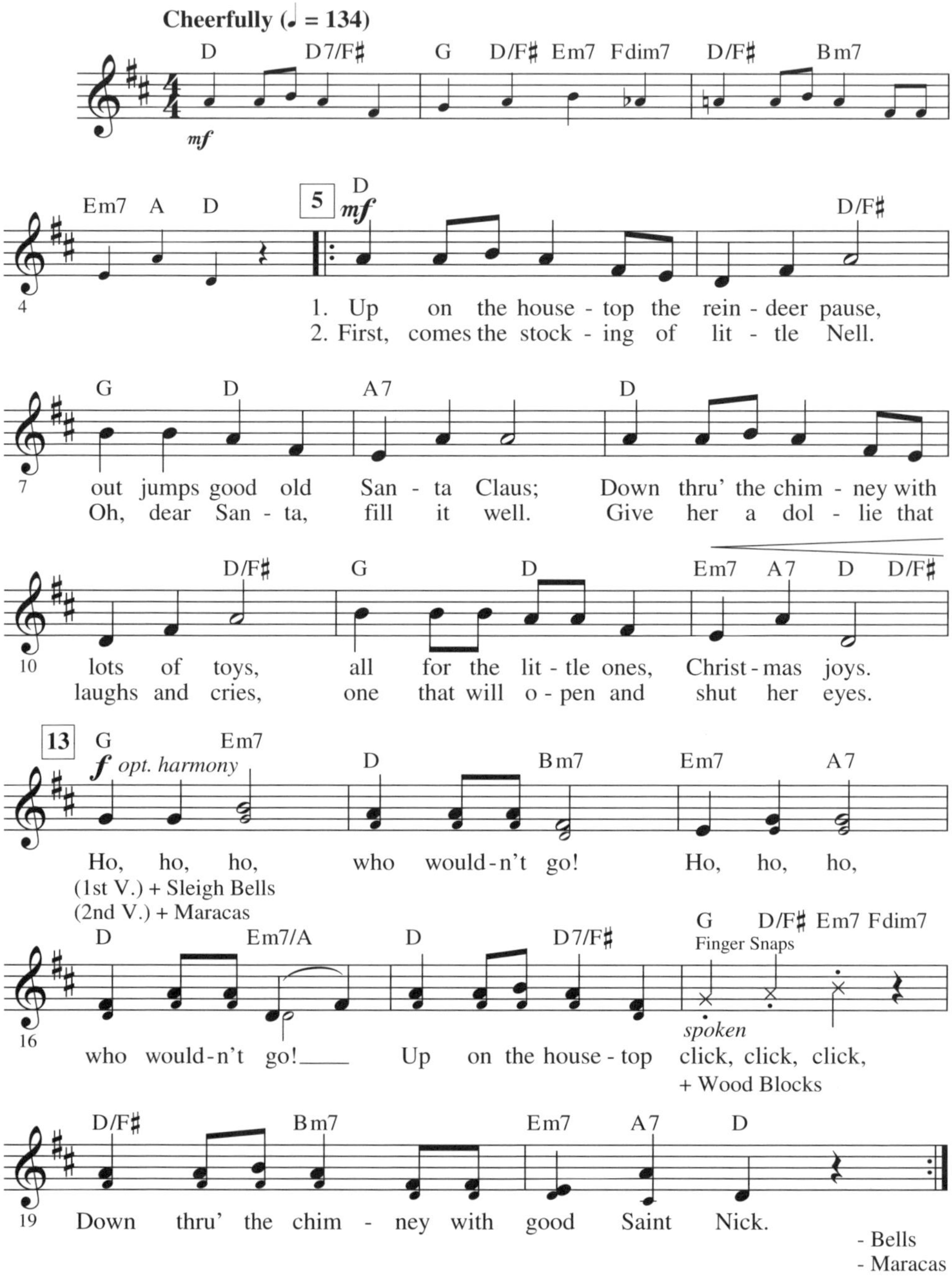

21
mf
D
D/F#
3. Next, comes the stock - ing of lit - tle Will;
G
D
A7
23
Oh, just see what a glo - rious fill!
D
D/F#
25
Here is a ham - mer and lots of tacks,
G
D
Em7
A7
D
Whip Crack
D/F#
27
al - so a ball and a whip that cracks.
29
f
G
Em7
D
Bm7
Ho, ho, ho, who would - n't go!
+ S. B. and Mar.
Em7
A7
D
Em7/A
31
Ho, ho, ho, who would - n't go!
Finger Snaps
D
D7/F#
G
D/F#
Em7
Fdim7
33
Up on the house - top click, click, click,
spoken
+ W. B.
D/F#
Bm7
Em7
A7
D
Whip Crack
N.C.
35
Down thru' the chim - ney with good Saint Nick.

We Wish You a Merry Christmas

Traditional English Carol
Arranged by TOM ANDERSON

Copyright © 2012 by HAL LEONARD CORPORATION
International Copyright Secured   All Rights Reserved

22
G   G/B   C   C/B   A7sus   A7
wish   you   a   mer - ry   Christ - mas,   We   wish   you   a   mer - ry
+ Tri./F. C., H. D., Tamb.
D   D/C   B7sus   B7   Em   G/B
25   Christ - mas,   We   wish   you   a   mer - ry   Christ - mas,   and   a
- Tri./F. C.
- H. D.
- Tamb.
C6   Am7   cresc.   Am7/D   D9
28   hap   -   py   New
ff   G   G2/B   C   Am7   D9   G6/9
32   Year!
+ Tri./F. C., H. D., Tamb.

We Wish You a Merry Christmas

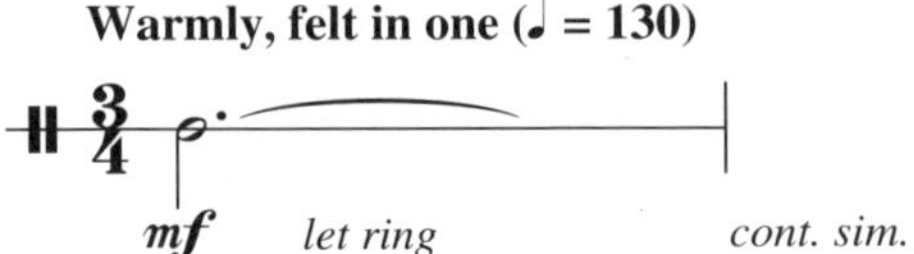

TRIANGLE/FINGER CYMBALS

Traditional English Carol
Arranged by TOM ANDERSON

We Wish You a Merry Christmas

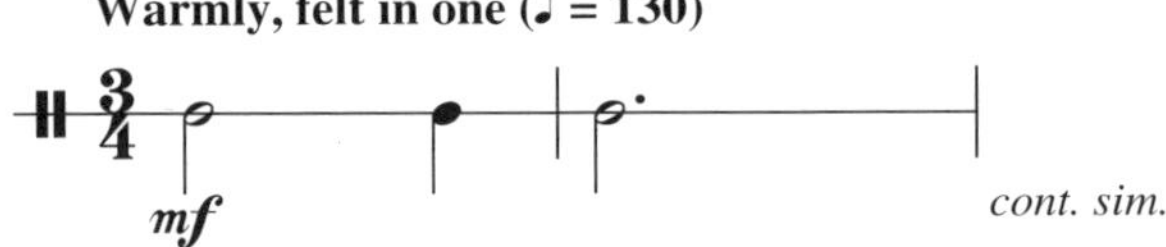

HAND DRUM

Traditional English Carol
Arranged by TOM ANDERSON

We Wish You a Merry Christmas

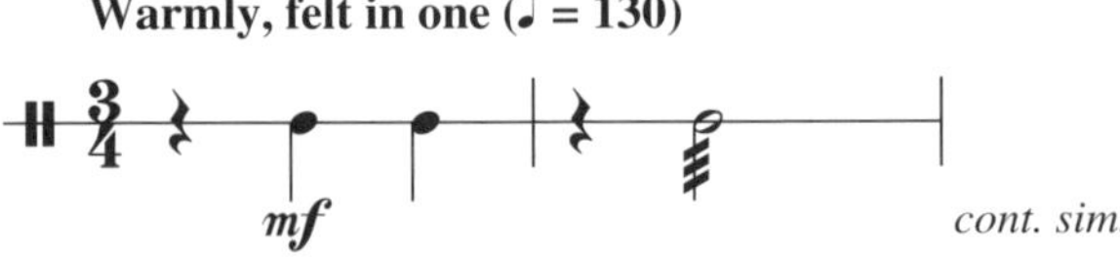

TAMBOURINE

Traditional English Carol
Arranged by TOM ANDERSON